CELEBRATING
## 50 YEARS
**Texas A&M University Press**
*publishing since 1974*

*The Ahern Home of Texarkana*

Red River Books, sponsored by
Texas A&M University–Texarkana
*Doris Davis, General Editor*

# The Ahern Home of Texarkana

Doris Douglas Davis

TEXAS A&M UNIVERSITY PRESS
COLLEGE STATION

Copyright © 2024 by Doris Douglas Davis
All rights reserved
First edition

∞ This paper meets the requirements of ANSI/NISO Z39.48-1992 (Permanence of Paper). Binding materials have been chosen for durability.

Library of Congress Cataloging-in-Publication Data

Names: Davis, Doris Douglas, 1946– author. | Cutrer, Thomas W., writer of foreword.
Title: The Ahern home of Texarkana / Doris Douglas Davis.
Other titles: Red River Valley books.
Description: First edition. | College Station : Texas A&M University Press, [2024] | Series: Red River Valley books | Includes bibliographical references and index.
Identifiers: LCCN 2024000350 | ISBN 9781648431982 (cloth) | ISBN 9781648431999 (ebook)
Subjects: LCSH: Ahern, Patrick Joseph, 1861–1932—Homes and haunts—Arkansas—Texarkana. | Mansions—Arkansas—Texarkana—History—20th century. | Owner-built houses—Arkansas—Texarkana—History—20th century. | Housing, Single family—Arkansas—Texarkana—History—20th century. | Architecture, Classical—Conservation and restoration—Arkansas—Texarkana. | Material culture—Arkansas—Texarkana. | Texarkana (Ark.)—Buildings, structures, etc. | Texarkana (Ark.)—Social life and customs—20th century. | BISAC: ARCHITECTURE / Historic Preservation / General | ARCHITECTURE / History / Modern (late 19th Century to 1945)
Classification: LCC F419.T49 D38 2024 | DDC 976.7/560904—dc23/eng/20240109
LC record available at https://lccn.loc.gov/2024000350

A list of titles in this series is available at the end of the book.

*Book Design by Kristie Lee*

*To my parents:*

William Harold Douglas
(1903–1968)

and

Florence Rachel Green Douglas
(1905–1990)

# Contents

Foreword, by Thomas W. Cutrer . . . . . . . . . . . . . . . . . . . . . . . . . . . ix

Preface . . . . . . . . . . . . . . . . . . . . . . . . . . . . . . . . . . . . . . . . . . . . . . . xv

Acknowledgments . . . . . . . . . . . . . . . . . . . . . . . . . . . . . . . . . . . . xix

**Chapter 1**
The Legacy of Patrick Joseph Ahern and Mary Olive Lansdale. . . . . . . 1

**Chapter 2**
Domestics in the Ahern Home. . . . . . . . . . . . . . . . . . . . . . . . . . . . . 43

**Chapter 3**
The Architecture of the Ahern Home . . . . . . . . . . . . . . . . . . . . . . . 54

**Chapter 4**
The Aherns' World of Print Culture and the
Turn-of-the-Century Home Library . . . . . . . . . . . . . . . . . . . . . . . 69

**Chapter 5**
Searching for the Fashionable in Early Texarkana:
Women's Clothing in Public and Private Spaces . . . . . . . . . . . . . . . . . 107

**Chapter 6**
The Music Room: A Space for Family and Song . . . . . . . . . . . . . 133

**Chapter 7**
The Nature of Privacy: Bedrooms and Beyond . . . . . . . . . . . . . . . 161

**Chapter 8**
Dining in Early Twentieth-Century Arkansas:
From Garden to Kitchen. . . . . . . . . . . . . . . . . . . . . . . . . . . . . . . . . 171

Conclusion .................................................. 183

Appendix: Ahern House Floor Plan
and Ahern–Lansdale Family Tree ............................ 187

Notes ....................................................... 193

Sources...................................................... 219

Index ....................................................... 233

# Foreword

Patrick J. and Mary Olive Ahern's grandson Brian Horrigan recollected the hours that he spent in his grandparents' library, perusing old etiquette books with their advice on how the young gentleman should deport himself in various social settings. Those books are "a window into the past," he said, which is "really . . . a different country."

*The Ahern Home of Texarkana* vividly recreates the domestic history of a small Southern town in the first half of the twentieth century through the lens of a particular family dwelling, the P. J. Ahern house, built in the Classical Revival style in the "Quality Hill" neighborhood of Texarkana, Arkansas, in 1905. It is now listed in the National Register of Historic Places and has become a showpiece of the Texarkana Museums System. This home preserves in concrete form glimpses of a way of life that has otherwise all but disappeared.

Texarkana, at the time the Ahern family built their new home, was a thriving young town, and, although only some thirty years old, it was located at the nexus of several railroads and was known as "the Gateway to the Southwest." Patrick Joseph Ahern, an immigrant from the Irish town of Dungarvan, and his bride, the former Mary Olive Lansdale, the daughter of a large upper-middle-class Catholic family from Washington, DC, moved to the new railroad town with great expectations. While Patrick Ahern had arrived around 1884 and had already helped establish the profitable O'Dwyer & Ahern Dry Goods Company, Mary Olive Lansdale came almost two decades later. Together they built this remarkable home, where they raised their six children..

In these pages Doris Davis, Regents Professor Emerita of English at Texas A&M University–Texarkana, explores the intersection of architecture, family life, culture, and technology.

This far-ranging book delves into almost every aspect of the domestic life of an upper-middle-class family in the first quarter of the twentieth century, creating a mosaic of art, music, literature, cuisine, couture, indoor plumbing, and the role of servants, and placing the Ahern family firmly into the context of its time and place. Drawing on exhaustive research in the documentary and oral history of the Ahern family and their community, Davis places the house, its furnishings, and its occupants in the context of the historical literature of the era, providing not only a minute description of the home—its architecture, decor, and furnishings—but also full biographical sketches of its occupants and their extended kinship groups and of their place in early twentieth-century America.

A room-by-room study of the Ahern house begins with the larger parlor or music room, which is the first room that a visitor would have entered. It was the setting for the social center of the family, dominated by Mary Ahern's massive Steinway. In this room, used for reading, writing, sewing, and conversation, the furniture was arranged for comfort and conversation, Davis maintains. Not only did it provide space for conviviality but also signified the family's socio-economic status.

Opposite this parlor is a smaller parlor where "the furniture was less comfortable and the north wind belted against the house." There, guests who Mrs. Ahern "didn't expect or want to stay long," as her daughter later revealed, "were always taken." These two rooms—one cozy and welcoming, the other stiff and formal—provide insight into how the Aherns structured their lives as well as their living spaces.

Bedrooms were located upstairs. In addition to the master bedroom were two bright, spacious bedrooms for the boys and for the girls, as well as a nursery that the youngest children shared with a live-in nanny, and a sleeping porch, popular in the pre-air-conditioned South.

Typical of the practice of subdividing a bedroom into a suite of two or more smaller rooms, P. J. and Mary Olive Ahern's bedchamber consisted of an antechamber that served as a sitting room and Mrs. Ahern's bedroom, and opened into a shared bathroom. The two and a half bathrooms in the Ahern house indicate the owners' upper-middle-class status, and the upstairs water closet yet maintains its original plumbing fixtures, boasting a utility closet, a sink, a claw-foot tub, and a toilet. In its day, Davis writes, this facility represented the state of the art in terms of "bathroom hygiene, aesthetics, and convenience."

Abigail Williams, in *The Social Life of Books: Reading Together in the Eighteenth-Century Home*, notes that "how books were used is as important as what's in them," and Davis lavishes an informed and loving chapter on the Ahern library—placing it in the context of the history of both public and private collections in America, and especially of the rural South of the first decade of the twentieth century.

At the end of the nineteenth century, only two or three small public libraries existed in all of Texas, and Texarkana was late in establishing its own library, not seeing one until 1924. The period of 1890 to 1930, however, saw the acme of private book collecting and the home library in America. Davis identifies the home library as "a place of retreat for the man of the house," and P. J. Ahern's collection contained an astonishing five hundred volumes, most of which remain in the Ahern house. These texts represent a vast array of subjects and provide evidence of their owner's intellectual curiosity. About a third of the books are such works of poetry as Alfred, Lord Tennyson's *The Idylls of the King* and Edgar A. Guest's *When Day Is Done,* and novels including William Makepeace Thackeray's *Vanity Fair,* Arnold Bennett's *The Old Wives' Tale,* and Charles Dickens's *Our Mutual Friend.* Such then-recent books that were to become classics of American literature as Edith Wharton's *The House of Mirth,* Willa Cather's *Death Comes for the Archbishop,* and William Dean Howells's *The Rise of Silas Lapham* are also represented on the Aherns' shelves, next to Edward Gibbon's monumental *The Decline and Fall of the Roman Empire.*

Biography, memoir, essays, letters, linguistics and languages, travel and geography, political science, medicine, mathematics, physics, business, and music and the arts are also generously represented, with almost 20 percent of the shelf space being dedicated to religious subjects, reflecting the Aherns' Roman Catholic faith.

In addition to literature and learning, music occupied a central spot in the Ahern home. An Ahern daughter, Ann, for many years gave piano lessons in the family home, and many of the book's anecdotes come from interviews with her former students. Professor Davis, herself a highly accomplished pianist, seems to take special delight in contextualizing the music room within the greater cultural importance of the role of music in America during the years that the Aherns occupied the house on Laurel Street.

Of great importance in the Ahern home was the place of food. The family employed a cook who was responsible for the family meals, but Mrs. Ahern greatly enjoyed baking and was especially well known for her cakes. One of the Ahern house's treasures is a well-used manuscript cookbook, compiled by Mary Olive Ahern herself, which dates from the earliest period of her marriage. In addition to recipes for numerous desserts, the book includes instructions for making breads, soups, vegetable dishes, salads and dressings, and entrees featuring ham, shrimp, cutlets, and spaghetti. In it she also calculated the cost of feeding a family of seven and the number of individual meals that she must prepare per year.

The Ahern kitchen, typical of the period, was located on the ground floor at the rear of the house, adjacent to the dining room and, in addition to the various work stations where food was prepared, gave access to a cool, dry cellar where the fruits of the family's canning efforts were stored, and a butler's pantry that provided storage space for cooking supplies and dishware. All of the Ahern meals were served and eaten in the dining room, a large room with seating for twelve adjacent to the kitchen.

The icebox, which had been introduced into American homes in the 1860s, was replenished by daily deliveries by the iceman. By the 1920s, however, General Electric was marketing an electric refrigerator with a built-in freezer.

Coal stoves made the transition to gas in the 1890s, but, although kitchen maven Christine Frederick wrote in the *Ladies' Home Journal* in the early decades of the twentieth century that "electricity could be the household's 'modern servant,'" the Ahern house never adopted an electric range or oven. The house did boast among its labor-saving devices a mangle, used to wring water from wet laundry and to press sheets, kitchen towels, and tablecloths.

The preservation of summer fruits and vegetables was an annual ritual in most American homes, and granddaughter Eleanor recalled "all of the burners going at once on the gas stove" during canning season. The Aherns had a large truck garden for squash, okra, tomatoes, beans, peppers, onions, and garlic, and the canning process consumed several days each autumn.

In addition to vegetables, much of the Ahern yard was dedicated to landscaping, growing such annuals as lilies, zinnias, marigolds, sunflowers, and yarrow, and flowering bushes such as roses, hydrangeas, and gardenias. One venerable fig tree survives from the days in which the Aherns were still in residence.

Clothing, especially women's clothing, reflects society's ever-changing sense of feminine beauty and represents a woman's personal taste, sense of style, and economic status, ranging from haute couture to everyday work costume. The Ahern house still displays four articles of its former mistress's wardrobe, which, in 1905, would have included morning dresses, carriage dresses, walking suits, evening dresses, and traveling dresses. Although her going away dress no longer exists, Davis cites an article in the *Washington Post* from 1904, giving a minute description of Mary Olive Lansdale's bridal attire—a gown of "white silk Brussels net, over ivory taffeta," with her face set off by a "large white picture hat," and accented by a "diamond crescent"—and her trousseau, which included her "going-away gown" of blue broadcloth with a "two-toned hat to match."

For more affluent consumers, dresses, hosiery, and the obligatory hats might have been purchased in such entrepots as New Orleans, New York, or even Paris or made to order by local dressmakers, seamstresses, modistes, and milliners. For those of lesser means, clothing could be purchased *prêt-à-porter* from such dry goods stores as O'Dwyer & Ahern, which advised to its shoppers that they could "buy garments of remarkable quality and beauty in the most popular models, ready to wear, at less than the cost of materials." Or—with the founding of Montgomery Ward in 1872, whose catalog helped to democratize American sartorial standards—ordering clothing by mail became increasingly common. But even well-to-do young ladies were trained in the art of needlework and were responsible for the production of much of their own clothing.

Davis also charts the kaleidoscopic changes in fashion that occurred between 1900 and 1950, offering fascinating glimpses into how such elements of style as cut, skirt lengths, fabric, and color evolved in the first decades of the twentieth century and how those fashions were marketed to the American consumer. In the 1920s, for example, as well as shorter skirts and less restrictive undergarments, women began to wear makeup—"powder, lipstick, rouge, eyebrow pencil, eye shadow and foundation cream" without fear of creating scandal or branding themselves as "painted women."

In the end, Davis's book offers an expertly guided tour through a bygone era with its seemingly primitive technology, its changing fashions, its arcane standards of decorum, and its evolving social customs. History is truly, as Patrick and Mary Ahern's grandson observed, "a different country."

—Thomas W. Cutrer

# Preface

In 1905, with Pres. Theodore Roosevelt in the White House, the Penn Railroad debuted the fastest train in the world, zipping from New York to Chicago in 18 hours. By then much of the nation's railway system was intact as well, tying the country together in important ways and opening sections of the nation to new development. In 1905, in Texarkana, Arkansas, one of the countless towns the railway system initiated, Patrick Joseph Ahern and his bride, Mary Olive Ahern, broke ground for their new residence, a spacious house built in the Classical Revival style, one that would fit in magnificently in the neighborhood, in an era of building large homes.

Mary Olive was a young woman from Washington, DC, with noticeably beautiful auburn hair and the mathematical skills of a computer. Patrick was an older man, honed by the hardships of a boyhood in Ireland and the toils of helping create the best dry goods store in town. Both were Roman Catholic; she loved beautiful things and he hated anything cheap. Together they built a house that has weathered the era of Urban Renewal, those decades of tearing down stately structures to make way for progress, often in the form of ephemeral fast-food businesses and the like. Built solidly and reflecting the love Patrick had for his young bride, the house stands today as a reminder of the gracious way of life possible for the upper middle class in early twentieth-century Texarkana, Arkansas.

Labeling itself the "Gateway to the Southwest," Texarkana may be best known today as the birthplace of Scott Joplin and Ross Perot. Divided down its middle by the Arkansas–Texas state line, it actually consists of two cities sharing only a municipal water and sewerage system, a library, and an airport. With separate mayors, police departments, schools, garbage collections, and convention centers, the city has struggled with its bifurcated origins. Without a town square, the old downtown follows the railroad lines and labors to redefine itself as an arts center, while the business part of the city clings to Interstate 30. Too often the downtown seems forlorn, belying the energy, beauty, and wealth of earlier periods.

A few substantial homes built during the turn of the century remain as evidence of the personal fortunes that allowed the construction of such costly structures. With wealth often made in the lumber industry, pioneering citizens took pride in their expensive homes and in the large and ornate churches they were able to build. Pictures of these earlier homes reveal bucolic scenes of flowering trees, well-kept gardens, and a variety of architectural styles, including that of the Ahern home.

I first toured this home sometime after the Texarkana Museums System began operating the house in 2011. Soon I became enamored with the style of the house, the artifacts of the wedding trousseau on display in Mrs. Ahern's bedroom, and the fact that she had insisted on having a Steinway piano in the music room. Also intriguing, the library contains most of the Aherns' books. Many with beautiful covers and colorful endpapers, the volumes possess the intrinsic lure of old books and attract the senses of any bibliophile. I am among those seduced by the attractions of this house and its history.

This book originated in that attraction and in the early encouragement from Dr. Emily Cutrer, President, Emerita of TAMU–Texarkana and a Professor of American Studies. Jamie Simmons, Curator of the Texarkana Museums System, graciously answered questions whenever possible. With the help of my husband, Robert Davis, who served as researcher of much of the material and as a reader of various drafts, I have completed *The Ahern Home of Texarkana*. The book focuses in part on the house itself, but also on the Ahern family wherever information was available. I have been able to interview a few people who knew or knew of Mr. and Mrs. Ahern and many others who knew their children, and I have profited from the unpublished history that Brian Horrigan, an Ahern grandson, has written about the Ahern clan. I have also been helped by extensive conversations with two other family members— Eleanor Horrigan Purcell, an Ahern granddaughter who lived in the house, and Dr. Frank Loda, a great-nephew who grew up next door. I have been hampered by the lack of any other family records, letters, or diaries. The only record I have seen is a small collection of recipes and notes, probably in Mrs. Ahern's handwriting, dating from about the second decade of the twentieth century.

# PREFACE

This book is in part a panegyric to a fine, pioneering family, to their way of life, their interests and activities as a family, and their contributions to Texarkana. In writing it, I am claiming not only an appreciation for the Aherns and their home, but also for the material culture left within the house—books, furniture, music, clothing, and other artifacts of early twentieth-century life. I have followed my own interests and instincts in writing the text with the aim of acknowledging what seemed to me to be what was good and true about the Aherns' way of existence. The discussions in each chapter are also informed by period theorists as well as modern critics of material culture studies.

The professional academic may find little that is new in these pages, but I hope the layperson, like myself, will discover useful information. My overriding research question has been how an upper-middle-class family was able to construct their way of life in an isolated area in early twentieth-century America. In essence, then, the book has a dual focus: the Aherns and their home and way of life in rural Arkansas and Texas.

Texarkana has had a number of texts written about its history, such as Barbara Overton Chandler and J. Ed Howe's 1939 *History of Texarkana and Bowie and Miller Counties*, William D. Leet's 1982 *Texarkana: A Pictorial History*, and Beverly Rowe's 2009 *Historic Texarkana: An Illustrated History* among other of her books. To my knowledge, however, no one has written about a particular house and the family who lived in it in Texarkana. The Ahern house is unique in that it is a single-owner property and remains almost as it was when completed in 1906.

Over forty years ago, Texarkana, Arkansas, City Director Margaret Dickey warned of taking historic structures for granted. With a keen interest in preserving city landmarks, in 1978 she selected the 400 block of Laurel—the block of the Ahern house—as one of the city's finest. "We have got to be aware," she said, "that this is one of the few neighborhoods left with large trees and fine homes."[1] The author of the accompanying article conveyed the street's appeal: "Ivy covered walls run the length of the 400 block . . . [with ivy] trailing up the trunks of nearby trees. Saplings planted 80 years ago by proud new homeowners now look down on Laurel's houses."[2] Of the five residences with large trees that made up this block of Laurel in 1978, only two houses remain—those built and lived in by the sisters from Washington, DC—Mary Ahern and Ella Kline. This book tells the story of the Ahern family.

# Acknowledgments

A book of this kind relies greatly on the help of numerous individuals whose knowledge, expertise, and generosity made this work possible. Foremost, I am grateful to the Texarkana Museums System for the use of their research holdings and facilities. Board President Velvet Hall Cool offered unconditional support as did TMS Curator Jamie Simmons, who gave graciously of her time, expertise, and understanding. She provided a wealth of information and brought many pertinent photographs to my attention. Her 2004–2005 interview of the late Eleanor Ahern Horrigan, the Aherns' youngest daughter, began my investigation of this remarkable family. The Board President and Curator also provided a reading of this manuscript in its early stages.

The extended Ahern–Horrigan family offered invaluable help. Eleanor Horrigan Purcell, daughter of the late Col. William K. and Eleanor Ahern Horrigan, kindly gave her time to several phone interviews during 2018. As the only Ahern grandchild to have lived in the Ahern home, she provided insight concerning the house and her grandmother, Mary Olive Ahern. She graciously introduced me to her brothers Brian and Patrick Horrigan, who also provided information. Brian Horrigan's unpublished manuscript on the Ahern family helped clarify my understanding of his grandparents' lives. Both he and Patrick read the manuscript in various stages, offering factual corrections and information. Their first cousins Cathy Ahern and Maureen Ahern Leahigh, John and Elinor Aherns' daughters, suggested more nuanced renderings of some material and provided a close reading of various iterations of the text. Maureen constructed an Ahern family tree for clarification. A family filled with Marys, Patricks, and Eleanors, demands a visual representation. I am also appreciative of the many family pictures shared by Catherine Purcell, great-granddaughter of Mary Olive and Patrick Ahern.

An additional reader of this manuscript Rachel Gunter, a professor of history at Collin College, offered numerous helpful suggestions concerning the text. Also, Thomas Cutrer, Emeritus Professor of History at Arizona State University, read and wrote about the text.

I am also appreciative of the staff at St. Edward Catholic Church for their help early on in my understanding of the important role the Aherns played in the church. Michael Naples, Director of Maintenance, provided facts as did Sister Miriam Miller. Also early on Pat Thomas, a graduate of Providence Academy, allowed me to use his yearbook and gave willingly of his time. The late Dr. Frank Loda, Mary Olive Ahern's great-nephew, offered additional information. I am also indebted to Susan Shaddox, Interior Design Consultant for Main Street Arkansas, who drew the house plans.

A chapter focused on the music that enveloped this house for decades would have been incomplete without comments from the piano students and musical friends of the Aherns' daughter Ann. They include Sandra Robertson Albright, Jana Atchinson Alexander, Teresa Howard Culling, Nona Culpepper, Jane Raffaelli Daines, Mary Ellen O'Dwyer Forte, Remica Gray, Marie Columbus Hagen, Delfina McGee Mays, Ann Atchinson Nicholas, and Judith Wright. Rosie Sanderson, Mary Ellen Forte, and Beverly Rowe, Professor of History at Texarkana College, provided details about fashion in early Texarkana. I am indebted also to Professor Rowe for her several books on Texarkana history and to Barbara Overton Chandler and J. Ed Howe's 1939 compilation of historical facts about Texarkana and Bowie and Miller counties. Additionally, J. T. Smith provided general information about the Aherns as did others whose names don't appear here.

I am appreciative of the librarians at Texas A&M University–Texarkana, in particular to former Director Teri Stover, for their willing support of this book and their help in procuring research materials. Finally, I appreciate the encouragement I received from Dr. Emily Cutrer, President, Emerita of Texas A&M University–Texarkana, and from my colleagues at the University.

I am grateful to my family who encouraged this work and especially to my husband Robert Davis, who gave much time to providing information and reading numerous drafts of the manuscript. Although I received help from many, any mistakes in the text are, of course, my own.

*The Ahern Home of Texarkana*

# 1

# The Legacy of Patrick Joseph Ahern and Mary Olive Lansdale

*Well, are you going to marry me or not?*

—P. J. Ahern to Mary Lansdale,[1] 1904

Patrick Ahern left southeast Ireland around 1881 at age twenty-one, the blue-eyed son of a farmer. He had been born on March 16, 1861, in the small coastal town of Dungarvan, in County Waterford. The town lies at the mouth of the Colligan River, which separates it into two parishes—Dungarvan on the west and Abbeyside on the east. A single-span bridge, built in the late 1700s by Lord Devonshire, links the two as does an old railroad bridge. Overlooking the bay stands the ruins of what must have once been an impressive turreted castle, commissioned by King John of England in the twelfth century.[2]

Patrick left behind his father, also named Patrick, born in 1811, and his mother, Anna, some eleven years younger, along with at least three siblings, Mary, Anna, and Johanna. He likely never saw his parents again, who died a few years after he left. Whether he ever saw his sisters again is unclear. They eventually emigrated to America, settling in Massachusetts, evidently not tempted to test their fate in the uncertainties of rural nineteenth-century Arkansas.[3] Such separation and longing as experienced by countless emigrants of the day gave rise to the wealth of popular Irish songs that became part of the canon of Irish American love songs and laments, such as "Danny Boy" and "My Wild Irish Rose," and provided much of the atmosphere in Irish literature, such as in James Joyce's poignant story "The Dead," the concluding narrative of *The Dubliners*, published in 1914.

But Patrick Ahern was a determined and an ambitious young man, and although his heart may have been conflicted at this separation, his mind directed him elsewhere as did the beckoning of his boyhood friend Roger Joseph O'Dwyer. Two years younger than Patrick and born in Tipperary, Ireland, O'Dwyer moved to Dungarvan sometime in his youth. Patrick attended St. Joseph's school, directed by the Christian Brothers, where he probably knew O'Dwyer. The school's principal Franic Brenan had worked in business before he joined the Christian Brothers and may well have encouraged both Patrick and Roger to consider the retail trade.[4] Whatever the details of their relationship and influence, a few things are certain. Both young men wanted to improve their lives and decided to pursue a livelihood through the promise of the mercantile business. And both joined thousands of other Irish emigrants who began leaving Ireland, even before the mass exodus of the famine of 1842 to 1845, and continued to do so throughout the century.

Whereas Roger O'Dwyer first settled in New York, Patrick Ahern made his way to London where he studied the retail trade, biding his time until he heard from his friend. O'Dwyer soon migrated south, first to Little Rock, Arkansas, working at the Quinn Dry Goods store, and then in 1883 to Texarkana, Arkansas, where he went into the dry goods business with J. J. O'Reilly at 204 East Broad. Within a year's time, Patrick Ahern journeyed to Texarkana and entered the O'Dwyer–O'Reilly business. When O'Reilly withdrew, Patrick became a partner in 1884 with his longtime friend, the two of them renaming the store O'Dwyer & Ahern Dry Goods Company.[5] Whether their circuitous journey had been planned in Dungarvan or evolved of its own accord, they would spend the next forty years or so living in the same town, going to the same church, and sharing the same friends. Roger had determined a retail establishment could thrive in Texarkana, persuaded his friend to believe so too, and together they made it happen.

## Early Texarkana

When Patrick Ahern arrived in Texarkana in 1884, he found a bustling young town, some ten years old, loud and boisterous, one eager to flex its muscles and humming with potential. Although the Civil War had reduced much of the South to rubble and had ended not quite twenty years earlier, the conflict had not devastated the area as it had done elsewhere where land had been gutted and properties destroyed. Granted, nearby cities of Jefferson and Marshall, Texas, had functioned as supply centers for the Confederate army and Washington and Rondo, Arkansas, served to drill and prepare men for battle, still the area escaped the battle-scarring destruction of being a site of war.[6]

Although settlers had long ago come to the areas of Bowie and Miller Counties, the creation of the national railroad system was the catalyst that brought the city of Texarkana into existence. In the late 1850s, the Cairo & Fulton Railroad inched steadily across Arkansas. By 1857, the Memphis, El Paso, and Pacific Railroad had reached the Texarkana area, but the Civil War halted the progress of the rails until the 1870s. In 1873, word spread of the imminent sale of lots where the Texas and Pacific and the Cairo & Fulton met on the line between Texas and Arkansas. Eager buyers appeared to stake out claims, and the following year, 1874, Texarkana, Texas, was incorporated as a city.[7] By way of endorsement, in January 1875, Texarkana's *Gate City News* rendered an enthusiastic promotion of the fledgling town:

> This being the shortest route from the North and East into Texas, Texarkana is the natural inlet for trade and commerce, and offers inducements that are unsurpassed for business houses of all branches of trades. Located here, with facilities for shipment to all points of Texas and Louisiana, merchants will control the trade of a very large section of country.[8]

Although O'Dwyer and Ahern were just boys in Ireland when the newspaper promoted the area, the two young men soon joined others to prove the accuracy of the statement. The following decades held great promise for some.

## The O'Dwyer & Ahern Dry Goods Company

The new business grew rapidly, thriving on the energy that Patrick Ahern added to the business enterprise begun by Roger O'Dwyer. Within three years, the firm moved to a new location, 110 and 112 East Broad Street, a three-story brick building with a basement. The additional space, the excellent location, and the prestige of brick helped ensure the company's financial success. After the costly fire of 1885, in which an entire block burned, the city required that any new construction be of brick instead of lumber.[9]

The firm soon became one of the most prestigious businesses in the area, earning a reputation for quality merchandise and reliable service. Consisting of both retail and wholesale trade, the store stocked men's, women's, and children's clothing and shoes. Additionally, the business included millinery, linen, sewing materials, and a fine china department. The dry goods business ran ads often, proclaiming the quality of the merchandise and the reasonable costs. Smart shoppers shop at this store, the ads implied. Later, O'Dwyer and Ahern opened a second store at 413 East Broad Street that focused on the needs of area farmers and housed less upscale merchandise. Both businesses prospered. The firm that started in 1885 remained intact for nearly fifty years.

## A Bride Comes to Texarkana: Mary Olive Lansdale

When Roger O'Dwyer encouraged Patrick to emigrate to Texarkana, he reportedly told him, "Don't bring a woman, there's plenty of them here."[10] Roger, on the other hand, had already secured a wife, marrying Bridget Mary Quillinan in 1885 in Chicago; she was also a native of Tipperary, Ireland.[11] Although Patrick finally did meet his future wife, Mary Olive Lansdale, in Texarkana, it was not until 1896, and they didn't marry until some eight years later. Mary Olive seems to have taken her time in weighing the merits of Patrick's proposal.

She came from an old Maryland family, and he was an Irish immigrant. In addition, he was forty-three and she just twenty-six, and by all accounts quite beautiful. In all, Patrick reportedly made seven trips to Washington, DC, to woo his would-be bride, and according to a family story, he finally exclaimed, "Well, are you going to marry me or not?"[12] In 1904, she finally decided in the affirmative. The wedding took place at St. Aloysius Church in Washington, DC, with a nuptial Mass. It was the same church in which Mary's parents had been married. According to friends and family, Patrick doted on his young wife, taking her to Niagara Falls for their honeymoon and giving her as a wedding present the grand house they would build together in Texarkana, Arkansas, at 403 Laurel Street.[13]

When Mary Olive first visited Texarkana, she came to see her older sister Mary Ellen Lansdale Kline, born in 1868 and called Ella by her family.[14] The two sisters had been born in Washington, DC, Mary Olive in 1877, into a large upper-middle-class family. It was a close family and understandably the sisters would want to spend time together. They also had five brothers, William, John, George, Walter, and Francis (born 1866, 1873, 1880, 1882, and 1888, respectively), and two other sisters—Catherine, born in 1866 (William's twin), and Annie, born in 1875, all hailing from DC. Their father, John Wesley Lansdale, was a financially successful builder and listed the value of his real estate and personal estate at $2,000 and $300, respectively, in the 1870 census. He could trace his family in Maryland back to the 1600s. Their mother, Mary Ellen Joy, claimed an "old" family on her father's side and a mother born in Scotland.

The Lansdale family ensured that their children had a good education, with all the girls going to "finishing" school after high school. With her studies completed, their second oldest daughter, Ella Lansdale, worked in the patent office in Washington, DC. It was there she met her future husband, John Peter Kline, the owner of a bakery in Texarkana and a future mayor. An amateur inventor, he had come to Washington to patent some of his ideas. When Peter and Ella married in 1892 and were on their way to Texarkana on the train, Ella supposedly looked out the window and said how poor all the people looked in the South. Kline reminded her to be careful about what she said because this was the Southerners' home and the people had had such a "hard time."[15] An emigrant from Luxembourg, Kline had come to Texarkana in 1879 and soon became one of the city's most prominent citizens, serving in many roles, including as director of the Merchants and Planters Bank for twenty-five years.[16]

When she first came to Texarkana, Mary Olive enjoyed time with her sister and decided that she, as her sister had done, would secure employment. Always a whiz in math, she became a bookkeeper at the most prominent dry goods store in town, O'Dwyer and Ahern. Years later, her granddaughter Eleanor remembered how her grandmother Mary Olive—or Mamie, as she called her—could add up a column of double- and triple-digit numbers in her head. "She was like a computer," Eleanor said. "I was always in awe of her." Eleanor remembered playing under the table as a child while her grandmother focused on family finances. "Mamie worked over columns of numbers with amazing speed," she added.[17] Mamie's daughter Eleanor said her ability in math was "beyond comprehension."[18] A talent for math ran in Mary Olive and Patrick's children, as two of them became accountants and a third specialized in tax law.

It was not long before Patrick Ahern noticed the young woman with the beautiful hair and a head for figures working in his store. In fact, he may have hired her. At any rate, Mary Olive was known for her beauty and personal charm. With long, reddish brown hair, a flair for wearing attractive clothing, and a lovely alto singing voice, she must have caught his eye early on. Several years later when they had first married and were living in a hotel in Texarkana while their house was being built, Patrick grew concerned about all of the men in the hotel who spent an inordinate amount of time trying to get acquainted with his pretty bride—so much so that Patrick decided to buy a small house near the construction site of his large house to ensure that hotel dwellers and those traveling through would not be staring at his young wife.[19]

## The Patrick and Mary Ahern Family

All the Ahern children were born in Patrick and Mary's new home except for the first, Joseph Patrick, born September 7, 1905. Their large, two-story house was not completed until 1906, as marked by Patrick himself in the porch's concrete on the left side. The Aherns wanted the home spacious enough to provide for a large family, and they weren't disappointed, in house or family. Mary Cecilia was born November 27, 1907; Ann Agnes, January 16, 1910; and the twins, John William and Catherine Elizabeth, born July 20, 1912. Finally, five years later on April 22, 1917, their last child, and by many admirers' opinion, the most beautiful, Eleanor Gertrude Ahern was born. The years prior to World War I were among the happiest for the family. As Patrick's business interests grew more lucrative, he became one of the city's largest property owners. Additionally, the city fathers credited him with helping Texarkana develop from a small village into the city it became. Although he focused largely on his mercantile concerns, he was also instrumental in helping other entities develop. These included Texarkana National Bank, Texas Cotton Oil Company, Miller Land and Improvement Company, and the Southern Furniture Company, among others.[20] As a prominent citizen, Patrick was proud of his success, his family, and his home.

Although Patrick Ahern had left Ireland to make a better life for himself, he returned there several times, including 1900 and 1907. During one of those trips, he placed gravestones at his parents' graves. He also had not forgotten the education he received from the Irish Christian Brothers at St. Joseph's school and gave them money throughout his life.[21]

In designing his residence, Patrick Ahern had initially purchased three lots in the 400 block of Laurel with the intention of centering his home on the middle lot. Mary Olive, however, wanted her sister Ella close to her. At that time, Peter and Ella Kline lived at 215 Elm Street (known later as Wood Street). While the distance was only about a quarter of a mile, in inclement weather and attendant muddy roads the sisters would not be able to see each other conveniently. Patrick offered Peter one of his lots to build a house on, and Patrick kept the middle and end lots. The Klines' house in fact was finished before the Aherns'. The two sisters loved living next to each other. Many years later, Ella's grandson Frank Loda recalled how close the houses were to each other with something like an "elastic" property line. He used to stand in the Klines' backyard and talk with his cousins and others through the Aherns' kitchen window.[22]

The Ahern children enjoyed living in such a large house. The youngest child, Eleanor, recalled playing there. "I can remember skating up and down the hallways," she said, although her mother was always concerned about the woodwork. Holidays were especially fun for the family, particularly Christmas. The children looked out the window to watch for the "wagon with the Christmas tree." "Oh, mama, here is the tree," one of them would yell to her. A couple of the men working at the O'Dwyer and Ahern store typically helped their boss put up the tree, always a huge one that stood in the spacious music room. And the decorations under the tree were unusual. Mrs. Ahern placed cotton under the tree to resemble snow. Within the snow rested a herd of delicate porcelain sheep and several porcelain watchdogs. The children loved looking at the bucolic scene. It seemed "wonderful," Eleanor said. "Mother always did her own decorations." Mrs. Ahern placed greenery on top of all the mantels. "Mother and daddy both enjoyed the Christmas season," Eleanor said. The family always went to midnight Mass on Christmas Eve. On Christmas morning, the music room doors were opened, revealing for the first time to the children the Christmas tree sparkling with lights and fully decorated. They opened their presents sitting around the tree. That morning they always had a Christmas breakfast and a big turkey later for Christmas dinner. "Mother made her own dressing with a special recipe," Eleanor remembered.

Another holiday the family enjoyed for years was Halloween. The priest at Saint Edward Catholic Church loved trying to guess the identity of the children dressed in their costumes. He entered into the fun by disguising himself as a ghost hung with chains. The children squealed while he clanged through the house looking for them in their hiding places. The mothers from Providence Academy came to help Mrs. Ahern with party affairs. They had taffy pulls, stretching the candy one way and then another until it was firm. The children bobbed for apples on the back porch, and apples also hung from strings wrapped around the door transoms. The children tried to catch an apple without using their hands. "We never went trick-or-treating in those days," Eleanor explained. The most fun was in fooling the priest. They all wore masks, and Eleanor was often dressed as a gypsy.[23]

The family also had a good time playing with their dog, a German Shepherd named Bob. He came to Arkansas fully grown as a gift from relatives in Washington, DC, brought on the train by John after he had finished his first year at Georgetown University.[24] Instead of growing accustomed to trains, Bob remained fearful of them for the rest of his life. That must have been difficult, as Texarkana had many trains coming through at all hours of day and night, and 403 Laurel Street was close to the railroad yard. Once one of the children decided to see how Bob would look as a lion and attempted to shave him accordingly. No picture seems to have survived of the lionized Bob, but one can imagine he didn't much appreciate his new look. Bob was also very fond of Patrick Ahern, and after Patrick died, he refused to enter his room.[25]

The Ahern children enjoyed living next door to their Uncle Peter and Aunt Ella, who had four children: Cyril born in 1893, Olive born in 1896, Vivian born in 1899 but dying as an infant, and Muriel born in 1905, who was only a few months older than Joe Ahern. The two families often shared meals and activities. Later, after Muriel married Frank Loda, the couple moved into the Kline house. After Peter Kline died in the early 1930s, Aunt Ella lived upstairs in the house with her own cooking and bathing facilities, and Muriel and her husband lived downstairs. Their son, often called Little Frank by the family, had many fond memories of the two families visiting throughout the years. Aunt Ella loved to bake, and the Ahern children sometimes went across the way to get something sweet to eat. In later years, the "Kline" house became the "Loda" house. Eleanor's children also recall visiting the Loda house. The many times they returned to Texarkana with their mother to visit, they always saw Muriel and Big Frank, who took them fishing and invited them over to see the fish in his backyard pond. [26]

Eleanor Ahern remembered her parents dressing up for the fiftieth anniversary of the town. Her mother wore a hoop skirt, and her father wore "tails." Her parents dressed up too for the opera house. Eleanor recalled thinking her mother looked beautiful. "And what pretty hair she had," Eleanor said. Her mother would sometimes let her help brush her hair. Eleanor brushed her mother's curls and helped her pull her long hair back and up for special occasions.

Eleanor remembered the house as a busy place where meals were a time for gathering. When one of the children celebrated a birthday they could choose the kind of cake they wanted as well as the menu for dinner that evening. Eleanor's favorite was chocolate cake and she loved her mother's recipe for it. The family had all their meals, including breakfast, in the dining room. Often there were guests eating with them, which made everything seem more festive. Eleanor remembered her parents as being quiet and kind individuals. Her mother was always giving handouts to anyone who needed food. Years later, after Mrs. Ahern was a widow, there remained a sense of goodness about the house. "Everyone in the area knew that Mrs. Ahern always gave out food at the backdoor," one commentator remembered. "There was such a feeling of good will that no one would ever harm those in the house as they grew older and more vulnerable to harm."[27]

A misfortune that struck this young family in these early years occurred around 1913 when little Ann, or Annie, as she was often called, suddenly grew ill. Only minutes earlier she had been playing in the house, running through the library. Suddenly, she fell on the floor and called to her mother frantically as her legs wouldn't support her. Mrs. Ahern immediately quarantined her from the other children since she had no idea what was wrong. When she didn't improve within a few days, they took her to New Orleans to see a specialist and were shocked to learn she had polio. Although the disease had existed for centuries, the first major polio epidemic in the United States didn't occur until 1894, with a larger outbreak in New York in 1916.[28] With polio being one of the most feared diseases in the country, the Aherns were understandably overcome in trying to care for Ann, whose prognosis was uncertain. Being faithful Catholics, they took her to a religious shrine for prayers and prayed themselves for her recovery. For many months, Mr. Ahern carried tiny Annie around the house and especially up the stairs to her room. Mrs. Ahern always thought that Ann had contracted the disease from a playmate who lived a few houses down from them on Laurel Street. Periodically Ann needed to visit the Ochsner Clinic in New Orleans for treatment of her polio.[29] Ann, however, became a resilient individual perhaps because of this tragedy, determined that polio would not define her as a person. She wore braces with special shoes and later had a car designed for her to drive with all controls on the steering wheel. She developed a successful career as a teacher and traveled wherever she pleased.

## The Aherns and the Michael Meagher Hospital

Patrick Ahern played a major role in bringing the Sisters of Charity of the Incarnate Word to Texarkana to establish and oversee the Michael Meagher Memorial Hospital. Another native of Ireland, Michael Meagher was a civil engineer and philanthropist who "witnessed the founding of Texarkana." He surveyed the Fulton and Cairo railroad and other areas of commerce in early Texarkana.[30] When Meagher died tragically in 1909, reportedly murdered in San Antonio, Texas,[31] Patrick Ahern, along with a board of other businessmen, became responsible for overseeing the provisions of Meagher's will. Always a charitable and unassuming man, Meagher had accrued a sizable fortune for the day of $75,000. As executor of the will, Patrick went to Ireland to settle Meagher's estate and had to argue with Irish officials who wanted the money to remain in Ireland. But Mr. Ahern prevailed and obtained the funds that Meagher had designated to provide health care for the indigent.[32]

Mr. Ahern also went to Galveston, Texas, to encourage the Sisters of Charity of the Incarnate Word to establish a hospital in Texarkana. In 1915, Mother Teresa O'Gara, CCVI, and the Council of the Congregation of the Sisters of Charity accepted a proposal from the Board of Trustees of the estate of Michael Meagher "to operate a hospital for indigent sick in Texarkana," Arkansas. In addition to Patrick J. Ahern, the board consisted of other prominent businessmen: F. W. Offenhauser, John P. Kline, Leo Krouse, W. Lee Estes, C. M. Blocker, Dr. J. A. Lightfoot, and Dr. R. L. Grant.[33]

When the Sisters arrived in the city in 1916, the Aherns invited them to stay at 403 Laurel Street while their convent was being built. Although the Sisters' Mother had initially instructed them to stay in the facility under construction for them, after one night of doing so and "hearing people walking in the house" while they tried to sleep, they decided to accept the Aherns' offer of hospitality and safety. The facility under construction lacked a lock on the front door, and hearing traffic in the house at night, the Sisters suspected transients were looking for a place to sleep. At the Aherns, the Sisters slept upstairs on the sleeping porch, and Mrs. Ahern oversaw the preparations of their meals so that the Sisters could eat together. During the day, Mrs. Ahern ensured that their lunches were sent to them while they were working in the hospital. The Ahern children—Mary and John—loved taking the lunch pails of food to the Sisters, in part because they got to ride on the elevators in the hospital. These were a novelty to the children.[34]

The Sisters often walked in the evening and would sometimes join Mr. Ahern sitting on the front porch. One night something potentially tragic happened that deserves mention because it testifies to Mr. Ahern's sense of justice and personal courage. That said, the story is probably apocryphal, as no family members recall having heard this version of it. Supposedly, one evening after dark everyone was still downstairs. Suddenly, all were amazed to realize that members of the Ku Klux Klan were on the front lawn, carrying lighted torches and concealing their identities under white hoods. Anticipating the impetus for the group's gathering, Patrick quickly hid the Sisters in the long hallway leading to the restroom downstairs and went out on the front porch to confront the group.

"What do you mean, coming on my property?" Patrick reportedly shouted to the mob. Just as he'd guessed, they were angry because the Sisters were staying in the house, plus they hated Catholics in general, they yelled. The dozen or so men had fired up each other's bitterness to a potentially dangerous boiling point. It seemed they had come to take the Sisters away or at least to make them leave town.

Tempers flared when Patrick went out on the porch. "All of you know me and know my family," he reasoned. "You know that I have contributed to this town." In short, he talked down the crowd, even calling out some of them by name. Interestingly, he recognized several by the shoes they wore since many had purchased shoes in his store. His somewhat jocular yet stern comments dispersed the crowd, and they left.[35]

Although powerful, this story possesses an inherently dramatic element, reminiscent of such films as *To Kill a Mockingbird*, and for this reason is probably not true. A version of the story that several family members have heard is that the Klan rallied on several occasions, erecting a burning cross, not on the Aherns' front lawn, but across the street in front of Miller County Courthouse. In this version, Mr. Ahern went out on his front porch and glared at the hooded men. With his hand in his pocket, he indicated that he perhaps had a gun. Such a stance on his part took courage, as most citizens would not have confronted Klansmen in this manner.

Both versions of this 1920s story not only underscore the omnipresence of the KKK in those days but also show Mr. Ahern's personal integrity. He was not a large man, but he was willing to confront an angry group to defend the Sisters and his family. The importance of this received narrative lies in its projection of Patrick Ahern as a person of values and courage. That it was passed on by some suggests the sound opinion held by many of this early pioneer of the city. The tale also highlights Mr. Ahern's financial power. With extensive land holdings in addition to ownership of a popular store, he signified the privilege and established wealth that may have intimidated the Klan.

With the help of the Aherns, the Sisters were able to supervise the renovation of the hospital. The trustees of the Meagher estate had purchased a hospital known as the Dale Sanitarium, and it was this building that the Sisters oversaw. The Michael Meagher Hospital originally had ten physicians, one dentist, ten nurses, and six Sisters. It functioned in this building until 1948 when a new hospital was constructed.[36] The two Sisters who stayed with the Ahern family never forgot their kindness. During the great influenza pandemic of World War I, Mrs. Ahern became ill with the flu. Although the hospital was very busy, as the town understandably was in a panic over the outbreak of influenza, one of the Sisters visited Mrs. Ahern once a day to help ensure her recovery.[37]

## The Aherns and Saint Edward Church

Catholic services began early in Texarkana, Texas, with priests initially coming from Galveston, Texas. Catholic archives indicate that the second bishop of Galveston, the Rt. Rev. C. M. Dubuis, D.D., came to the Texarkana region on October 8, 1871. Father Theodore Bufford, a native of France, celebrated the first Mass in a small building where the Hotel McCartney was later constructed. He became the first priest of Sacred Heart Catholic Church, which was completed in 1874 on Spruce Street between West Broad Street and Clinton Street, later renamed West Third Street. This building also housed St. Agnes Academy, supervised by the Sisters of St. Agnes. This church was rebuilt in 1890 on the same site with beautiful stained-glass windows and a magnificent steeple bell.[38] The Aherns may have attended Sacred Heart periodically early on, and their eldest son Joseph went to St. Agnes Academy.

Because the diocese of Little Rock wished to establish a Catholic church in Texarkana, Arkansas, it sanctioned the founding of St. Edward under the Most Rev. Edward Fitzgerald on June 20, 1903. It celebrated its first Mass in the Miller County Courthouse, across the street from where the Aherns would build their home. On December 25, 1903, St. Edward dedicated its first Mass in a frame building constructed at East Fourth and Hickory Streets. St. Edward School opened in 1908, overseen by the Olivetan Benedictine Sisters.[39] A priest especially important to the Ahern family, Father, later Monsignor, Oliver B. Clarendon, arrived in Texarkana from Little Rock on September 23, 1918, to assume the duties of pastor of St. Edward. With the church originally at East Fourth and Hickory, Father Clarendon wanted to construct a more substantial church between East Fourth and Fifth on Beech Street. He raised the funds to add to the lots already purchased by his predecessor, Father Boyle. Mr. Ahern along with others contributed funds to help construct the church. Father Clarendon also established Providence Academy, overseen by the Sisters of Divine Providence from Our Lady of the Lake College in San Antonio. The Ahern children received an excellent education at Providence Academy. In 1924, Father Clarendon established Calvary Cemetery, the Catholic cemetery of Texarkana, Arkansas. Members of the Ahern, Lansdale, and O'Dwyer families are buried there.[40]

The Rt. Rev. John B. Morris, Bishop of Little Rock, dedicated the new St. Edward Church on April 8, 1923. Constructed in a magnificent Romanesque style, with dimensions of 120 feet by 60 feet, the church reflects the dedication of early members and their willingness and ability to provide substantial funds for a lavish building. The music program for the dedication reveals the participation and cooperation of these pioneer families in the church. Mrs. Patrick J. Ahern directed the choir and Mrs. John C. O'Dwyer, Roger O'Dwyer's daughter-in-law, played the organ. Among the choir members listed on the program, five members of the O'Dwyer family appear as well as the names of Mrs. J. P. Kline (Ella Kline, Mrs. Ahern's sister) and Mrs. George Lansdale (Mrs. Ahern's sister-in-law).[41]

The Ahern and Kline families also donated funds for two beautiful stained-glass windows in the nave of the church. One, given by the Kline family, depicts the Nativity of the Blessed Virgin; the other, donated by the Ahern family, reveals the Nativity of Christ. Both windows show the family names below the window. The families also provided funds for memorial windows. One is a memorial to Catherine Ahern; four windows memorialize members of the O'Dwyer family. The beautiful window over the main altar depicting the sacraments was a gift from the O'Dwyer family. The Lansdale family donated an impressive window of Saint Francis.[42] In a long-held family tradition, Mr. Ahern was instrumental in the acquisition of the beautiful Carrara marble altar.[43]

## The Aherns Acquire an Automobile

Mr. Ahern refused to own a car until the 1920s. He purchased a Ford and built the detached garage to house it. Joe's sister Eleanor recalled how much her dad relied on Joe to drive him around to the various farms and investment properties they owned. Mr. Ahern himself never learned to drive. After Joe went off to college, the task fell to Mary to chauffeur her father to the farms.[44] Although her husband never learned to drive, Mrs. Ahern did, and evidently liked to drive rather briskly. Once she was driving and Joe saw her ahead of him on the road. He tried to catch up but couldn't. She made that Model T zip along, although she always fussed at her sons for driving fast.[45]

When Joe was still at home to drive, Eleanor would often want to go, bumping around in the backseat of an open car as they drove through

Miller and Bowie Counties.[46] The roads were not paved in rural areas, and an open car provided a rough ride. "You had to have a light car," Eleanor explained, "and you'd better not get off track or you'd be down in the mud. You'd need someone to help you get out. We'd bring tow sacks and put those on top of the mud for traction. You can't believe the roads," she said, and then repeated, "You can't believe the roads." The car was always open if it wasn't raining. "Branches would brush your face," but Eleanor said she always wanted to go. She enjoyed going down into the bottom lands. Most of the streets were not paved. Eleanor remembered when the pavement went only as far as Ninth Street. When the pavement finally extended to Twentieth, Eleanor said, "Oh, it was nice when it got that far!"[47]

## The Aherns: Prohibition and the 1920s

Although Patrick Ahern had always been something of a teetotaler, he thought that Prohibition was a stupid idea and decided to circumvent it himself. His actions reveal a man with a quirky sense of humor and a penchant for thinking for himself. Before Prohibition went into effect, he bought a large quantity of alcohol, in particular bourbon, from a local liquor store along with many bottles of wine. The new law did not prevent people from drinking what they already had purchased. With his large basement, he had plenty of space to store an inventory of bourbon that he must have thought would last a decade of legislative foolishness. On special occasions, he liked to serve liquor from his inventory to his guests, which must have heightened the merriment of all. In addition, Mrs. Ahern enjoyed spiking the eggnog that she served during the holidays, including that offered to the young men who were studying to be priests.[48]

The eldest son, Joseph, told a family story about Prohibition. When still in college, he and some friends visited Atlantic City, New Jersey, a major resort in the 1920s. In search of something to drink, they asked their cabbie for a recommendation, which he gladly provided, giving them a card on which appeared, what seemed to Joseph, to be Chinese characters. When they couldn't find the place, they showed the card to an Irish policeman on his beat who easily directed them to a "plain door." Inside, a large mirror extended the length of a bar, which in turn covered the entire width of the room. When they asked the bartender for a drink, he said all he had was sarsaparilla. But when Joe presented the card, the bartender's demeanor changed. He promptly pushed a button whereupon the mirror rose revealing a large collection of various types of liquor that had been brought in from a ship outside of the three-mile limit prescribed by law. The young men enjoyed a drink, and had a story to tell for years to come.[49]

A funny family story also developed relating to the Aherns and alcohol. Later in the 1940s Frank Loda, the Aherns' great-nephew, remembered guests being served bourbon and water on several occasions at the Aherns as their typical before-dinner drink. When their youngest daughter Eleanor was on a first date at college in San Antonio with the young man who later became her husband, he asked her what she wanted to drink. "Bourbon and water," she promptly responded as though that was what *anyone* would want to drink. While her future husband thought that was a peculiar drink for a young woman to desire, he complied with her request.[50]

By the 1920s, some of the older Ahern children were ready to attend college. For the boys, the Aherns' first choice was Georgetown University, a four-year Catholic college, while the girls headed to Georgetown Visitation Convent, a two-year college for young women. Since both schools were in Washington DC, close to Mrs. Ahern's family, they had an additional appeal. In 1924, Joseph had his bags packed to return to Georgetown when Mr. Ahern seems to have suffered his first stroke. Joe never returned to college and never completed his degree. Instead, as first-born, he stayed in Texarkana to help his father run the family business. After completing two years at Georgetown Visitation Convent, Mary earned a baccalaureate degree from Trinity College in Washington DC in 1929 and as a single woman began a long and successful career in accounting. John completed a Bachelor of Arts degree in 1933 and remained in Washington to attend Georgetown Law School, where he earned Bachelor of Laws, Master of Laws, and Doctor of Laws degrees. He began what would become a distinguished career as a tax lawyer. And Ann completed a degree in 1930 at Georgetown Visitation Convent; when she returned home, she attended Texarkana College and taught music to generations of Texarkana children. At a time when a large percentage of the populace lacked even a high school diploma, Ann, John, Mary, and Eleanor all held college degrees.

## The Ahern Family Business and the Great Depression

Despite Mr. Ahern's possibly suffering a stroke as early as 1924, he decided in 1925 to buy out the O'Dwyer interest in the dry goods store. His friend Roger O'Dwyer had died in 1924 and with five O'Dwyer sons who might want to be brought into the business, Mr. Ahern thought it better to buy them out. Some of O'Dwyer's sons had already started their own ladies' fashion store, ostensibly in competition with their father's business. Mr. Ahern's decision proved to be a great financial tragedy for him and his family. Instead of selling some of his properties to purchase the O'Dwyer interest, he decided to take out a bank loan, his rationale being that he could reasonably pay back the loan with profits made by the store.[51] What he didn't foresee, nor did most Americans, was the devastation just beyond the horizon.

While historians continue to debate exactly why the stock market crashed in the fall of 1929, the result proved devastating for millions. By 1933, seventy-five percent of American stock securities—about $90 billion—had evaporated.[52] By 1932, unemployment reached an unprecedented twenty-four percent of the labor force.[53] Well-to-do Americans—such as the Aherns—were no longer able to buy expensive furniture, cars, or other luxuries, while less affluent Americans had to cut all unnecessary items from their budget, such as new clothes, shoes, and hats—that is, the bulk of the items that the Aherns' dry goods store sold. The Great Depression affected both their retail and wholesale businesses, sending it into a downward spiral. When the bank loan came due, Mr. Ahern was not able to generate the cash to pay. He attempted to borrow from both local and regional banks, but without success. Even though he was a stockholder in the local bank that held his loan and had had excellent business dealings with them in the past, the bank refused to extend credit and foreclosed on the loan. Whether the foreclosure was one of absolute necessity or prompted by other motives, such as anti-Irish Catholic sentiments, as Mr. Ahern suspected, its decision meant financial ruin for his business.

In short, he lost the store. He also lost much of his extensive land holdings. But his house at 403 Laurel Street was safe because it had always belonged to Mrs. Ahern, given as a present, and was never used for collateral.[54] Mr. Ahern's business belongings were auctioned off on the courthouse lawn across from the house. The Ahern children Mary and Eleanor watched the proceedings from a parked car, and Mrs. Ahern watched through the front windows of the house. Although he had had more strokes by then and was unable to work, Mr. Ahern was cognizant of what was happening.[55] Eleanor later said, "I'll never forget the feeling of seeing our business holdings sold at a public auction. It was awful." The occurrence stayed with her for the rest of her life.[56] Economic loss was a plight common among the populace with many facing far worse conditions, however, than the Aherns, who at least had a home to call their own.

But the era of the Great Depression was difficult for the Aherns for more than just financial loss. It was a period of personal loss. Catherine Ahern, John's twin, had suffered respiratory problems and had had several treatments for tuberculosis. She died in a sanitorium in El Paso, Texas, in January 1931 with Mrs. Ahern by her side. She was only eighteen. It was an unfathomable loss for all of the family. Catherine was a beautiful, young women with many charms. She and twin brother John had been the best of friends, sharing each other's secrets and spending time together. Both loved to dance and often they walked to dances together in the evening. They would split up at a dance and then walk home together. Some family members feared that John might never completely get over Catherine's death. It was an awful blow to all and a loss that Mrs. Ahern talked about to the end of her life. She never really got over losing Catherine.

Death continued to haunt the Aherns. John Peter Kline, the Aherns' brother-in-law who lived next door, died in September of that year. The happy times the Lansdale sisters had shared with each other would never be the same now that Ella was a widow. The next year proved no respite from grief. The Aherns' much beloved priest Monsignor Clarendon of St. Edward Church died in June 1932. He had seemed a member of the family, often joining them for holiday dinners and for informal visits throughout the year. In the evenings, Monsignor Clarendon loved to walk from the church and join Mr. Ahern sitting on the front porch. Bob, the Aherns' dog, liked Monsignor Clarendon a lot. Whenever he saw him coming, he loped across the street to meet him. He would also often escort him back to the rectory.

The Aherns' eldest son, Joseph, or Joe, married Mary Pearle Brannan in January 1932. The union produced two daughters: Mary Pearl, called

Little Mary, born in 1933, and JoAnn, born in 1944. Mary Pearl was the first of the Aherns' grandchildren, but Mr. Ahern did not live long enough to see her.[57] On July 30, 1932, Mr. Ahern died; over the years, he had suffered several strokes, but Catherine's death probably hastened his own. Still grieving for her husband, Mrs. Ahern lost yet another relative that year—Annie Agnes Lansdale Mess, one of her older sisters, died in November.

Mrs. Ahern remained a widow for almost forty years. She continued living in the house that she and her husband had designed, but she wasn't alone. Her daughter Ann, who had returned from Georgetown Visitation Convent in 1930, started classes at Texarkana Junior College and began a long and successful career as a piano teacher, living and teaching in her parents' house for the rest of her life. Despite the personal losses of the Great Depression, the house was filled with music. Eleanor, Mrs. Ahern's youngest daughter, only fifteen when her father died, loved to dance and sing, as did her mother. Mrs. Ahern continued to direct the choir at St. Edward Church, and she organized the church's Altar Society for over half a century.

Mrs. Ahern's mother, Mary Ellen Joy Lansdale, also lived with her during this time. A widow herself since 1907, Mrs. Lansdale chose to spend most of her later years with her daughter Mary Olive and son-in-law Patrick. He was genuinely fond of her and welcomed her to extend her visits for as long as she wanted to stay. Both Mr. Ahern and Mrs. Lansdale valued each other's company and loved to talk with each other. Mrs. Lansdale always relished her heritage of an "old family" in Maryland. Once, years before she came to live with the Aherns, she and Mr. Ahern reportedly had been in a discussion about immigration, with Patrick shoring up his argument in favor of the immigrants. She smiled and supposedly said to him, "In all deference to you, Patrick, the immigrants are of course ruining the country."[58] In retrospect, the irony of her statement is obvious, as she came to depend on her son-in-law, the Irish immigrant, for much of her livelihood in her later days.

## The Aherns: 1940s

Eleanor, the youngest daughter, grew into a beautiful young woman in the 1930s. She had the same good looks that her mother had possessed years ago that made the salesmen turn their heads in the hotel where she and Mr. Ahern had stayed as newlyweds. With beautiful auburn hair, flawless skin, and model good looks, she also possessed the intellect and fortitude that enabled her to graduate as valedictorian from St. Edward's Providence Academy. A contemporary of hers in town said, "We were all just goggled-eyed" about Eleanor. "She was the prettiest thing and also pretty with her ways."[59] Receiving a full scholarship for her freshman year, she elected to attend Our Lady of the Lake College outside of San Antonio, Texas. She may have wanted to break with family tradition at Georgetown and go elsewhere. Or as an independent young woman, she may have wanted to escape the presence of all her Washington, DC, relatives. In addition, Mrs. Ahern probably wasn't financially able to send Eleanor to Georgetown for college. It was the Depression, and money was tight. Eleanor did well at Our Lady of the Lake. After her freshman year, she got a job working in the library as a bookbinder. She rebound books in the school's library as well as texts that the nuns brought her—journals, prayer books, hymnals, and others. During her junior and senior years, Mrs. Ahern paid Eleanor's college expenses with money from oil leases. She graduated in 1939 summa cum laude with a major in history.

Eleanor met her husband in an interesting way. One day the nun in charge of her college dorm got a call from an individual who said that a number of military officers stationed at nearby Randolph Field, the US Army Air Force base, wanted to meet young women at the college. The nun rounded up all the young female students she could find, and Eleanor was among them. She and handsome William Kienle Horrigan, a young officer and a West Point graduate, hit it off immediately and began dating in the fall of 1938. After only a few months, the couple became engaged. Mrs. Ahern was excited about the wedding until she learned that it would take place in Manila, Philippines, where her future son-in-law was now stationed, and she wouldn't be able to attend.[60]

In fact, Eleanor's daughter said her grandmother "had a fit. She was so disappointed." Mrs. Ahern had always excelled at organizing social events, and as it turned out, Eleanor was her only daughter whose wedding she might help plan.[61] But such was not to be. She was able, however, to help her daughter select a wedding dress.[62] Mrs. Ahern was able to hold a lovely reception at 403 Laurel Street announcing the engagement. She escorted Eleanor by train to San Francisco, where her daughter boarded a boat to the Philippines. The vessel stopped in Tokyo, Shanghai, and

Hong Kong, before docking in Manila, a three-week trip. The couple married on March 14, 1940, at the Archbishop's Palace with the groom's uncle Fr. Alfred Kienle presiding over the ceremony.[63] Col. Lawrence K. Churchill, the commanding officer at Nichols Field, and his wife arranged a beautiful wedding breakfast as a surprise for Eleanor. "If she has to come all this way for her wedding," Mrs. Churchill reportedly said, "she's going to have something lovely."[64]

After their marriage, Eleanor and William lived on the army base where their first child, a daughter named Eleanor, was born, on April 3, 1941. But just five weeks later on May 13, mother and child had to evacuate the Philippines. The US government determined that all dependents of servicemen had to leave and published a list every two months of evacuees. If your name was on the list, and you didn't leave, you "were on your own." When Eleanor had doubts about leaving, William argued his point. "It's going to be really bad, and we want to be sure the baby is all right," he said. "I can't help you when this starts. I'll be flying planes, and that's the last ship we know for sure that's leaving."[65]

William was right in his advice. In fact, "the worst American loss in these early months [of the war] was the Philippines." In December, the Japanese took Manila and overwhelmed the troops under Gen. Douglas MacArthur. On May 6, 1942, the US and Filipino troops surrendered and were forced into prisoner-of-war camps where many would die of "beatings, disease, and starvation."[66] Over forty years later, a son and grandson, Patrick and Michael, narrated his experience:

> He was stationed in the Philippines from March 1939 to February 1942. He was at Clark Field when the war began. In early February 1942, he and his unit, the Nineteenth Bomber Group, flew from the Philippines to Darwin, Australia, prior to being assigned to Java in the Dutch East Indies to support resistance to the Japanese invasion. Flying primarily against Japanese naval targets for one month, his squadron was sent back to Australia in March 1942 when the Japanese successfully invaded; however, his compromised B-18 crash landed in Java on March 9, and he and his crew were taken prisoner.[67]

After the Dutch and US prisoners were consolidated, they were sent to Singapore and then shipped to a Nagasaki prisoner-of-war camp at a shipyard. Serving as the ranking allied officer in the camp, William was there from December 1, 1942, until April 15, 1945. Then he was transferred to another POW camp in Mukden, Manchuria, until liberated by the Russian army on September 11, 1945. In mid-September he traveled via hospital ship USHS *RELIEF* to Okinawa and then was flown to San Francisco to reunite with his wife, Eleanor. In total, he had spent forty-one months as a prisoner-of-war. He was separated from his family for four years and four months.[68]

Meanwhile, in 1941, Eleanor had made her way back home to Texarkana, a two-week journey, first on a ship being sent back stateside. Many on board would never see their husbands or fathers again. Just a few days out, their ship turned so abruptly that had Eleanor been on deck, she would probably have fallen off. She heard that their ship was headed to rescue a sinking vessel. But shortly thereafter, their ship turned around again, as a ship closer to the distressed one helped with the rescue instead. It was an arduous journey over water to San Francisco. Alone with a baby only a few weeks old, Eleanor struggled through the days. Finally at port, she had the business of securing her trunks and making transportation connections. She took baby Eleanor home to 403 Laurel Street, where the little girl acquired the nickname of "Scamp." Living in the house at the time also were Mrs. Ahern, and her daughter Ann, Eleanor's sister.

Eleanor soon went to work in Texarkana. The small city was hopping with activity and needed people to work for the war effort. Lone Star Army Ammunition Plant and Red River Army Depot needed places for people to live who came to work at the plants. Eleanor was employed for about a year in an office that oversaw transforming houses into apartments to address the area's need for additional housing. Then she worked for the national War Manpower Commission, which was charged with helping to balance the labor requirements of industry, agriculture, and the military. In a local office, housed next to the Hotel Grim, Eleanor completed reports on various government labor statistics. Eleanor's oldest brother, Joe, also found employment at the defense plant. The homefront efficiency ultimately enabled the military success. "By 1944, the last full year of war, American factories and fields were producing 30,000 tanks; 100,000 planes; 2,000 ships; and vast quantities of munitions, guns, supplies, and food for American military forces and for its United Nations allies. No soldier, sailor, or airman was as well-equipped as the American GI."[69]

And while Joe and Eleanor worked in the war effort, sister Ann was busy on the musical front, teaching piano lessons to countless children, including her niece, Scamp, who spent her first five years of life at 403 Laurel Street. Mrs. Ahern must have reveled in having a child in the large house once more. All day, she was the one who cared for Scamp. It was Mamie and Scamp in the huge home—Scamp following Mamie around, trying to do many of the things she did. Scamp had a dog, a collie named Lady that looked like Lassie in the movies.[70] But there must have been many hours of unhappiness as well. Ann broke her leg at the beginning of the war, and Eleanor and Mrs. Ahern took care of her. She was bedridden for a long time, and her food had to be taken up to her on a tray. Mrs. Ahern's granddaughter Scamp remembers it as a difficult time, but she would have been just a toddler then and must be thinking of stories she heard later.[71] Money was not plentiful, and Eleanor didn't know when or if she'd ever see her husband again. And then when he came back to the states, and after months of rehabilitation, William, Eleanor, and Scamp left; Mrs. Ahern must have missed them immensely.

William Horrigan served a distinguished career in the military for more than twenty years, and Eleanor seemed to have enjoyed all their traveling. "You're just like your father," Mrs. Ahern accused her daughter. He was always happy traveling around seeing the world, whereas Mrs. Ahern had no wish to risk her life crossing the ocean.[72] Besides their first-born daughter, little Eleanor, William and Eleanor had four sons: William Patrick, Brian Richard, Joseph Michael, and Neil Alfred, born 1947, 1951, 1957, and 1959, respectively.

The Aherns' son John also married during the 1940s. He married Elinor Shea Oliver in February of 1946 in Sacred Heart Church in Washington, DC. Like Eleanor's husband, William, John, who was practicing law in New York City when the war started, served in the military as an attorney at the Pentagon during the war, but he elected to leave the service once the war ended and practice law as a civilian. A wedding picture of John and Elinor graces the mantel in the library of the Ahern home, 403 Laurel Street. John stayed in Washington, DC, after the war, where he specialized in tax law and enjoyed a successful career with the firm Nash, Ahern & Abell. The marriage produced four daughters and one son: Elinor Genevieve or Ellie, born in 1948, Catherine Ann or Cathy, born in 1950, Patrick Joseph II, born in 1953, Maureen Elaine, born in 1955, and Eileen Carol, born in 1959.

# CHAPTER 1

## The Aherns: 1950s and Beyond

By the end of the 1950s, Joe had separated from his wife, although the marriage was never annulled by the church nor were they ever divorced. In 1959, Joe moved back into 403 Laurel Street and lived there for the next forty-three years of his life. During the 1940s, his niece Eleanor or Scamp remembered her Uncle Joe living close by with his wife and daughters. He was always dropping by the house to check on his mother, she recalled. To his niece Scamp, he seemed to be a happy man who liked to tease people.[73] One of Miss Ann's piano students called him the "gentleman of the house." He always wore a hat of Homburg style. He was "soft spoken" and dressed "in suits." She remembered him as having investments in the stock market.[74] Another piano student remembered him as a "very nice man" and "friendly." That student studied with Miss Ann from 1953 to 1958 and recalled Joe stopping by occasionally to eat with the family.[75] One student described him as "businesslike" and "always dressed in suits." Once when Miss Ann sent this student upstairs to practice, she peeked into Joe's room. She found it neat with dozens of shoes lined up along the walls in a uniform manner. "He was a snappy dresser," she noted, "a handsome, well-dressed man." Later she recalled him from his having worked the elections for Miller County Courthouse.[76] Someone who knew him from church thought of him as "well dressed, well mannered, reserved."[77]

His family recalled Joe as a "meticulous individual," one with "very exact habits." For example, he consistently hung up "his hat just so," and he placed his belongings in such measured ways that if anyone moved one of his items on a dresser in his bedroom, he noticed. He had a sharp, dry wit about him and greatly admired the humor of Will Rogers. He loved playing bridge, as did his wife, Mary. After his father's store closed, he ran for tax collector in Texarkana and won once. But in a future election, things went awry. When ballots had not been received from an outlying town, he drove out to see what the problem was. On his way there, he met his political opponent heading toward Texarkana with the ballot box in hand. Clearly the integrity of the election had been compromised. Joe felt, as his father had several years before about his business dealings, that anti-Catholic sentiments cost him the election.[78]

Most summers in the 1950s, Mrs. Ahern, in her seventies, and Ann, in her forties, took to the highway on lengthy road trips. Ann had an

Oldsmobile, especially designed for her, that she made good use of. Off to Washington, DC, to visit relatives, Ann frequently took at least one summer course there in music, once even a course in Gregorian Chant.[79] They also sometimes rode the train to Washington. And the relatives came to see them as well. Eleanor and her children were frequent visitors during summer vacations. All the children loved the house, the cellar, the stairs, and the sun porch. "All the children slept out there. It was a wonderful place in summer time," Eleanor remembered about the porch. All the children stayed there in the summer of 1959 as their parents looked for a home and employment following Bill's retirement from the air force. In the summer of 1966, Brian, Joe, and Eleanor took an "epic bus trip" together, touring from Los Angeles to San Antonio, where they met Ann and Mrs. Ahern, and drove back to Texarkana to spend much of the rest of the summer there. In 1968, they flew to San Antonio, again met Ann and Mrs. Ahern, and saw the 1968 World's Fair, called the Hemisfair, together before driving to Texarkana to spend several weeks.[80]

John and his wife, Elinor, also visited several times and brought all five of their children with them to celebrate Christmas with the family in 1961 and 1967.[81] And Mary came home as well, always for Christmas and in the summer. She was "very close to her mother."[82] At Christmas she loved to help Ann with the Christmas recitals.[83] Although Mary never married, she was never a "wall flower." She was "not afraid to speak her mind" and had something of a "feisty" personality. Like her mother, she was good at math and excellent in music.[84] She considered being a concert pianist and studied music at great expense in Washington, DC, but in the end decided she didn't want a life of the constant touring typically associated with a concert pianist and gave up the idea. She continued to enjoy piano, though, throughout her life.[85] When she came home for visits, she would play the piano after dinner. Sometimes she'd play songs and others would sing. She was the "best pianist of the group."[86] One of Miss Ann's piano students remembered Mary as being "quite the dresser." She recalled that "Mary always wore a full-length mink coat home for Christmas."[87]

After Mary completed her undergraduate degree in English and Latin from Trinity College in Washington, DC, she later took a B.C.S. from Columbus University, also in DC and completed graduate hours toward a master's in accounting there. In the early 1930s, she worked as a statistical clerk and assistant section supervisor at the US Census Bureau. Late in 1932, she began her career at the National Lumber Manufacturers Association in DC. "She computed the first edition of 'Wood Structural Design Data,' published in 1934," and worked for this firm, later known as the National Forest Products Association, for forty years, retiring in 1972 as assistant treasurer. In late 1973, she took another job at the International Snowmobile Industry Association where she worked until 1988. Mary was happy, leading a busy, professional life in a major city. But in the late 1980s, she left her apartment in Washington for the last time, moved everything back to her parents' house, 403 Laurel Street, and lived her final years in Arkansas.[88]

Mary always had a knack for finding out what was going on. When she was a kid and Saint Edward Church was being constructed, she knew how many bricks had been laid in the structure daily and reported to her parents what had been done. She was always someone who took charge of situations. "Mary made everyone get in line. She wouldn't have it any other way."[89] Eventually Mary traveled to her father's ancestral home in Ireland in 1973. She went to find her paternal grandparents' grave at the cemetery in Kilgobnet, a few miles outside of Dungarvan, Ireland.[90]

By the time Mary returned for good in 1988, her mother had been dead for almost two decades. Mary Olive, or Mamie as her children and most of her grandchildren called her, died on March 4, 1970. She became frail at the end, and when exposed to the flu, died within a week. Ann, who had lived an independent life herself, died on November 26, 1988. She was almost seventy-nine and struggled all her life to overcome her bout with polio. In spite of it, she was able to attend college at Georgetown Visitation in Washington, DC. For several years she also went to Johns Hopkins Hospital in Baltimore, seeking help for her physical condition. She had a great deal of medical work completed there relating to her polio, including "transplants of muscle tissue in her legs," which resulted in lengthy scars. Several times she stayed at that hospital for various treatments, none of which did much good. Mr. Ahern once commented, "I could have built another 403 Laurel with the money spent on Ann's treatments."[91] In the end, she assumed a stoical attitude and determined she would do what she wanted to anyway. It might be just a bit more difficult. A piano student of Ann's in the 1950s and 1960s remembered her climbing the steps into 403 Laurel Street (there are ten steps), and climbing the steps into St. Edward Church (about twenty). And for many years, she managed to climb the stairs in the house (over twenty) and the attic. When she was a kid, she walked home with the other children from the Catholic school. She seemed never to have been coddled, or perhaps her determination to be independent wouldn't allow much coddling.

In the end, all the Aherns living in the house had to move their bedrooms downstairs because they couldn't manage the stairs. Ann and her mother, Mary, shared a bedroom in what had been the smaller parlor. Mr. Ahern had had his bed there as well after strokes prevented him from going up and down the stairs. When Mrs. Ahern grew ill, the family placed her bed in the dining room against the back wall, and nuns came to the house periodically.[92] Toward the end of Joe's life, his bed was set up in the library, but he never came home from the hospital.[93]

Patrick, Mary Olive, and three of their children—Joe, Mary, and Ann—all had the privilege of living in their home until the end of their lives. One of Miss Ann's piano students remembered the Rosary services that Mrs. Ahern and her children had in the house for the deceased. The night before the church service, the body was laid out in front of the bay window in the music room. After a series of prayers, family and friends shared their memories of the loved one.[94] The family remained close throughout their lives, a close-knit fabric of love and regard.

They were, as one of their contemporaries said, just "outstanding members of the community."[95] One of Miss Ann's piano students summed it up well: they were a "fine family living in a way that was not the norm anymore," for they "were able to hang on to family rituals." For many years, there was no television set in the house; and TV sets added later didn't seem to have made much difference in terms of the family's interests.[96] Instead, they continued to retain the style of living they had when they were children and their parents were young. They valued talking to each other, reading, making music together, and the marvel of recalling memories with laughter, good will, and the grace of God. Determining the legacy of such a family involves not only considering their children and their children's children, but also the many ways they touched the history of this town and other places as well as the lives of the people who knew them. And finally, their legacy is also the excellent structure at 403 Laurel Street itself. As one commentator noted, "It is a treasure!"[97]

Roger O'Dwyer and Patrick Ahern, courtesy of the Texarkana Museums System, Wilbur Smith Research Archive

O'Dwyer & Ahern Dry Goods Store, 1920s, courtesy of the Texarkana Museums System, Wilbur Smith Research Archive

Interior of O'Dwyer & Ahern Dry Goods Store, Patrick Ahern first on the left, courtesy of the Ahern, Horrigan, and Purcell families

O'Dwyer & Ahern business card, courtesy of the Ahern, Horrigan, and Purcell families

1904 wedding of Patrick Ahern and Mary Lansdale with family members, courtesy of the Ahern, Horrigan, and Purcell families

1904 Ahern–Lansdale wedding, courtesy of the Ahern, Horrigan, and Purcell families

Peter Kline, the Aherns' brother-in-law, courtesy of Ricky Keith

Ella Lansdale Kline, Mary Ahern's sister, courtesy of Ricky Keith

Mary Ahern as a young adult, courtesy of the Ahern, Horrigan, and Purcell families

Ahern home, 1916, courtesy of the Texarkana Museums System, Wilbur Smith Research Archive

Patrick and Mary with children from left to right front row: John, Catherine, Eleanor, Ann; back row: Joseph and Mary, courtesy of the Ahern, Horrigan, and Purcell families

Mary Ahern with children, courtesy of the Ahern, Horrigan, and Purcell families

Joseph, Mary, and Ann Ahern, courtesy of the Ahern, Horrigan, and Purcell families

Catherine Ahern playing with pet dog, courtesy of the Texarkana Museums System, Wilbur Smith Research Archive

Ann Ahern, courtesy of the Ahern, Horrigan, and Purcell families

Joseph Ahern, standing by the side of the Ahern home, courtesy of the Ahern, Horrigan, and Purcell families

Ahern children with friends and St. Edward's nun, making a snowman, courtesy of the Ahern, Horrigan, and Purcell families

St. Edward's school dramatic production, 1925; play cast in front of the Ahern home: Catherine in front, Ann on step, John in sailor costume on right, and Mary, queen at top, courtesy of the Ahern, Horrigan, and Purcell families

Michael Meagher Hospital, courtesy of CHRISTUS St. Michael Health System

Fiftieth Anniversary of Texarkana, courtesy of the Texarkana Museums System, Wilbur Smith Research Archive

Ahern Window, St. Edward Catholic Church, photograph by Doris Davis

Wedding of William Horrigan and Eleanor Ahern, courtesy of the Ahern, Horrigan, and Purcell families

Eleanor Horrigan and daughter Eleanor, called "Scamp," courtesy of the Ahern, Horrigan, and Purcell families

John Ahern's college 1933 graduation photograph, "Ye Doomsday Books," Georgetown University, courtesy of the Texarkana Museums System, Wilbur Smith Research Archive

Wedding of John Ahern and Elinor Oliver, 1946, from left, Joe Ahern, Eleanor Horrigan, William Horrigan, Elinor Ahern, John Ahern, Mary Olive Ahern, Ann Ahern with Eleanor Horrigan, and Mary Ahern, courtesy of the Texarkana Museums System, Wilbur Smith Research Archive

Ahern family—clockwise top left, John, Joe, Eleanor, William (Eleanor's husband), Elinor (John's wife), Ann, and Mary, courtesy of Maureen Ahern Leahigh

# 2

# Domestics in the Ahern Home

*Mother never had any trouble getting help.*
*She was always very nice to people.*

—Eleanor Ahern Horrigan, 2004

*I never had a child get hurt I cared for . . .*

—Hettie Williams, 1920, quoted by Eleanor Ahern Horrigan,[1] 2004

In her study of domestic servants and the expectations of households between the World Wars, Phyllis Palmer found that though middle-class women increasingly had more labor-saving devices at their disposal and the help of various domestics, these years "witnessed the perpetuation and heightening of household standards designed for a servant-aided home." Although not everyone could afford to hire domestics, "well-tended domestic space was upheld as the ideal center for social life."[2]

The nature of the Ahern house—both in terms of size and style—required domestic servants to ensure the household functioned well. Domestics or "the help," as they grew to be called in the South, might be employed for numerous reasons: to cook, to care for children, to clean, to do the laundry, to manage yards and gardens, and to nurse the ill. The Aherns employed individuals throughout the twentieth century in all these categories and no doubt grew dependent on their relative expertise. With a family of six children and the assumption that the home would be ready to entertain others on short notice, Mrs. Ahern had to be organized and flexible. She would not have succeeded without "the help." But absent family records, diaries, or letters, writing about these domestics, some of whom spent many years serving this family, is difficult. For a few individuals, I have been able to secure little more than their names and for others, not even that much. Nonetheless what I have been able to learn about them constitutes the bulk of this chapter.

## An Overview of Domestic Service in the United States

A country founded on the equality of all had ironically from the beginning various types of indentured workers and slaves. This contradiction between ideology and action resulted in a tension that sullied the relationship between master and servant then and throughout the history of servitude in this country. And service in the South was quite different from that in the Northeast or the West.[3]

In the colonial period, indentured white servants, transported convicts, Native Americans, and Blacks performed service. The largest number of convicts and indentured white servants were in the middle and southern colonies, while the Indigenous servants were mostly in New England and Black slaves in the South. By the end of the period, "black enslaved labor began to displace white servitude in the South and native-born free laborers displaced Native Americans and indentured whites in the North."[4]

In the North, the American Revolution emphasized issues of freedom and democratic ideals, where service was now performed largely by free wage-laborers. By the middle of the nineteenth century, however, the large influx of immigrants from Ireland and elsewhere affected the attitude of some employers who found immigrant laborers to be lacking in skill and fortitude. The resulting tension between employer and employee began to appear in popular magazines and other materials for housewives as "the servant problem."[5]

In the South white slave owners used enslaved labor to displace nearly all kinds of white domestic laborers. The harsh and cruel conditions resulted in what W.E.B. Du Bois termed "a despised race to a despised calling."[6] In writing about household service in the nineteenth century, Faye E. Dudden excluded the South in her work because she said, "[S]lavery took the place of free service and where even after emancipation service took forms that cannot be understood apart from the heritage of race slavery."[7]

Black women also were far less likely than other groups to be able to move from a domestic position in the early twentieth century into another occupation or to stop performing domestic work once they married. When World War I caused more nonservant jobs to become available to both men and women than ever before and those who could do so left the service industry, Black women were far less likely than others to secure a nondomestic-service position. By 1920, Blacks comprised 82 percent of all servants in the South.[8]

Social historian Evelyn Nakano Glen points out that most view the period of 1890 to 1920 as the "nadir of black citizenship in the South," an era with more oppression and the loss of Black rights.[9] To understand the nature of Black domestic service in the early twentieth-century South, it's necessary to realize the contextualized aspects of such service. A combination of forces such as white supremacy, Black disfranchisement and intimidation, and the unfair conditions imposed by Jim Crow segregation resulted in the 2,585 lynchings documented in the South from 1885 to 1903. Such public lynchings constituted "voyeuristic spectacles," at times drawing crowds of several hundred or even thousands of viewers.[10] In Texarkana as well, public violence against Blacks and lynchings took place. The city's history of race relations shares the dark past of the South as a whole. It is within this social and racial context, thus, that we look at the topic of domestic service in the Ahern house.

From all accounts, Mrs. Ahern appears to have been an especially kind individual; and growing up in the urban area of Washington, DC, in an upper-middle-class family, she had been exposed to ways of thinking that supported an inherently charitable disposition. As a young adult she married an immigrant from Ireland, who, although he had been successful in accumulating property and wealth, represented Irish Catholics, two groups that had been and continued to be persecuted by some in this country. And, of course, Mary Ahern was Roman Catholic herself. These circumstances no doubt broadened her way of thinking and deepened her response to the plight of others less fortunate. Her great-nephew Dr. Frank Loda noted that Mrs. Ahern was "by far the most gentle of the family; the glue that held them all together." In fact, he said that Mrs. Ahern "was more gentle, more loving, and more flexible" than his own grandmother.[11]

And as her youngest daughter, Eleanor, recalled almost a century after her mother's wedding in 1904, "Mother never had any trouble getting help. She was always very nice to people."[12] Mrs. Ahern was also not afraid of working hard herself. Working alongside of help in the kitchen took on what Faye E. Dudden terms a kind of "lyrical dignity" about other examples of employer and employee working together.[13] Few actions made an employer more palatable to the "help" than that person's willingness to understand and share the work.

## Rank and Uniforms for Domestics

In extremely wealthy households, domestic servants wore uniforms or liveries that indicated their rank, from the butler to the maid-of-all-work, each with a designated role and space. The butler, for instance, worked wholly in the drawing room and dining room, in command of the other servants and serving at the table.[14] In upper-middle-class homes, such as the Aherns', no butler was employed despite the house possessing an area known as the butler's pantry. Instead, the property functioned with fewer servants—usually the maid-of-all-work or parlor maid, the cook, and the nursemaid.

In households that adhered strictly to dress, each employee wore a slightly different uniform. For instance, in the morning, the parlor maid wore an unadorned print gown and a long apron with a bib and straps over the shoulders as well as a cap of definite dimensions.[15] In winter, the nurse maid wore a black gown with white apron, cuffs, and collar and a "full white muslin mob cap that for the morning [had] short muslin strings." In the summer, she sported a print gown with her apron.[16] A more relaxed style of dress ruled in the Ahern house, especially as the twentieth century inched toward midpoint. While some wore a fairly typical maid's outfit, others donned a simple apron.

## Domestic Service in the Ahern House

### *The Laundry*

Studies show that women hated the laundry task more than any other and whenever they possessed any discretionary funds, even poor women spent it on their laundry.[17] Women who earned money by washing other people's laundry generally took it to their own home rather than washing in an employer's home. Provided they had the equipment, a laundress had more autonomy in doing so.[18] The Aherns used both on-site and off for their laundry needs. For the items washed on premises, the Aherns had a clothesline located in the northwest corner of the middle lot, as far out of public view as possible. In the cellar sat a large, deep, galvanized washtub where a domestic servant washed some of the family's personal items. Attached to the north wall, the washtub had three sections with faucets for each section and is a reminder of the huge amount of laundry a family generated. For that reason, much of the rest of the laundry was sent out either to a professional laundry service or to a laundress, or perhaps to both.

Commercial laundry services had grown rapidly after the Civil War. Initially, they laundered "men's shirts, collars, and cuffs . . . and flatwork," such as sheets and tablecloths.[19] By 1900, several general-purpose soaps—Ivory, Borax, Sapolio, and Gold Dust—were known nationally. In 1906, Lux Flakes was the first soap for laundry available in any form other than a bar. Granulated soaps originated for use in electric washing machines, which appeared about 1914 for use in the home.[20] As Thomas J. Schlereth observes, "A piped-in water supply and a water-carried sewerage system, along with new washing machines, gradually centralized the work of soaking, rinsing, soaking, sudsing, scrubbing, scalding, bluing, starching, and drying clothes in the basement."[21] After 1914, ads in magazines, journals, and newspapers associated cleaning products with "female users, modernity, and social improvement."[22] Not only was cleanliness next to godliness, but an ad for Unilever Soap declared that "soap is civilization."[23]

A few commercial laundries are listed in the 1906 Texarkana City Directory: Brackman Brothers, State Line Avenue; Hannon Brothers, 203 West Broad; Lee Sing, 316 Vine Street (later Olive); and Memphis Pressing Club, Elm Street (later Wood). Under "Steam laundries" appear The Ralph Brothers, Elm Street and Texarkana Steam Laundry, Elm and West Broad. By 1910, Gate City Laundry appeared at 308 State Line and Clyde Hannon on East Broad. The 1915–16 Directory lists Crow's Laundry on West Oak and Lelia, Jin Key on East Elm, and Red Cross Laundry. Constant on all listings are Lee Sing and Ralph Brothers.

Mrs. Ahern, however, probably sent her clothes to a laundress rather than to a commercial laundry.[24] Without any records left in the house, however, it's impossible to tell who that laundress might have been. Even determining who the laundresses were in 1900 poses problems. Since the laundresses are not identified in the business section, checking each individual listing is the only way to determine their identity. A sampling of laundresses from the 1899–1900 *City Directory* under the alphabetical listing of A and B reveals eight laundresses, of whom all but one seem to be working out of their homes. Under Section A appear Emma Adams, Texarkana Troy Steam Laundry; Josephine Adams, 903 Wood; Priscilla Adams, 421 East Eighth; and Lulu Addison, 416 North Oak. Under Section B appear Josie Bell, 1302 Laurel; Lucy Bell, 803 State Street; Dovey Bazell, 613½ Elm; and Mollie Blackmre, 716 Elm. A telling detail is that all of them are listed as "C," meaning "Colored." The laundress was the most common type of domestic worker in the nineteenth century,[25] and in the South, the majority of them were Black, marking them as part of the hardworking poor. In Zora Neale Hurston's compelling and aptly named short story "Sweat," washerwoman Delia Jones rations each minute of her day. The story opens:

> Any other night, Delia Jones would have been in bed for two hours.... But she was a washwoman, and Monday morning meant a great deal to her. So she collected the soiled clothes on Saturday when she returned the clean things. Sunday night after church, she sorted and put the white things to soak. It saved her almost a half-day's start.[26]

Hurston offers a vivid portrayal of Delia's arduous work and illustrates the common practice of the Black washerwoman laboring over white people's clothes in the early twentieth-century South.

### *Child Care: Work as a Nanny*

That domestic who was the most highly valued by the mistress and the family was typically the person who took care of the children. These servants, referred to as "nurses," on census reports and city directories,[27] took on an intimate knowledge of the family. Usually they lived with the family, as was the case with Hettie Williams, who had a bed in the Ahern house in the upstairs nursery. Nursemaids typically bathed and dressed the children, fed and played with them, and put them to bed for naps and at night. Since Hettie's bed was in the nursery, she also would have gotten up in the middle of the night to care for them. Of the servants working in the house, Hettie Williams seems to have served the longest and to be the one most often mentioned by others as a domestic. That said, specifics about her are few and uncertain, gained largely through census reports, which are sometimes inaccurate, and a few comments made by the family and others.

The first systematic national information on women's occupations began with the federal census published in 1870. On this report, compilers were mandated for the first time to list the occupation and gender of each person, no matter the age or marital status.[28] This census was also the first national record made after emancipation in the South. It is on this report that Hettie Williams's name first appears. She is listed as "Hettie Williams," twenty-two years old, married, and Black; she appears on the Savanah, Georgia, Chatham County, Federal Census along with the name of her husband, James Williams, age twenty-six. She is "keeping house"; both are illiterate. While I can't claim with certainty that this listing is that of the person who worked in the Ahern house several decades later, I do know with some certainty that Hettie Williams, living in Texarkana, was born in Georgia either in the late 1840s or early 1850s, and that this is the listing in Georgia that most nearly matches what I know about her. Although there were a few free Black individuals in Georgia in the 1840s and 1850s, it is highly probable that both Hettie and her husband, James, were born in Georgia as slaves. They had been living as "free" individuals for about five years at the time of the census. Both had probably labored on a plantation in the Savannah area. On various national census reports, their parents are listed as being born sometimes in Georgia and sometimes in Florida. Probably they were unsure themselves about the place of birth of their parents.

Ten years later in the 1880 Federal Census, Hettie appears as living in Augusta, Georgia, Richmond County. Her address is 1355 Elo Street. She is listed as married and living with a "W. Williams," a laborer. The census collector notes that her husband is "sick." Unfortunately, most of the 1890 Federal Census was destroyed in a fire, so there is no record of her again until the 1900 Federal Census. In 1900 she appears as "Hattie Williams," age forty-four, born in 1855 in Georgia, currently living in Texarkana, Arkansas, Miller County, Ward 4, at 1315 Ash. She is a "widowed housekeeper," the mother of one child, who is deceased. She is boarding with Henry Wheeler, age thirty-seven, and his son Silas Wheeler, age six. This is the first record of Hettie living in Texarkana.

When, how, and why she came to Texarkana are all speculative. Most likely she came by wagon with others moving westward to gain better living conditions. Sociologist Stephen Steinberg notes that numerous ex-slaves headed toward Texas and other southern and western areas in search of jobs as laborers.[29] Her husband, who was listed as ill on the 1880 census, evidently died, as she is now a widow.

On the 1910 Federal Census, she is "Hetty Williams," age sixty, living on Lengel Street, with the "O'Hern" family, Patrick, Mary, Joseph, Mary, and Anna. For the first time, Hettie is listed as a "nurse," and the mother of two children, with only one living. Mistakes are obvious on the report. She is living, of course, with the Ahern family and, as the 1910 *City Directory* indicates, at 403 Laurel. Whether she had had one or two children is unclear. On the 1920 Federal Census, Hettie appears as Hettie Williams, age seventy, born about 1850. She is "widowed" and lives with the Aherns as a nurse for the Ahern family: Patrick and Mary and children: Joseph, age fourteen, Mary, age twelve, Anna, age nine, Catherine, age seven, John, age seven, and Eleanor, age two.

Hettie Williams seems to have worked for the Ahern family as a nanny from about 1906 to about 1920. The children called her "Aunt Hettie," "aunt" being an epithet often applied to Black nursemaids and other domestics in the South. The youngest of the Ahern children, Eleanor stated that Aunt Hettie had worked for her Aunt Ella Kline, taking care of her children, who were born before the Ahern children; then she worked for Mrs. Ahern. Sometime after the 1920 Federal Census, Hettie "resigned" as a nurse with the Ahern family. According to Eleanor, one day she took off down the hall and Hettie couldn't catch her. Perhaps Eleanor fell and though she didn't hurt herself, she might have. Eleanor was three. From that day on Hettie refused to take care of children. She said she had never had a child get hurt that she cared for, so she refused to risk it now. Hettie was getting old. Her resignation was "a terrible blow to her mother," Eleanor said. Mrs. Ahern had depended on her for so many years.[30] Hettie clearly took her work seriously and realized the tremendous responsibility vested in her to ensure that a child was safe. She could no longer do that. Mrs. Ahern must have been comforted that Hettie would still be around, as she found a place for her elsewhere in the house. Plus, Hettie must have needed and wanted to work. At that point, Hettie Williams became a cook for the Aherns.

By 1920, Hettie Williams was probably at least seventy, she had toiled during slavery for twenty years, labored as a housemaid for thirty years, and worked as a nursemaid for twenty years. She is listed in the 1920 *City Directory* as being a cook at 403 Laurel; in 1924–25 she appears as living at 1214 Laurel St. That is the last entry on Hettie Williams in Texarkana. A "Hettie Williams" appears on the 1930 Federal Census, living in Prescott, Arkansas, with a Black school teacher and her grandson. Hettie is listed as eighty-four and born in Georgia. Whether this is the same Hettie is not known but it seems likely this reference is to her. There is no record of her after this entry.

Hettie seems to have died sometime in the 1930s, but there is no death certificate for her in Arkansas or Texas, and she is not listed in any of the area cemeteries. Dr. Frank Loda, a grandson of Mrs. Ahern's sister Ella Kline, remembered family comments about Aunt Hettie. "The whole [Ahern & Kline] family worshipped her," he said, "and looked to her as a great source of strength and love."[31] No doubt there are countless stories, both comic and sad, about her taking care of the Ahern and Kline families, but at this point they seem to be all forgotten. We can only imagine the stories she might have told. For years she slept in the nursery taking care of the most recent of the Aherns' children. An intimacy must have evolved among her and Mrs. Ahern and the children. While we don't know the depths of Hettie's heart, we do know that Mrs. Ahern by all accounts was a gentle, kind person. Had she not been so, then Hettie would have sought employment elsewhere, as plenty of households needed nursemaids in early twentieth-century Texarkana. That said, the work of a domestic, no matter the capacity or the conditions, was arduous and often unpleasant.

### *Domestic: Cook and Maid*

The most difficult type of domestic work is that which is categorized as a maid-of-all- work. Lillian Pettengill, a Mount Holyoke graduate who set out to investigate service at the turn of the century, praised it as "healthful" work, but had to "admit that when she worked as a domestic her hands became so tired and sore that she could scarcely move them in the mornings."[32] Another hardship for live-in domestics in some areas was that they might have problems seeing their own family, but this situation was mitigated in the South. As historian Faye E. Dudden comments, "Relatively integrated residential patterns" allowed domestics to return home for lunch to check on their own children.[33] This residential pattern was replicated in Texarkana with domestics often living two or three blocks from the houses where they worked. These neighborhoods were not integrated in the current sense but designed for the benefit of the white household. The proximity of the domestic to the workplace ensured that the white mistress was not hindered by having to transport the help.

On the 1920 Federal Census, Julia Holt, age fifty-five and widowed, is listed as working for the Ahern family as a cook. Although Mrs. Ahern often liked to plan the meals and prepare desserts, the cook's job was to ensure that the family had three hot meals a day, all served in the dining room. Mrs. Ahern insisted the evening meal consist of meat, vegetables, salad, bread, and dessert. The cook sometimes served the meal and helped clean the kitchen with the maid after the meal. Julia Holt lived fairly close, residing as a boarder at 512 Mary Street with Harry Elliott. Much younger, Mary Duckett, age eighteen, worked as a maid, cleaning rooms, furniture, woodwork, floors, bathrooms, and other surfaces. She is listed on the 1920 Federal Census as residing at 209 Preston Street as a boarder with a Major Washington. Other domestics who worked in the house through the years include William Branch, who had a restaurant in 1915 on Ash, and probably worked for the Aherns in the 1920s and 1930s as either a gardener or chauffeur; his wife, Mamie, who worked as a maid and perhaps a cook; and Rosie Lee, their adopted daughter, who worked as a live-in maid.[34] Finally, a longtime and highly regarded housekeeper named Martha worked for the Aherns for many years and is remembered fondly by grandson Patrick Horrigan, who recalled going with his Aunt Ann on several occasions to take Martha home when he visited in the 1950s.[35]

These years must have been difficult ones for Mrs. Ahern in some ways, particularly during the 1930s. As her granddaughter Eleanor stressed on more than one occasion, the 1930s were hard years for her family.[36] With the loss of the Ahern business and Mr. Ahern's declining health and death in the early 1930s, trying to maintain certain household standards with a reduced income must have taxed her mathematical and emotional skills.

In her study of the popular iconography embedded in the era of domestic service in the South, Kimberly Wallace-Sanders includes a photograph made about 1903 of two white children at play—a little boy perhaps four and his younger sister, around two. In front of them is a child's tea service with two dolls. The scene seems idyllic and innocent until examined closely. In front of the children a white doll sits at a small tea table and a black doll stands, attending to her role of serving tea. Depicting a kind of rehearsal for adulthood, the photograph reminds modern viewers of how racial attitudes are internalized, caught in this indelible image of white privilege and Black servitude.[37] The relationships in the South involving the Black domestic servant and her white mistress and children were fraught, as in this photograph, with a mixture of joy and pain, with the inevitable despair wrought by inequality and the tremendous capacity of the human heart to love. That love may well have resided more in the white mistress and her children than in the heart of the Black domestic, but the mystery of love cannot be reduced to a simple equation.

Hetty Williams with Ahern children, courtesy of Patrick Horrigan

# 3

# The Architecture of the Ahern Home

*The man is only half himself, the other half is his expression.*
—Ralph Waldo Emerson,[1] 1844

*A house that has been experienced is not an inert box. Inhabited space transcends geometrical space.*
—Gaston Bachelard,[2] 1958

In building their home in Texarkana, Arkansas, Patrick and Mary Ahern were also inevitably building their lives, as what they built would in turn influence their way of living. Such an intricate and critical endeavor involved not only artistry but also intuition and courage. Building a house is a public act in which the builder presents their work for others to judge. As architectural historian Joseph Rykwert points out, every building is "necessarily an act against nature."[3] The building invades the natural world and to be worthy must successfully compete with what was there before. Fruitful architecture requires two elements that must complement: utility and aesthetics. Or as architectural historian Mariana Griswold Van Rensselaer succinctly notes, successful architectural products are "useful objects made beautiful."[4] In essence, in designing their home, the Aherns had to consider both the practicality and beauty of their construction.

The binary of *practical* and *beautiful* may be nuanced to include *reliable*, for objects are not useful if unreliable. The resulting triad resonates with a definition approximating that of architecture's earliest theorist, Vitruvius, active in the first century BCE, who argues that architecture has three attributes: *firmitas, ultilitas,* and *venustas,* or strength, utility, and beauty.[5] This well-known maxim remains a critical architectural principle, whether building a skyscraper or a domestic structure, and informed the construction of the Aherns' home in the early twentieth century.

Built in 1905–06, the house's structure refers to the earlier architectural style of Classical Revival, marked by expansive columns and symmetry, but it also shows evidence of Modernity in its straight lines and lack of excessive ornamentation. By the date of its construction in 1905, with the emergence of scientific, economic, and technological attitudes of the turn of the century, the use of ornamentation or structural decorative elements was questioned. Only two years after their house was completed, the well-known architect Adolf Loos published a seminal essay entitled "Ornament and Crime," in which he argues that ornamentation is a waste of labor, health, and money.[6] In essence, for him ornamentation is a crime. Simplification became a dictate of the twentieth century, as evidenced stylistically in the Aherns' home.

One of the best-known architects writing prior to the construction of their house—whose work appears in their collected library—was John Ruskin. His essay "The Lamp of Truth," published in 1849, considers elements of reliability or truth in architecture. He recommends that structural materials be the same as that suggested, that surfaces not be painted to represent other entities, and that machine work not be substituted for handcrafted items.[7] Ruskin's essays were widely collected and presumably known to the Aherns. That they elected to mimic stone with their house's concrete façade suggests, however, the practicality of using what was close at hand as a building material.

The dialectics inherent in architecture add to the complexity of any structure, including the domestic. Such dialectical pairs as "enclosure and opening," "light and shade," "natural and constructed," "inside and outside," "movement and repose," and "mass and void" contribute to the complexity of construction. And that they consist of gradients along a continuum adds depth to such elements. Additionally, they can influence each other.[8] As architect Robert Venturi writes, "[E]ven the house, simple in scope, is complex in purpose if the ambiguities of contemporary experience are expressed."[9] Although he wrote that in 1966, it is applicable to various settings.

The popular late nineteenth-century Michigan architect of domestic structures D. S. Hopkins advised those who were planning to build a house to study plans carefully and "take plenty of time to satisfy yourself of your wants."[10] He acknowledged, however, that exteriors of homebuilding can be problematic. He suggested that homeowners let the architect design much of the exterior "in good taste" and "substantially."[11] Hopkins also recommended that architects achieve good proportions and effective roof lines. Appropriate paint coloring or staining was essential as well. Clearly Hopkins saw the role of the architect as crucial, both in terms of craft and aesthetics.[12]

The majority of styled American houses fall into one of four categories, depending on their architectural elements: Ancient Classical, Renaissance Classical, Medieval, or Modern. The architectural style of the Ahern house falls generally within the first of these—Ancient Classical, a type of structure that in turn consists of three styles: Early Classical Revival (1780–1830), with "side-gabled or hipped roof houses" and high entry porches; Greek Revival (1820–1860), with columns often resembling Greek temples; and Neoclassical (1895–1940), with two stories and elaborate, high columns.[13]

Late nineteenth-century home builders had at their disposal pattern books showing various styles and architectural plans. These books became especially popular the latter half of the nineteenth century with *Village and Farm Cottages* by Cleveland, Backus, and Backus, published in 1856. This publication offered mail-order plans, one of the earliest to do so. Soon mail-order companies appeared in many large cities; some businesses, such as Sears, Roebuck, and Company, even pre-cut all materials, making the carpenters' work easier.[14] Whether Mr. and Mrs. Ahern had any of these illustrated books is uncertain, but judging from their popularity, one would think it highly likely.

One in particular might have caught their eye: *Suburban and Country Homes* published by William T. Comstock in 1893. It printed clear designs and pictures of twenty-four homes with the addresses of the architects should a reader want to contact them.[15] Helpful essays address various aspects of building a house, including how to plumb one. "Suggestions on House Building" by architect A. W. Cobb provides clear steps in planning a house. For instance, he recommends home builders consider the necessity of privacy yet accessibility of each room and the cheerfulness produced by direct sunlight; plus, he suggests that dining rooms have easterly exposure for "cheer of the morning sun at breakfast time" and offers information on how to achieve various finishes of the interior wood.[16] He also recommends "successful grouping of rooms," to ensure attractive scenes as one looks from one room to another or, as he termed it "disposing their features so as to make the most of them."[17]

The Aherns followed the first commandment of the world of house building, at least for upper-middle-class dwellings: secure an architect. Although they had in mind the style, features, and details of what they wanted, they procured an architect to ensure the house's perfection. They chose William Burdsal, an architect who had come to Texarkana from Lebanon, Ohio, as early as 1882.[18] His office—the Burdsal Architects and Builders Company—was located in the triangle across the street from St. James Episcopal Church near Fifth and Olive Streets. Born in Ohio in 1845, Burdsal was an experienced architect and knowledgeable about the style that the Aherns selected—Classical Revival. Both Burdsal in Ohio and Mrs. Ahern in Washington, DC, would have seen a variety of houses built in this architectural style.[19] It was a design that enjoyed various revivals throughout the nineteenth and early twentieth centuries. Burdsal, however, never lived to see the completion of the house in 1906, as he died in the latter part of 1905.[20] The Aherns must have been saddened that he did not live to see the results of what was probably his last architectural work, for the house is a magnificent example of Classical Revival.

## The Exterior of the House

The exterior of the Aherns' Classical Revival house appears massive to most contemporary eyes, and the structure *was* "built to be a showplace of huge proportions."[21] Situated on two lots, an interior and a corner, the house attracts the eye with its weighted presence. The northern section sits close to the property line, allowing open spaces on the front and south side of the house. Adding to the grandeur of the structure, a concrete retaining wall of about 3.5 feet encases the yard and elevates one's perception of the height of the property. Five concrete steps, set into the wall, lead up to the front walk, which in turn leads to another five steps opening on to the front porch. The steps have a black, wrought-iron railing, added at a later date, that matches the railing of the balcony over the front door. Beyond the retaining wall, a public sidewalk follows the boundary of the yard in front and along the side. On the front side, the original rock street extends from the modern pavement about 2 feet, adding to the historical dimension of the house.

With an extensive columned front porch that wraps around the south side of the house and symmetrically placed windows, the house offers classically detailed Ionic columns and a central door flanked by windows along its sides and overhead, with the door of the balcony similarly fashioned. Although possibly locally made, these intricate windows consist of beautiful beveled leaded, crystal that suggest a skilled craftsman and add to the rich intricacy of the house. The height of the porch extends to the roofline, with four columns in front and two along the side that seemingly hold the roof and porch's dark, wooden ceiling in place. Enclosed by concrete balustrades, the porch consists of immense concrete slabs, one of which on the porch's far southeast side contains the indentation of "P.J.A. 4/10/06" that Mr. Ahern made in the concrete before it had dried. On this same side, a balcony extends to the second level, which in 1918 was enclosed to make a sleeping porch.[22] With windows on three sides of the sleeping porch, the circulating breezes offered a welcomed respite from the searing heat of southern summers.

The outside of the house consists of concrete blocks with a pattern reminiscent of rock. Made on site, the blocks reflect a grayish light and may have suggested to Mr. Ahern architectural materials he had seen years ago as a young man in Ireland. Some of the original forms used to make the blocks remain in the cellar with measurements of 10 inches deep, 10.75 inches wide, and 22 inches long. A number of companies advertised the strength of concrete at the time; for instance, Atlas Portland claimed that its concrete blocks chosen as building materials should "insure permanency as well as comfort and architectural beauty and strength."[23] This same company pointed out that insurance rates are often lower with concrete houses; plus concrete structures tend to be warmer in winter and cooler in the summer. Finally, this company claimed that concrete meets the three essentials that the Roman architect Vitruvius demanded: "stability, utility, beauty."[24]

The five chimneys also consist of concrete. The roof of the house is slate and enhances the house's aura of consisting of natural substances. The hipped slate roof falls to a "boxed-eave overhang, decorated with dentils."[25] Centered above the doors, a dormer "contains two double-hung, one-over-one windows" with "a boxed-eave overhang."[26] On the southwest side of the lot, stands a rectangular stucco garage. This later structure, built around 1925, reminds us that the Aherns would not have had a car in 1906.

The house was built in a section of Texarkana, Arkansas, called Quality Hill, the name based on the pioneering families' perception of fine architecture and well-to-do citizenry. Quality Hill covered a downtown area of about twenty square blocks. Most of the houses are now gone. The Ahern home is one of only a few of the original structures that surrounded the original Miller County Courthouse, a brick structure that sat in the same location as the current one that dates from the 1930s. The neighborhood in those days contained much activity. With Central School located where Beech Street Baptist Church is today, there were many school children walking through the neighborhood. The Aherns' youngest daughter, Eleanor Horrigan, remembered it as a "very pretty area, the old homes together—the Fouke home, the Offenhauser, and others ... red brick houses with white trim. They were lovely old places. And the Buchanan homes on both the Arkansas and Texas side. It breaks my heart," she said, "that they have all been torn down. They were very, very pretty ... the prettiest block."[27]

## The Interior of the House

The house's interior is truly extraordinary. Mr. Ahern "despised anything cheap,"[28] an attitude that becomes apparent as one walks through the spacious rooms of the structure. From the beautiful wooden floors to the individualized carved mantels, the house offers the finest materials then available. The floors, for instance, consist of "virgin edge cut pine." The yellows and reds of this "closely-grained" wood appear beautifully through the wood's light stain. The woodwork, pocket doors, and staircases contain a slightly darker stain. All of the woodwork has its original finish, the beauty of it being one of Mrs. Ahern's special treasures.[29] Mrs. Ahern selected the various mantels from magazines. On one occasion, she found one that she particularly liked but dismissed, thinking it too expensive. When the shipment came in, she was thrilled to see that mantel. Mr. Ahern had bought it for the Music Room as a surprise for her.[30] Additionally, each mantel has at its base hand-cut ceramic tiles that are individualized in color and design. Mrs. Ahern was also particular about maintaining their integrity. One of Ann Ahern's piano students from the 1950s remembered that students were not allowed to step on the tiles surrounding the fireplaces.[31]

The house contains six of the original eight ceiling lights, which worked with either gas or electricity. The upper tier of lights functioned with gas and resemble candles, while the lower tier consists of electric lights with a hand-blown, translucent glass shade. In 1906 electricity was available primarily for the benefit of Texarkana businesses and was turned off at night. The Ahern house was upscale in having electricity, but it also had to have gas to ensure lights at all hours. By 1910, Texarkana maintained a more modern electric power plant, which soon made gas lights passé, a relic of the Gas Light Era.[32] With ceilings of 12 feet and huge windows throughout, the house receives much natural light during the day and plenty of fresh air, which was important. Air conditioning did not appear in the South until the 1950s.

The layout of the house replicates the traditional design of the Classical Revival style, popular throughout late nineteenth and early twentieth centuries. For example, the wide central hall cuts the house into two sections and provides the central axis of the structure. This central corridor contains over 300 square feet and functions as a reception room as well as an opening to the other parts of the house. Almost 10 feet wide and over 30 feet long, it allows the placement of several large pieces of furniture. Also typical of Classical Revival, the house contains a music room, front parlor or reception room, and a butler's pantry. These areas were eliminated "from all but the most elaborate houses of the period 1910–1930"[33] and suggest a more formal style of life associated with the Victorian and Edwardian periods, replete with live-in servants. The small parlor, music room, library, and dining room have wide doorways, with pocket doors, that open into the central hallway.

The Aherns' stairs, located in a central position in the entrance hall, contain twelve steps leading to a midlevel platform; ten steps then lead in the opposite direction to the second floor. The back stairway leads from the kitchen and suggests an earlier style. The Ahern house, however, has something of a compromise design; the stairs leading from the kitchen meet those from the central hall at the designated turning point. Anyone taking the back stairs would use the same upper staircase to the second floor. This "compromise" version accomplishes the same goal: the "help" can maneuver the stairs without being seen by the homeowner or any guests on the first floor.[34]

A feature of the Ahern house that points to twentieth-century Modern appears in Mrs. Ahern's selection of divan and matching chair, placed in the central hall. Upholstered in red leather, the furniture appears to be of the Mission style, a simplification of previous styles and reminiscent of Gustav Stickley, one of the best-known leaders of the reform movement in furniture design, who "tried to . . . do away with all needless ornamentation."[35] These two pieces remain in the collective memory of many visitors to the house. Former students of Ann Ahern frequently ask, "Is that red couch still there?" The couch served as a holding place for students waiting for their piano lessons.

Although the Aherns hired an architect, they had already drafted a basic design for the structure. Mr. Ahern wanted his wife involved in every aspect of planning and often asked her advice on the arrangement of rooms.[36] Mary Ahern knew certain features that she especially wanted in the house. For instance, she wanted closets and plenty of them. She was quite forward in her thinking here. At the time, wardrobes were still in vogue for most homes, and bedrooms typically had no closets at all. In the Ahern house, each bedroom has its own closet, and the bathroom along the central hall upstairs has a utility closet. Mrs. Ahern was especially proud of the long cloak closet that leads to the bathroom on the first floor. About 3 feet wide and over 12 feet long, the closet can accommodate the coats of many guests. When visitors came to her new house, she was proud to show them this extensive closet. In later years when family members could no longer maneuver the stairs, this long closet served as their regular clothes closet.

Mrs. Ahern also wanted a built-in china cabinet in the dining room. It is a large cabinet that extends nearly to the ceiling. The height provided a safe place for her china and crystal. She also designed the butler's pantry with shelves and cabinets that match the china cabinet in the dining room. Picture rails, made to match the woodwork, appear about a foot from the ceiling. These are long, horizontal pieces of wood that hold pictures, mirrors, or other objects. By using these, Mrs. Ahern could easily change the placement of any ornamentation on the walls and avoid putting holes in the plaster. Generally, though, Mrs. Ahern's minimalist approach did not include decoration on the walls. She also wanted wooden corner guards to protect the corners of the plastered walls. These corner guards are vertical pieces of woodwork that match the other woodwork in the house.

The Aherns were prescient in designing a house with a half bathroom on the first floor and two full bathrooms on the second. Many period houses had no bathroom on the main level and typically only one on the second. Most of the original bathroom fixtures remain in the house and reflect the Edwardian period. The bathrooms on the second floor contain pedestal sinks and one contains a claw-foot tub. As mentioned earlier, one of the bathrooms opens onto the long, central hallway. The other bathroom sits between the master bedroom and that belonging to Mrs. Ahern. Transoms appear above most of the doors for air circulation in the pre-air-conditioned South. Their woodwork matches that of the doors. Additionally, to send instructions to the cook or others in the kitchen, a long tube connecting the kitchen with the master bedroom remains, an early style of intercom.

The first floor contains about 1,730 square feet, not counting the built-on back porch later designed as a laundry room or the circular porches. In addition to the 240 square feet of the smaller parlor, the 345 square feet of the music room, and the 225 square feet of the library, the dining room, kitchen, and butler's pantry add more than 500 square feet to the combined footage. The five upstairs bedrooms replicate the square footage of the first floor along with the bathrooms and closets. The master bedroom is the largest, measuring about 264 square feet. It also contains a mantel as does the other front bedroom, which is about 248 square feet. Each also contains a closet as well as symmetrical front and side windows. Mrs. Ahern's bedroom is about 210 square feet. Her bedroom connects with the main hall of about 320 square feet and the sleeping porch, which adds more square footage. The first and second floors have a combined square footage of over 3,500 feet without considering the cellar, attic, porches, and other areas. Miller County lists a total of 5,223 square feet.[37]

The house contains an extensive cellar with entrances leading to the backyard as well as the kitchen. The cellar encompasses an area to store garden utensils as well as shelves for various items including preserves and canned vegetables. The attic was "very well made"; at one point, Mr. and Mrs. Ahern had planned to finish it into another room. With wallpaper in place and a solid floor, the space clearly suggests the intention of use as an additional room.[38] Eventually however, the attic seems to have functioned as most attics do, as a place to store outgrown clothing, various business papers, tax records, and lots of school records and awards accumulated by the six children who grew up in the house.

Sound domestic architecture involves a number of sciences and several arts, as outlined above. It is never *simply* simple, as contemporary architect Mark Wigley notes in his study of the relationship between architecture and deconstruction: "The architectural figure is . . . never simply that of the well-constructed building. It is also the decorated building, one whose structural system controls the ornament attached to it. In the end, the edifice is as much a model of representation as presentation."[39]

## Landscape Gardening

At one time giant oak trees stood in the parkway between the outer sidewalk and the street. Of the more than half a dozen trees that graced the side and front of the house, none remain. Giant oaks with 10-foot girths towered above the house, framing the structure in a majestic manner. Decades ago, tall oaks and pines framed the houses up and down Laurel, offering shade during the sweltering dogdays of summer and into the warm afternoons of southern autumns. The Aherns' well-designed yard complemented the house as a place of retreat and comfort. With flowerbeds of roses, lilies, cannas, gardenias, hydrangeas, perennials, and annuals, the blooms must have perfumed the yard and created scenes of beauty. In her analysis of landscape gardening, architectural historian Mariana Van Rensselaer argues that masterful gardening can be a form of art: "When [a person] grows plants for their beauty as isolated objects he is a horticulturist; but when he disposes ground and plants together to produce organic beauty of effect, he is an artist with the best."[40] Just as the Aherns carefully chose the style and details of their architecture, they also selected a landscape to enhance the visual effects of the whole.

# CHAPTER 3

## The Philosophy of Architecture

In many ways, Mr. and Mrs. Ahern saw their house as a retreat for their family. The home was a place to nurture those growing to maturity, develop their creative and intellectual pursuits, and foster their ethical and moral fiber. The unchanging white walls of the home remained steadfast throughout the years for the children.

Some cultural historians see interior architecture as a potential factor of influence. Social historian Candace M. Volz offers the residential library as an example of an interior that fostered the inculcation of values and learning. It was a place where children were encouraged to regard books as objects of worth and to become readers to learn about the world and its various disciplines. It was also a place where parents might share books with their children and a "signal to visitors that this household valued intellectual curiosity."[41] Volz suggests that the evolution of the library into the contemporary study depicts how society's values have changed. The study, now associated largely with the man of the house, is no longer a place for books, but provides an area for displaying the acquisition of trophies and various accolades. The study may reveal something about the personality and goal of its owner but typically has little to do with fostering ethical principles in children.[42]

In his study of geography and space, geography theorist Yi-Fu Tuan considers how all of us become attached to a particular place, especially that of a home. "What begins as undifferentiated space," he explains, "becomes place as we get to know it better and endow it with value."[43] He argues that all individuals appear to have personal belongings and all seem to need a personal space, no matter how small—perhaps just a personal chair will do, but something to claim.[44] French philosopher Gaston Bachelard also writes about the psychological and spiritual aspects of personal space and suggests that our homes, particularly that in which we are born or grow up, become an essential aspect of our memories. "But over and beyond our memories," he argues, "the house we were born in is physically inscribed in us."[45] Bachelard sees the house as not only a place of memory and security but believes the house we grow up in resonates in us in meaningful ways *throughout* our lives. We retain the emotion we have associated with this house in unconscious ways.

Architectural philosopher Edward Hollis points out, what we all know, that many buildings outlive the purposes for which they were originally constructed. Residential homes sometimes become offices, retail establishments, schools, or, in the case of the Ahern home, museums. Well-made and attractive buildings, if valued by the society that made or inherited them, take on a life of their own, evolving into different versions of their original selves. Hollis speaks of this evolution as a kind of storytelling. Each change in a building, he writes, "is a retelling of the building as it exists at a particular time—and when the changes are complete, it becomes the existing building for the next retelling."[46]

In light of this philosophy, the Ahern home has taken on a different story that it tells. It preserves in concrete form glimpses of a way of life that has disappeared from contemporary society. But just as it at one time served as a place of nurturing values and learning for individuals of an earlier era, today it tells its own story to those who visit. It is a story, in part, about the integrity of its own architecture. As Hollis argues, "Buildings are gifts, and because they are, we must pass them on."[47]

Front door of the P. J. Ahern home with surrounding leaded windows, Texarkana Museums System, photograph by Doris Davis

Patrick Ahern's initials in the concrete on the front porch, 1906, P. J. Ahern home, Texarkana Museums System, photograph by Doris Davis

P. J. Ahern house, courtesy of the Texarkana Museums System, Wilbur Smith Research Archive

Staircase of upper stairs of the P. J. Ahern home, Texarkana Museums System, photograph by Doris Davis

Music room mantel of the P. J. Ahern home, photograph by Doris Davis

P. J. Ahern home on a summer day, Texarkana Museums System, photograph by Doris Davis

# 4

# The Aherns' World of Print Culture and the Turn-of-the-Century Home Library

*No man acquiring money enough to build a house making any pretentions, would dare to omit the library, so called. The woman of the house would not permit it.*

—Lillie Hamilton French,[1] 1908

That Patrick and Mary Ahern included a room designated as the library in their 1905 home is not surprising. Upper-middle-class citizens commonly included a library in fashioning their residences. In fact, historian Harold M. Otness points out that rooms "dedicated to the keeping and using of books have been features of upper-and-middle-class American life over the last two centuries."[2] What is surprising is that most of the Aherns' original library is still intact—almost five hundred volumes plus various pamphlets along with the furniture and architectural features of the room.

An examination of the library's collection allows an understanding of some of the intellectual pursuits of the Aherns in early twentieth-century Texarkana. As book historian Robert Darnton notes about the library of Thomas Jefferson: "To go over the list of books in [his] library is to inspect the furniture of his mind."[3] And because the period 1890 to 1930 constituted the height of book collecting and the home library in the United States,[4] the Aherns' library affords the historian information about the intellectual resources and design of a home library in a small turn-of-the century town in southwest Arkansas.

Historians of this area—Barbara Chandler and J. Ed Howe—describe Patrick Ahern as a "great reader,"[5] and his brother-in-law John Kline, who lived next door, as one who "devoted his spare time to reading the classics and other good literature."[6] Both men collected books and evidently made good use of them. The Aherns' youngest daughter, Eleanor, claimed that the library was always her father's room[7] although many of the books, especially those on music, reflect Mary Ahern's interests. Historically, the home library typically constituted a place of retreat for the man of the house. An unidentified author in a 1912 edition of *House Beautiful* claimed that no space "so distinctly and entirely belongs to the house-owner himself as his library."[8] Much as in Jane Austen's comic novel *Pride and Prejudice* wherein Mr. Bennet declares to his wife: "I shall be glad to have the library to myself as soon as may be,"[9] Patrick Ahern must have enjoyed reading in the confines of this well-lit and attractive room.

Home libraries were in fact practically a necessity for anyone who wished to pursue an intellectual life prior to public libraries, which did not develop in rural areas until the early twentieth century. While Benjamin Franklin's subscription library, which he shared with a group of friends in Philadelphia, might be considered the first public library in America, libraries open to the general public did not appear until the nineteenth century. Boston established one as early as 1854 with others appearing by 1875 in 257 additional cities.[10] Texarkana was late in establishing its own. In our own time where, as library historian Wayne A. Wiegand notes, the "United States has more public libraries than McDonald's restaurants,"[11] it's easy to forget the lack of public facilities in early twentieth-century Texas and Arkansas.

Considering the Aherns' book collection in the context of Texarkana and the nation's print culture of the period encourages both an appreciation for the collection and an understanding of *why* and *how* the Aherns may have purchased many of the books resting on these shelves.

## Overview of Print Culture in the Texas and Arkansas Regions

### Public Library in Texarkana

In 1909 the *Texas Libraries*, a publication of the Texas Library and Historical Commission, offered a report on the progress of the public library system in Texas prepared by Benjamin Wyche, president of the then newly established Texas Library Association. He claimed that in 1899 only two or three "small" public libraries existed in the state. By 1909, over twenty-five had been established, including sites at Tyler (1899), Bastrop (1900), Dallas (1901), Fort Worth (1901), Brenham (1901), Temple (1902), Belton (1905), Clarksville (1905), and Jefferson (1906), with additional sites being started in 1909 in Paris, Nacogdoches, Winnsboro, Ballinger, and Denton, among others.[12] Early libraries in Arkansas appeared in Fort Smith (1906), Little Rock (1906), Eureka Springs (1906), and Morrilton (1915).[13] Texarkana is noticeably absent from this list. In fact, as late as March 1914, the *Texarkana Courier* reported that "a library and reading room" might share a space with a Confederate monument to be erected on State Line Avenue.[14]

The bulk of these early libraries in Texas and Arkansas reflected the Carnegie philanthropic program. Between 1886 and 1917, the Carnegie Foundation established 1,689 libraries, "many of them in small towns."[15] Thirty-two existed in Texas and four in Arkansas.[16] Clearly much of the growth of the public library system depended on the support of wealthy benefactors. Between 1880 and 1899, public libraries received $36 million, mainly from "manufacturers, merchants, and politicians," while Andrew Carnegie alone contributed $41 million to the building of libraries between 1886 and 1917.[17] In all, Carnegie gave $649,500 to Texas and $138,600 to Arkansas.[18] The terms of these Carnegie Foundation grants provided for the construction of a library building if the town acquired the books, oversaw the building, and employed a librarian. By 1923 almost a third of the US populace benefited from the Carnegie libraries.[19]

That Texarkana elected not to receive a Carnegie grant for a public library suggests either the inability of the city leaders in Texas and Arkansas to agree to or provide for the conditions of the grant or simply the town's lack of sufficient interest or both. That Carnegie required a town to maintain the library through taxes in the amount of 10 percent annually of its original award may have dissuaded some. The requirement that the town provide for a site may have caused disagreement as well. Certainly citizens could have shown that the area needed a library, which constituted another requirement.[20] While at first Carnegie's representative James Bertram required only a statement from the community indicating all requirements had been met, later he requested formal documents and letters of intent signed by the mayor or city council.[21] And because Texarkana was a racially segregated town, it would have received a grant based only on the number of people actually permitted to use the library. The "grant equation of $2 to $3 per citizen" would have reflected only the white population, which would have considerably reduced any possible allocation.[22]

In addition, some Texarkana citizens may have been afraid of having a library because they thought the public use of books would spread disease. Citizens worried about such illnesses as tuberculosis, infantile paralysis, diphtheria, and smallpox and with good reason. Over five hundred thousand Americans died in the great influenza pandemic of 1918 and 1919.[23] Others may have been self-righteous about accepting "tainted" money from Andrew Carnegie, resentful of a tycoon who had accumulated such wealth from the back-breaking labor of others. The "tainted" objection received national notoriety when Mark Twain, upon being asked if he thought Carnegie's money was tainted, replied, "Yes, it is—'taint yours and 'taint mine."[24] By 1917 the development of the public library system had lost considerable momentum. In that year Andrew Carnegie ceased his philanthropic program because an investigation revealed "lack of interest, rather than lack of money" to explain the failure of many communities to provide the Carnegie-built libraries with the required tax support they needed.[25] This failure may have been Texarkana's as well.

Without the benefit of the Carnegie program, Texarkana was not able to establish a public library until 1924. Historians Chandler and Howe credit the Young Women's Christian Association, organized in Texarkana in 1918, with establishing the city's first public library. When first organized, the YWCA had provided a library for its members, including a reading room, which, according to former Texarkana Library Director Alice Coleman,[26] was located above Bryce's Cafeteria at 215 Pine St., and had collected "a large number of books." The YWCA members donated these books later to the new public library, which formally opened on December 1, 1925.[27] Texarkana's first public library existed in a "two-story house on State Line Avenue at Seventh Street in Texarkana, Arkansas."[28] When Josephine Wright Post, valedictorian of Texas High School's 1922 class, entitled her address "Why Texarkana Needs a Public Library," Texarkana's newspaper of the day—the *Four States Press*—printed her entire speech under the headline: "It is especially appropriate at this time because of the movement for a local library."[29] The momentum for a public facility did not falter, and the Texarkana Public Library finally opened its doors. It was, however, seventy years after the nation's first public library had begun in Boston.

## Traveling, Social, and Subscription Libraries in Texarkana

Without access to books in a local public library, Texarkana citizens had to rely on other means of getting reading materials. An early method of distributing books occurred in the so-called traveling library movement. Initiated by Melvil Dewey in New York in 1892, traveling libraries eventually existed in some thirty states,[30] including Texas. But the 1914 quarterly publications of the *Texas Libraries* indicate difficulties in the acquisition of sufficient funds to send books to needy areas. The traveling library consisted of several books and magazines packed in a container suitable for being transported by wagon, mule back, or freight.

The libraries served towns lacking a library, clubs requesting books for study, and small public libraries and cost "$50 each." They would benefit "isolated communities where the books are not only read, but talked over again and again, and often change the whole current of neighborhood thought and talk." This idealistic passage ends in an equally idealistic quotation from the *Chautauquan*: "It is after all, not the few great libraries, but the thousand small ones, that may do the most for the people."[31] Although the traveling library movement succeeded in some states, it seems not to have been effective in Texas. After 1920 the traveling libraries generally became book wagons, or in some places county or branch libraries.[32] The traveling library program probably never reached Texarkana, or if it did, it was ineffective and short lived.

Two kinds of libraries, however, did exist in Texarkana prior to the establishment of the public library system: the social and circulating libraries. The first group generally combined the function of a library with the social aspects of a club, while the latter was typically associated with a bookstore or other commercial enterprise and had a different financial structure.[33] In other words, procuring books from a circulating library typically required money, not membership.

In her overview of the status of women in Texarkana during the Progressive Era, historian Beverly J. Rowe notes that the Current Topics Club, an organization for women, was initiated as "a literary improvement group" in 1920 and "had a circulating library of books," bought by and limited to the twenty-four members of the group.[34] Although the books "circulated" among members, only members, who were elected, could use them. This library seems more like a social library as does the early library that the YWCA formed for its members' use. On the other hand, the First Church of Christian Science established a reading room and a "circulating library" that was free and did not require church or social membership.[35]

An example of the more traditional circulating library occurred in Texarkana's early book and stationery stores and possibly in other businesses. In this model, individuals paid a subscription fee to borrow books over a period of time or simply rented individual books. For example, J. S. Gaines, a book and stationery store at 312–14 State Line Ave., ran several ads in the *Daily Texarkanian* in the spring of 1910 promoting its "Circulating Library." It claimed to offer "All latest Fiction," providing citizens the chance to rent a book for a dime.[36] The practice of offering books for rent in a store that also sold books was long standing, finding origin in this country in William Rind's fledgling bookstore in Annapolis in 1762.[37] Although his venture failed, the concept of the circulating library caught on in the colonies with owners of coffeehouses and other businesses operating circulating libraries on their premises.[38] In fact, in Great Britain, the practice was common. In all, some 365 circulating libraries existed there, with most operating between 1750 and 1850.[39]

## Early Book and Stationery Stores in Texarkana

Although Texarkana lacked a public library until the mid-1920s, it claimed bookstores. The 1899 *Texarkana City Directory* lists three businesses under "Books and Stationery," all on East Broad: E. D. Lingold, J. S. Ragland, and Smith Drug Company.[40] An advertisement in the 1901 *City Directory* touts Ragland's early establishment in 1876 and promises a

"Complete Line of Blank Books and Office Supplies."[41] Ragland, in fact, was quite popular. Beverly Rowe notes that E. A. Warren, editor of the *Daily Texarkana Independent*, encouraged readers to support this business. "Go to Ragland's for your Sunday reading materials," Warren wrote. Rowe adds: "Ragland Stationery must have been the gathering place of Texarkana's early literati."[42] Those who gathered there may have included Patrick Ahern and his future brother-in-law John Kline. Patrick's dry goods store—O'Dwyer & Ahern—was on East Broad, close by.

An ad that Ragland Stationery ran several times in the *Daily Texarkanian* in 1905 illustrates its prominence as a bookseller. "Just Received the Following New Books," the headline proclaims in bold type. The ad then goes on to list fourteen texts with their authors, the most prominent one being Edith Wharton's now classic *The House of Mirth*, first published in 1905.[43] Throughout this period, customers generally depended on the knowledge of salesclerks to recommend books. Although "new arrivals" were typically displayed on tables for customers' easy viewing, in most retail bookstores, unlike in a modern bookstore, most of the stock was housed on shelves and in cupboards, typically separated from the area open to browsers.[44]

The 1912 *City Directory* lists even more businesses under "Books and Stationery": Brown News Company on West Broad, DeFee and Adams on Buchanan, T. J. Elrod on Dudley, J. S. Gaines on State Line Avenue, and Ragland's. Also listed is the Presbyterian Book Store along with its advertising slogan: "FOR THAT BOOK OR GIFT."[45] The Presbyterian Book Store ran an ad on June 10, 1910, announcing "Commencement Gifts" that consisted of "Graduation and High School Books from 50 cents to $6.00." The store promised a large assortment of "illustrated Gift Books, Standard Works and Poets, bound in leather, at prices that please."[46]

That a few Texarkana bookstores enjoyed considerable longevity attests both to a local populace that bought books and to the businesses selling other items as well. For example, both Ragland and J. S. Gaines sold fishing tackle among other items. Historians have documented the difficult role for booksellers in Texas and neighboring states. Although Austin claimed some fifteen or sixteen bookstores between 1870 and 1900, most closed within a couple of years. Only one bookstore offered a circulating library, charging $7 annually for a customer's renting one book at a time.[47] Most of the bookstores in both Austin and Houston also sold other goods. In addition to books, Miss Lizzie I. Moody's bookstore in Houston sold "jewelry, hair goods, toys, bric-a-brac, and Butterick sewing patterns" as well as newspapers, periodicals, and stationery.[48]

## Door-to-Door Salesmen and Reading Groups

Although early bookstores in Texarkana sold reading materials, not all books published during the period were available in retail stores. Instead, subscription publishers often relied on book agents to canvass door to door to sell their publications and waited until orders were received before printing and binding the books. Usually subscription books were big, heavy texts bound in ornate styles. Their price depended in part on the binding style a customer chose. These books tended to be sold in sets, such as encyclopedias, memoirs, handbooks, and collections of writers' works. Beginning in the 1870s and 1880s, a number of specialized publishers produced series of the classics in this manner. In 1878 Harper Brothers, a trade publisher, began publishing the Franklin Square Library to compete with Lakeside Library in Chicago and Munro's Seaside Library in New York. Publishers often labeled these sets a "library."[49] The Aherns' home library includes a number of books published as sets or as a "library."

Door-to-door book agents were so plentiful during the period that they gave rise to numerous jokes, most of them focusing on book agents' pushy spiels and sometimes unlawful shenanigans. As late as 1905, a story circulated about an agent in New England who sold subscriptions at a hundred dollars each for a book on opera, the proceeds of which would be spent to lobby Congress to create a national opera company. Neither the book nor the company materialized for these hoodwinked customers. By 1900, well dressed canvassers, with above-average educations and suitcases of samples in hand, might earn $3,000 a year, a solid salary for the period.[50] Texarkana had its share of these salesmen. The history of the door-to-door book agent includes names of prominent individuals, such as Mark Twain, Longfellow, Daniel Webster, and future president Rutherford B. Hayes, the latter selling subscriptions to Butler's *Lives of the Saints* throughout southern Ohio.[51]

Texarkana citizens also received publishers' catalogs in the mail encouraging them to order books through the postal system. The postal laws of the period allowed the cheap mailing of books in a series as long as texts were "dated, numbered, and published regularly in uniform style."[52] Plus, with the creation of the Book-of-the-Month Club in 1926, the largest and most successful of these reading clubs of the era, customers could receive promotional catalogs and texts in the mail as members of a "club." With the establishment of Rural Free Delivery and parcel post in the early twentieth century, these clubs reached thousands of potential readers in outlying areas across the nation, including Texarkana.[53]

Another reading group that some citizens in Texarkana may have joined was promoted by the Chautauqua program, founded in 1878 as the Chautauqua Literary and Scientific Circle (CLSC). It offered a four-year study of designated home reading and appealed to many. Especially designed to involve citizens living in small towns, by 1898, it boasted 10,000 reading groups with a fourth of them being in towns of fewer than 500 people and half in cities of no more than 3,500. In fact, even "train crews on western railroads" conducted reading circles, and one can reasonably assume some of those crews traveled through and stopped off in the early days of Texarkana. With a monthly publication titled the *Chautauquan* (quoted earlier in this chapter), the CLSC promoted the serious kind of reading that the Aherns' library reflects.[54]

Finally, the earliest of Texarkana's citizens had access to reading materials at the Union Depot and on the trains. This genre—known as "railroad literature"—appeared by the 1870s and garnered fans. Generally inexpensive reprints, these publications catered to railroad travelers. Such publishers as Boston's A. K. Loring with its Railway Companion Series, New York's Putnam and Appleton, Philadelphia's Peterson, and the prolific Frank Leslie of New York, produced large editions. The American News Company distributed many of these publications, which were priced at 10 and 29 cents each, sold at newsstands and "hawked through the trains by train boys."[55]

## Newspapers and Magazines

During the 1880s through the early twentieth century, US culture was quickly changing into one of print, connecting various social and political threads of the nation and seemingly bent on weaving these into a collective cultural fabric. Aside from libraries and books, newspapers played a crucial part in creating this tapestry. Helped by the advertising revenues they increasingly collected, newspapers "became the print form most responsible for leading the United States into a new mass-media era."[56] Patented in the nineteenth century, telegraphs provided the news to papers everywhere, and the Associated Press became the main carrier of these news stories.[57] With the advent of newspaper "chains," in the early 1900s owners could print the same material—news stories, women's pages, serial novels, and so on.—in almost a hundred different newspapers on the same day.[58]

The *Daily Texarkanian* of 1905, however, shows little evidence of having received canned pages from national sources or being affiliated with the Associated Press. For example, on October 9, 1905, the paper ran a front-page story with the headline "Formal Invitation for Roosevelt to Come to Texarkana,"[59] on October 19 it ran the local story and headline "Woman Horribly Deformed Died at Poor Farm,"[60] and on October 23, it ran a front-page narrative about five "drunks" appearing before a local magistrate. This latter writer notes: "They were a dejected crew and it was clear from their woe-begone looking countenances that conscience was busy at work gnawing on their guilty souls."[61] These stories offer a microcosm of the tumultuous journalistic heritage of the day and range from the lively to the salacious. Overall, they depict a cacophony of topics and styles with a noticeable lack of journalistic design.

The history of Texarkana's newspapers in fact offers a narrative as convoluted as the layout of its early papers. The story begins with G. H. and F. G. Wootten's weekly—*The Texarkana Democrat*—created in 1875 in Texarkana, Arkansas. By 1883, the *Democrat* added an afternoon daily and changed ownership several times; in 1892 under new ownership, it merged with the *Daily Texarkanian*, which had begun in 1891, and now offered weekly and daily publications. Changing ownership several times in the early 1900s, in 1926 the paper was bought by D. W. Stevick, who also purchased the *Four States Press* (earlier named the *Texarkana Courier*) and *Texarkana Journal*. Stevick published the *Texarkana Daily News*, an evening Arkansas paper, along with the morning *Texarkana Gazette*, based in Texas. In 1933, C. E. Palmer, who had earlier owned the *Four States Press* and the *Texarkana Journal*, bought both papers from Stevick and began the newspaper dynasty that still exists today, one that would eventually win state and national awards.[62]

Besides newspapers, residents of Texarkana also enjoyed having access to a wide variety of magazines. By 1880, about 3,000 periodicals existed in the United States. Some of these entered Texarkana homes via the mail system, getting to this area by rail. Unlike newspapers, periodicals tended to identify with special interests—fashion, religion, occupation—and generally not with a certain area. Of the ten most popular magazines of 1880, four produced "literary" readings, one fashion, and three agricultural. The most popular of these was the *New York Weekly* with a circulation of 200,000 with Harper's and Scribner's holding fourth and fifth place. The *New York Weekly* printed mostly serialized novels, including romance, Buffalo Bill stories, and those by Horatio Alger. Aware of the popularity of these story papers, the Catholic Press began the weekly *Illustrated Catholic American* in 1880, running a series on "eminent Catholic Americans" and serializing the novel *Victor's Crucifix*.[63] Based on the Aherns' collection of Catholic publications, one can reasonably assume Patrick Ahern became a reader of this weekly.

Publishers of magazines soon began a practice that newspapers pursued too. Although previously magazines had had a modest circulation, aiming to attract "cultivated and relatively affluent readers," all of this changed with a price war begun by *Munsey* with *Cosmopolitan* and *McClure* in 1893. *Munsey* began selling for 10 cents at the newsstands and offering a subscription for $1.00 a year; it thereby increased its circulation from 40,000 to 200,000 in less than six months. Soon magazines generally began marketing publications at a cost below that of production, making money on advertising instead. Such a practice improved circulation dramatically, increasing from 18 million in 1890 to 64 million in 1905. In other words, US publishers circulated almost four magazines per month for each US household, an amount that surpassed "weeklies, newspapers, or books."[64] They also helped secure readers of books by running serializations of novels and by profiling authors as celebrities.[65]

The *Daily Texarkanian* ran an ad for *Munsey* in February 1906 that touts its current monthly publication as "one of the finest and most finished numbers in all that goes to make a high-grade magazine that we have ever issued." It claimed "[N]o better magazine of the month at any price—none better anywhere" existed.[66] The very next day, the *Daily Texarkanian* published an ad for the *Delineator*, which claimed it published the "Authoritative Fashion News."[67] Clearly Texarkana residents of the period were part of this burgeoning culture of print.

# CHAPTER 4

## The Aherns' Book Collection

The Aherns' library reflects the era's growing interest in printed materials covering a vast array of topics, but it also provides a portrait of an intellectually curious individual. In an interview in 2005, Patrick Ahern's youngest daughter, Eleanor, described her father as a "quiet" man, but also one who loved to travel, to experience the thrill of seeing things first hand.[68] Historians Chandler and Howe describe his "modest, quiet, retiring nature" and emphasize his "charity . . . extending in all directions, irrespective of race or creed."[69]

Such a demeanor suggests a thoughtful, sensitive man, much like that described by seventeenth-century Francis Bacon in his famous essay "On Studies": "Read not to contradict and confute; nor to believe and take for granted; nor to find talk and discourse," he advises, "but to weigh and consider."[70] The Aherns' library—particularly in its initial form—seems the essence of Bacon's words. It reflects the love of learning instilled in Mr. Ahern by the Christian Brothers and a tradition of reading that he maintained all his life.

Of the almost five hundred volumes found in the Aherns' book collection, a little over a third of them constitute books published in series or sets. The vast array of subjects in these texts underscores the family's intellectual curiosity. About a third of the books are literary—poetry, fiction, drama, biography, memoir, children's literature, essays, and letters—with almost 20 percent, religious, reflecting the Aherns' Roman Catholicism. About 17 percent focus on music, representing both Mary Ahern's enthusiasm and later that of her daughter Ann, who became a well-respected piano teacher in the Texarkana area. Additionally, almost 10 percent pertain to history, indicating the Aherns' interest in both political and cultural studies.

Other topics include linguistics and languages (around thirty volumes), travel, geography, political science, medicine, math, physics, art, and business. Highly acclaimed general encyclopedias of the period appear as well. Finally, the Ahern children's school and college yearbooks find a place on these shelves along with their son John Ahern's 1940 dissertation at Georgetown School of Law: *Credits and Refunds—Income Taxes*. In addition, various pamphlets and souvenir memorabilia contribute to this print culture.

Such an impressive personal library brings to mind the scene in F. Scott Fitzgerald's famous novel *The Great Gatsby*, contemporary with the Ahern volumes. One of the novel's characters wanders into Gatsby's "high Gothic" library one night during one of his vast parties and is shocked to find the books are real with "pages and everything," instead of being "durable cardboard," although the pages were not cut.[71] Some books of the period came from the publisher with pages attached at the top or side and had to be cut or opened before reading. The Ahern collection, however, has "cut pages," as the books were read.

To sum up, the Aherns' library constitutes not only Patrick and Mary's original selections but also the contributions made by their children. With publication dates of the complete library ranging from the 1860s through the 1980s, over half of the library—about three hundred volumes—have dates no later than 1919, with over one hundred of these printed in the first decade of the 1900s. Over thirty books predate the twentieth century with about fifty texts from the 1930s. Since Patrick Ahern died in 1932, one can reasonably assume that the books published from 1860 through the early 1930s constitute the original collection. That only one family but two generations lived in this house and purchased and shared books complicates knowing exact ownership of much of the unsigned material. Their daughter Ann, born in 1910, spent most of her life in the house and another daughter Mary, born in 1907, returned to the home in retirement. Ann remained in the house until her death in 1988 and Mary, until her death in 2003. Youngest daughter, Eleanor, with her infant daughter lived in the house for five years during World War II, waiting for her husband to return from the war, and often returned for vacations later; and son Joseph, born in 1905, moved back into the house later in life and remained there until his death in 2002. Printed materials that are undated—about fifty books and pamphlets—constitute some of the oldest materials as well.

## Patrick Ahern's Book Collection

### *Religious Book Sets: The Catholic Encyclopedia and others*

Foremost, the original library consists of a number of noteworthy book sets, published as compilations of scholarly treatises and reference articles. Among these appears the highly regarded *The Catholic*

*Encyclopedia*, initially published in fifteen volumes, dating from 1907 to 1912 with an index and explanation of purpose following in 1914, 1917, and 1922. Published for the Catholic Press by the New York firm the Robert Appleton Company in large leather-bound folios, the work offers "authoritative information" on all Catholic concerns and doctrines.[72] The board of directors consisted of five eminent Catholic scholars of the period.[73]

Before 1880, the Catholic Press had focused largely on poor and recent immigrants, but beginning in the late nineteenth century, Catholic publications for families had a decidedly more middle-class tone.[74] This change exemplifies the movement in US Catholicism from the "immigrant mission" to a more "assimilative subculture."[75] *The Catholic Encyclopedia* reflects this shift in emphasis, as it sought to elevate "the taste of the Catholic reading public" with European high culture "as the rightful heritage of American Catholics."[76] By 1911, a Catholic Press Association was formed to organize all communications nationally.[77] Since books were believed to be essential to "Catholic life and worship,"[78] a vast array of Catholic publications came into being throughout the nineteenth and early twentieth centuries.

What is perhaps most intriguing to a contemporary reader of these volumes of *The Catholic Encyclopedia* is their inclusion of discussions of various art forms and scientific discoveries rendered through a Catholic lens. According to the editors, the work details what Catholic educators, poets, artists, scientists, and others have achieved in their various areas.[79] For example, a laudatory article on Johann Wolfgang Amadeus Mozart ends: "What Mozart, with his Raphaelesque imagination and temperament, would have been for *church music* had he lived at a different time and in different surroundings or risen above his own, can easily be imagined."[80] Similarly, after praising French dramatist Moliere's style and comic genius, the article ends by suggesting that although "it was his wish and duty . . . to be of service to *morality*, he has been severely censured in this regard."[81]

Such comments notwithstanding, one can appreciate the laudatory remarks of its contemporary reviewers. London's *Saturday Review* terms it a "model of reference works" and the *Athenaeum*, a "thorough and learned enterprise."[82] Replete with fine illustrations, some in large color plates, of such items as maps, art, architecture, and portraiture, the work abounds in scholarly detail. With several hundred authors and all articles approved by the editorial board, the work is an impressive composite of information published by the Catholic Press. These were expensive volumes, published by subscription. Their well-worn condition no doubt reflects not only the Aherns' reading but also that of friends, including members at St. Edward and Sacred Heart Catholic Churches who could not afford to buy a set.

The Aherns' library also includes *The New Catholic Dictionary*, published in 1929 and sold by subscription, which aims to be "A Book of Life, of Catholic life, past and present, in every part of the world,"[83] as well as Alban Butler's *Lives of the Saints*, undated. The "Very Rev. James Doyle," author of its preface, explains that this publication will make this "inestimable work" accessible to all, whereas its earlier publication in twelve volumes was quite expensive.[84] Published in both Dublin and London, this leather-bound set may well have been among the materials Patrick Ahern brought with him from Ireland to Arkansas in the early 1880s. Other religious works include two copies of Thomas à Kempis's *Imitation of Christ*; *Father Burke's Sermons and Lectures*, a three-volume green leather-bound work with gold lettering, published in New York in 1872, 1888, and 1896; and the two-volume *The Monks of the West* by Count de Montalembert and published in Boston by Marlier, Callanan. Though undated, the text includes Montalembert's preface, dated 1860. The table of contents of Father Burke's collection notes the extensive nature of his lectures, including such titles as "Catholicity as Revealed in the Character of the Irish People," "Catholicity not the Danger, but the Safety of the Great American Republic," and the "Future of the Irish Race at Home and Abroad."[85]

## Other Book Sets

Like the previous work, *Irish Literature*, a ten-volume set, reflects Patrick Ahern's Irish background. Published in 1904 in Philadelphia by John D. Morris, the collection contains the works of Irish writers still read today, such as Edmund Burke (volume 1), Oliver Goldsmith and Lady Augusta Gregory (volume 4), and Oscar Wilde and William Butler Yeats (volume 9) as well as writers whom most of us have forgotten, such as Mary Elizabeth Blake along with her poem, "The First Steps," in which she records the happiness "That only to mothers is known, / For the beautiful brown-eyed baby / Took his first steps alone!"[86]

## CHAPTER 4

Born in 1840 in County Waterford, Ireland, Blake came to America as a child, attended Emerson's private school in Boston, and, according to the editors of this volume, became the mother of a daughter and five sons, "all Harvard men." These are attractive volumes (6 × 8) bound in brown leather and green cloth, supplemented with intricate illustrations of people and places. If Emily Dickinson is correct in saying, "There is no Frigate like a Book / To take us Lands away"[87]—then reading these volumes must have transported Patrick to his homeland. Published in the United States, the collection had special appeal for Irish American readers.

Also gracing these shelves is a five-volume set of Gibbon's *The Decline and Fall of the Roman Empire*, published in New York by Belford, Clarke and edited by H. H. Milman. Bound in red cloth with gold lettering on the covers, these quartos (4 × 6) fit nicely in the hand. Though this edition is undated, the original appeared between 1776 and 1788 and contained about 1.5 million words, 10,000 references to historical personages, and 8,000 footnotes.[88] It is not surprising that *The Guardian* recently listed it among the one hundred best nonfiction books ever published.[89] The musicality of Gibbon's famous opening—"In the second century of the Christian æra, the empire of Rome comprehended the fairest part of the earth, and the most civilized portion of mankind"[90]—appears throughout this monumental work that spans over a thousand years. It is the style of a storyteller who possesses what *The Guardian* calls a "staggering erudition."[91] Many authors—Winston Churchill and Evelyn Waugh, for examples—admired Gibbon's style. "It has always been my practice," Gibbon explains, "to cast a long paragraph in a single mould, to try it by my ear, to deposit it in my memory; but to suspend the action of the pen till I had given the last polish to my work."[92]

Another set of historical texts designed to be accessible appears in John Clark Ridpath's *History of the World*, a four-volume set first published in 1890 and initially sold only by subscription.[93] Bound in red leather with gold printing on its cover, these large folios enjoyed much popularity among turn-of-the-century readers and were reissued numerous times. In the preface to volume 1, Ridpath parses words carefully both to praise and upbraid fellow historians. In fancy words, Ridpath claims these other texts were too erudite.[94]

Born into a poor family in Indiana in 1840, Ridpath excelled in academics, eventually teaching and becoming vice president at his alma mater Asbury College (now DePauw University) before he resigned to focus on writing. Although he strove to present well-written and accurate historical accounts, today's readers will notice within his works a strong influence of "Social Darwinism, imperialism, and nationalism" and "explicit notions of racial hierarchy." That said, his work still proves valuable in determining how these views shaped American and European notions of "history, progress, and the world."[95] To what extent Mr. Ahern agreed with these ideas is unclear, but some aspects of the book may have shaped his thinking.

Various other historical works appear on the shelves of this library: *The National History of Ireland* by Abbe MacGeoghegan and John Mitchell, published in 1884 in New York; *The Story of Ireland* by Alexander M. Sullivan, published in Dublin and undated; *The Parochial History of Waterford and Lismore*, published in 1912 in Waterford; and *The Romance of Irish History* by John G. Rowe, published by the Talbot Press in Dublin and Belfast and undated, among many others. The wealth of historical information offered in this library would have served the most inveterate of late Victorian and Edwardian readers.

Yet the acquisition of so much information may have seemed staggering to some. In a text designed to promote scholarly pursuits and organize home reading, *The Standard Question Book and Home Study Outlines*, published by Frontier Press in Buffalo, New York, in 1914, aimed to help readers become scholars of texts. It opens, "The days of the cave man have passed" and, "what the twentieth century demands is the trained intellect."[96] Meant as a study guide to Henry Ruoff's 1914 *The Standard Dictionary of Facts*, this slim volume categorizes topics, offers ways to study, and presents questions for home use. Its approach underscores the turn-of-the-century belief in progress.

A quite different approach to learning history appears in the thirteen-volume set *The Real America in Romance* by John R. Musick. Published by William H. Wise in New York in 1908, the work is supplemented by a study guide in a final volume "Prepared under the Advice and Direction" of Edwin Markham, the American poet. These attractive volumes sport brown leather, with embossed gold-leaf lettering on the spines with gold on the edges and a hand-tooled embossed front and back cover. Musick's stated goal was to use the techniques of fiction to write history though he wasn't interested in producing historical fiction, which he thought often distorted facts. Pursuing this idea, Musick determined to use more the style of Victor Hugo in *Les Miserables* than that of Boswell in *The Life of Samuel Johnson*, wherein Boswell employs recorded conversations, letters, and observations to give an impression. Claiming that "if one reads at all, he reads fiction,"[97] Musick sought to stay true to history in his narrative approach. "History," he proclaims, "is the most broadening, stimulating, and instructive of all studies."[98] Although the modern reader appreciates his admiration of history, the lofty task he set for himself probably required the gifts of a Victor Hugo for success.

## Encyclopedia Britannica

A far more engaging set of texts exists in the library's inclusion of the highly praised eleventh edition of the *Encyclopedia Britannica*, published in 1910 and 1911. Twenty-nine slim leather-bound volumes (6 × 8) resonate with some of the best turn-of-the-century prose ever written. The *Guardian* relates the story of the American journalist A. J. Jacobs who read through the *Britannica* and offers an assessment: "Compared to more modern editions," he notes, "reading the 11th is like reading a Faulkner novel instead of an instruction manual."[99] Instead of presenting the "single-treatise plan" that earlier editions had offered, the eleventh edition doubled the number of articles—about 40,000—and used headings for a reader's easy reference.[100]

Moreover, it employed notable contributors to provide entries. For instance, the well-known authority and fairytale author Andrew Lang wrote articles entitled "Apparitions," "Ballads," "Fairy," and "Mythology," among others. In the first of these, after considering *illusion* as a type of apparition, Lang provides the intriguing yet succinct example of Sir Walter Scott's vision of the poet Lord Byron, "then lately dead," which "proved to be a misconstruction of certain plaids and cloaks hanging in the hall at Abbotsford, or so Sir Walter declared."[101] English editor, suffragist, and poet Alice Christiana Meynell wrote the entry "Elizabeth Barrett Browning"; Sir Donald Francis Tovey, British musicologist, composer, and conductor, wrote "Opera" and "Music"; and Sir James Jeans, English physicist, astronomer, and mathematician, wrote "Molecule." The Aherns' copy of the eleventh edition is the "Handy Volume" issue, a 1915–16 photographic reprint of the original sold via the

Chicago mail-order house of Sears, Roebuck and Co., which enabled it to achieve a wider audience.[102]

*Orations*

The Aherns' penchant for selecting informative reading material appears as well in *The World's Famous Orations*, a ten-volume, green leather and cloth-bound set of quartos published by Funk and Wagnalls in New York in 1906. William Jennings Bryan, nineteenth-century orator and politician from Nebraska, served as editor-in-chief with Francis Halsey, American writer and historian, serving as associate editor. The publication garnered a brief notice August 4, 1906, in *The New York Times*, which describes the work's structure: "one volume each for Greece and Rome, three for Great Britain, one for Ireland, one for Continental Europe, and three for America."[103] The Nebraska newspaper *The Commoner* ran an advertisement for the set some ten years after its initial publication, calling it a collection of "Speeches That Have Made History." The ad asks readers to imagine "The Whole Set on Your Library Table—All Carriage Charges Paid by Us, and Without a Cent from You."[104]

Bryan's Preface clarifies that in addition to already acclaimed masterpieces, the volumes contain oratories that he considered most valuable to those interested in history and forensics.[105] To that end, appear British author Charles Dickens's "As the Literary Guest of America" delivered in New York City, February 18, 1842 at a dinner in his honor, Washington Irving presiding;[106] Washington's First Inaugural address at Federal Hall in New York on April 30, 1789;[107] and Theodore Roosevelt's "On American Motherhood," delivered in Washington in 1905 to the National Congress of Mothers.[108] In the latter, Roosevelt, reflective of his time, defines the woman's sphere, except in "exceptional cases," as that of the "home-maker," but then goes on to say that no typical work done by a man is as hard or as important as that of a woman rearing a group of children.[109] There are orations from Native Americans, such as "Red Jacket on the Religion of the White Man and the Red," delivered at a "council of chiefs of the Six Nations" in 1905 by Sogoyewapha of the Senecas as a response to a missionary who proposed to work among them.[110] "We do not wish to destroy your religion or take it from you," Sogoyewapha reportedly stated. "We only want to enjoy our own."[111]

## Lexicons

One of the most intriguing sets in the library appears in the twelve-volume *The Century Dictionary: An Encyclopedic Lexicon of the English Language*, published in 1902 in New York under the direction of William Dwight Whitney, whom the editor of *American Dictionaries* identified in 1913 as "the leading philologist in America" of his generation.[112] Whitney, Professor of Comparative Philology and Sanskrit at Yale University, planned a three-tiered approach as outlined in the Preface: to offer the public a "serviceable" and "practical" general dictionary; a composite of technical terms; and finally much "encyclopedic matter" with illustrations.[113] Large folio volumes bound in black and blue leather, these books show the wear associated more with use than age. The dictionary, which began its preparations in 1882 and first appeared in 1889–1891, contained 200,000 words, required nine years of work, and cost $980,000 before the first plates for printing were created.[114] By 1909 two supplements to the dictionary resulted in a collection of 530,000 words and phrases.

A contemporary advertisement for the *Century Dictionary* touted it as the best dictionary available. "The best books are useless," the ad proclaims, "if not used." Further, it argues that this dictionary will enhance every other text in the library. And finally, when reading anything, "your *Century* should be at your elbow."[115] With such a promotion, it's easy to see why the Aherns added the set to their library. A glance at one of the entries underscores the set's versatility and erudition.

Consider, for example, the entry on *cadence,* used as a noun. There first appears an extensive etymology, followed by eight definitions. As illustrations of the third definition, which begins "A regular and agreeable succession of measured sounds, " four literary examples from Chaucer, Milton, Oliver W. Holmes, and Tennyson appear. Lines chosen from *Paradise Lost* provide the example for Milton: "Blustering winds, which all night long / Had roused the sea, now with hoarse *cadence* lull / Sea-faring men."[116] Several definitions of *cadence* as pertaining to music complete the entry, supplemented by illustrations of musical staves indicating among others "perfect," "imperfect," "interrupted," and "plagal cadence."[117] Clearly, the *Century* aimed to approach the thoroughness of the famous *Oxford English Dictionary*, which today is considered the best dictionary of the English language. The *Century* offered a remarkable dictionary for turn-of-the-century home use.

## Classics & Belles-Lettres

Another serviceable and attractive set appears in the seventeen red and green leather-bound volumes of the *Universal Classics Library*, published in 1901 by M. Walter Dunne in Washington and London, under the direction of Appleton Prentiss Clark Griffin, a highly respected librarian and bibliographer. The set is an excellent example of the type of publications as discussed earlier that indicate by title an entire library of materials. Each volume is edited by an authority in the appropriate field. Among the works in this "library," which are largely of a political and philosophical nature, appear *The Federalist Papers* by Hamilton, Madison, and Jay; Plato's *The Republic* and *The Stateman*; and the Earl of Chesterfield's celebrated and highly controversial correspondences, *Letters Written to his Natural Son on Manners and Morals*, dating from 1757.

Two volumes entitled *English Belles-Lettres* and *French Belles-Lettres* give variety to these otherwise mostly political discourses. In the former of these appears for instance, Elizabethan poet Sir Philip Sidney's "An Apologie for Poetrie," written around 1579, and Romantic English poet Samuel Taylor Coleridge's *Biographia Literaria*, an autobiographical discourse published in 1817. The *French Belles-Lettres* offers among other works humor in Paul Scarron's *The Strolling Players*, a picaresque novel that creates comedy through parody. Finally, the historical novel *Salammbo* by Gustave Flaubert proved to be shocking as a tale of lust, sensuality, and cruelty, yet highly popular. Flaubert's novel prompted many operatic versions of the story as well. It's difficult to tell whether the Ahern family read all of these, including *Salammbo*, but the latter would probably have been a welcomed change for some readers from these otherwise mostly difficult political discourses.

### *An Art Edition of Shakespeare, a Gazetteer, and a Travel Book*

Shakespeare, of course, appears in this library, represented by a couple of editions. *An Art Edition of the Most Popular Dramas of Shakespeare* offers a synopsis of the plots of some of the best-known of Shakespeare's plays written by famous nineteenth-century English essayists Charles and Mary Lamb with outlines offered by Mary Seymour. A large folio edited by C. A. Gaskell, the text was published by US Publishing House in Chicago in 1889, as a family edition. With mixed motives, editor Gaskell wants all to have a familiarity with these plays to prevent "embarrassment and regret" for those ignorant of the classics, but he also offers a bowdlerized edition, excising parts he deems unsuitable for family reading.[118] Bound in red embossed leather with the title in gold leaf on the front and gold on the book's edges, the work has marbleized endpapers and shows much use, presumably by all of the Aherns.

Certainly belonging to Patrick Ahern, *Rand, McNally & Co.'s Encyclopedia and Gazetteer* published in 1889 reflects his interest in geography and travel, a fact that the Aherns' youngest daughter Eleanor emphasized about her father.[119] Published in Chicago, the book has eighty full-page colored maps and almost two thousand engravings. A large text bound in embossed dark red leather with the title in gold on its cover and spine, the book promises the inclusion of many new works focusing on American subjects.

A book complementing this text appears in a pocket-size edition of *How to Travel* by Thomas W. Knox, published by G. P. Putnam's Sons in New York in 1887 in a "revised edition." Its subtitle offers "*Hints, Advice, and Suggestions to Travelers by Land And Sea All Over the Globe.*" Among the more intriguing chapter titles appear "Special Advice to Ladies, by a Lady," "Traveling with Camels and Elephants, "and "Traveling Without Money—Round the World for $50." In the first of these—"Advice to Ladies"—after many paragraphs focusing on what to bring and how to organize one's belongings, the chapter concludes with advice "for a becoming head-covering to wear in railroad carriages" when not wearing a hat. Simply "take a gentleman's small-sized silk pocket handkerchief, of becoming color, and trim the edges with some cheap black Spanish lace." The author suggests it will fit the head nicely and be easily carried in a bag.[120]

This little text also has front end papers advertising Crosby's Vitalized Phosphites for "Mental or Nervous Derangements," Jeremiah Skidmore's Sons' Coal Dealers, J. C. Gillmore & Co.'s "Fine Traveling Trunks," and Hall's "'Between the Acts' all-Tobacco Havana Cigarettes, For Sale Everywhere," among others. One assumes these ads helped finance this small book. The text does not appear to have had great use. According to daughter Eleanor, although her father tried to persuade her mother to travel, she remained hesitant to go abroad.[121]

## Mary Olive Ahern's Books

A set of books that Mary Ahern no doubt selected—*Modern Music and Musicians*—constitutes what Louis C. Elson, its editor-in-chief, terms "a musical library in itself."[122] Seven large folios, bound in green leather with gold lettering on the embossed covers, offer a rigorous study of music that consists of two volumes of piano music, one of vocal songs, and three of religious music, musical theory, and history. These well-worn volumes date from 1912 and offer the sound scholarship and selection of pieces as overseen by Elson, who was Professor of Music at Boston's New England Conservatory and a celebrated author and musicologist in his own right. The Aherns' edition of these books—labeled the Philharmonic Edition—offers the writings of a wide-ranging group of authorities in music as well as various portraitures of famous composers.

In contrast with the solemnity of the prose and portraits of learned men, a few wistful illustrations of young women at the piano also appear in these volumes. One of them, entitled "A Reverie," a painting by Frank Dicksee, depicts a sylph-like young woman playing a grand piano, with presumably a suitor sitting close by, one of his legs seemingly touching a leg of the piano. A single light shines down on the intimacy of the two.[123] Another picture of a painting by R. Poetzelberger labeled "Old Songs" depicts a solitary maiden sitting at a spinet, her left hand caressing a music book on the piano and her right holding another book at which she gazes intently. With drooped eyelids, she seems both demure and sensual. Another illustration labeled "An Egyptian Singing Girl" depicts a young woman dressed in a gauze-like smock, bejeweled with earrings, bracelets, and necklace. Reclining on the floor, she strums a harp as an incense burner floats whiffs of smoke upward.[124] Such pictures complement many of the emotionally evocative pieces included in the volumes, such as those by Chopin, Liszt, Rachmaninoff, and others, and remind us of the nineteenth century's view of music as potentially sacred but often inherently dangerous in its appeal.

Also highly evocative, *The Cavalier* by George Washington Cable bears the name of "Mary Olive Lansdale" on the inside cover. This first edition, published in 1901 in New York by Charles Scribner's Sons, sports a dark red cloth cover with decorative design by Margaret Armstrong and illustrated plates by Howard Chandler Christy. It relates a story of love and adventure during the Civil War between a young Confederate soldier and a lovely and daring Confederate spy. After a series a harrowing adventures, they find love in each other. The text constitutes an example of Lost Cause literature in its attempt to romanticize the bravery of Confederate soldiers in the midst of unwarranted loss. Cable's talents lay in evoking the "exotic aura of old New Orleans, and the Spanish-French Creole society," but his support of human rights for all people prompted him to leave the south and settle in New England in 1884, where he continued to write novels as late as 1918.[125]

Another book inscribed with "Mary Lansdale" on the inside cover, *The Mirror of True Womanhood: A Book of Instruction for Women in the World*, offers a guide to proper decorum for young women, as its title promises. Published by the Excelsior Catholic Publishing House in 1895 and written by Bernard O'Reilly, the book includes chapter titles such as "The True Woman's Kingdom: The Home," "How the Home Can Be Made a Paradise," "Special Training for Girls and Boys," "The Mistress of the Home and Her Social Duties," and "Maidenhood." In the preface, O'Reilly explains that his purpose in writing the book, first published in 1877, was to withstand "the spread of the prevailing naturalism."[126]

In a chapter that opens with "The Divine Comforts of Poverty and Toil," O'Reilly offers advice to women in various professions: shop workers, teachers, and dressmakers, among others. With the latter, he acknowledges their "cruel responsibility" and "toil without cessation." Further, "the strongest constitutions soon give way, and the ruin thus wrought is irreparable." But physical devastation pales beside "dangers . . . to which we would fain not be forced even to allude." The section ends in his adding: "Respect yourselves . . . and, precisely because you are poor, dependent, and constrained to do hard work for very little money, never permit any one placed above you in your labor, so much as to breathe a word capable of bringing a blush to your cheek."[127] Although O'Reilly's circumscribed world would not permit him to include a more forthright discussion of sexual harassment, to his credit he is more direct in his condemnation of how women and children were abused though factory work, estimating some 500,000 women and children employed in factories in 1878. Additionally he rails against "Heartless Industry" and the lack of legislation protecting women and children.[128]

*Etiquette, Politeness, and Good Breeding*, another guide to decorum, adds to the Aherns' collection of texts on acceptable behavior. Because the book was published in Scotland, it may well have been a book that Patrick brought with him to Arkansas. A pocket-sized work with "Etiquette" written in pencil on its paper cover, the book also includes a "Variety of Model Letters." Published in Glasgow by Dunn and Wright Printers without a date or author, this little book covers the gamut of social etiquette, including such topics as "Balls," "Concerts," "Drawing Room Etiquette," "Dinner Parties," "Dress," Letters of Introduction," "Morning Visits," and "Salutations and Leave-Takings." In a chapter titled "Dress, Manners, and Personal Appearance," the author laments that "far too much time is often engrossed by dress," and further, "The Beauty of dress" . . . resides "in not being conspicuous, in neither distorting, nor yet concealing the human form with unnatural additions."[129] This author laments the liberties some take with being alone in public: "Time was, when private gentlewomen rarely, if ever, walked in the streets unattended by a footman; but times are changed, and a degree of liberty is allowed."[130]

### The Ahern Children's Books

An especially beautiful yet haunting book, Dante's *Inferno*, bears the inscription "To Joseph Ahern from Dr. Nettie Klein 1921," designating the Aherns' oldest son, Joseph, born in 1905, as the owner. This large folio, bound in dark red cloth with illustrations on the front in black and gold-leaf, was published by P. F. Collier, in New York, translated by Henry Francis Cary, and illustrated by Gustave Doré. Its hauntingly beautiful opening from Canto I—"In the midway of this our mortal life, / I found me in a gloomy wood, astray"—has become famous to generations of readers. Exceptional as well are Doré's illustrations rendered throughout the text. A nineteenth-century French painter and sculptor, Doré illustrated both children's literature and the classics.[131]

*The Light in the Clearing* by Irving Bacheller constitutes another intriguing text, with the inscription "Joseph P. Ahern." This best-selling novel, written in first-person, depicts the adventures of a young man who is the main witness of a murder. Published by Grosset & Dunlap in New York in 1917, this first edition sports a red cloth cover. Joseph also owned Bacheller's *A Man for the Ages*, published in 1919 with the subtitle "A Story of the Builders of Democracy." This historical fiction was the first in a three-volume set about Abraham Lincoln, often required as high school reading in earlier periods. Bacheller was an American journalist who knew American novelist Stephen Crane and like Crane pursued fiction to much popular acclaim. In fact, the great popularity of his fiction practically made him a household name in the early twentieth century. He was also instrumental in creating the New York Press Syndicate, the first main metropolitan press syndicate that existed. Crane's *The Red Badge of Courage* first appeared in print as a serial novel in Bacheller's syndicate.[132]

Two classics that bear the inscription "Mary C. Ahern," the oldest daughter of the Aherns, are Willa Cather's *Death Comes for the Archbishop*, published in 1927 in New York by Alfred A. Knopf, and *The Rise of Silas Lapham* by William Dean Howells, published in 1928 by the Riverside Press. A valuable first edition, the Cather text has the original green cloth cover with the title and author printed on its cover and spine. The novel is based on the lives of Bishop Jean Baptiste L'Amy and his vicar, Father Joseph Machebeut. The framework of the story allows Cather to include what she especially loved—biographies, miracles and saints' legends, descriptions of landscapes, and the rituals and beliefs of Catholicism.[133]

The other novel owned by Mary C. Ahern, *The Rise of Silas Lapham*, has a blue cloth cover with "Riverside Literature Series" embossed on its front. On its spine appears "New Edition" in black along with the title and author. Originally published in 1885, this "New Edition" represents the fashionable trend of publishers to offer a "library" of the classics. It also offers a guide for teachers, replete with questions on chapters and entrance exams for college, as well as "Scenes for Dramatization," "Topics for Themes," and "Word Study."[134] The most popular of Howells's many novels, this one depicts a collision of social classes made possible by the rise of self-made tycoon Silas Lapham in the paint business. When he moves to Boston to introduce his two daughters to society, his fortunes wane but not before he is snubbed by the well-to-do Coreys. Howells was quite successful as a writer and critic, and in his editorship with the *Atlantic Monthly* helped shape American taste in fiction for his generation.[135] "The novel I take to be the sincere and conscientious endeavor to picture life as it is," he writes, "to deal with character as we witness it in living people and to record the incidents that grow out of character."[136]

A French novel *Abbé Constantin* by Lodovic Halevy bears the inscription "For Mary and Anna Ahern with X'mas love … 1920." Published by

H. M. Caldwell in New York with no date, the quarto is bound in brown leather with gold-leaf on its spine. On the front appears a picture in the color of trees and a meadow with pink and yellow flowers. It's an attractive book that would have appealed no doubt to the Ahern daughters. With characters the antithesis of French naturalist Émile Zola's typical character of evil inclination or mishap, *Abbé Constantin* offers remarkably likeable and honest personalities. The book was quite popular and seems to have prompted the Académie française to have elected Halevy to their midst in 1884. It remained popular not only because of its support of Catholicism but also because of its highly flattering portrayal of Americans.[137]

British novels that appear in the Aherns' collection include W. M. Thackeray's *Vanity Fair*, published by J. M. Dent in 1920, Arnold Bennett's The *Old Wives' Tale*, published in 1911 by George Doran, and Charles Dickens's *Our Mutual Friend*, published by Rand, McNally in Chicago, without a date. First published in 1847, *Vanity Fair* takes its title from Bunyan's *Pilgrim's Progress*, a title suggestive of the shams and greed of a money greedy society.[138] Subtitled *A Novel without a Hero*, the work follows the schemes of penniless Becky Sharp. In a famous scene wherein upon leaving Pinkerton's school for girls in a carriage and having just received a copy of Johnson's Dictionary, Becky "put[s] her pale face out of the window—and actually f[lings] the book back into the gardens."[139] As critics have argued, the novel clarifies that the psychological natures of the characters mimic the corrupt society they populate.[140] The spunk of Becky Sharp constitutes the antithesis of Father O'Reilly's focus on meekness in *The Mirror of True Womanhood*.

That the Aherns sometimes approached reading literature in a scholarly manner is suggested by the library's inclusion of literary histories. For example, *American and British Literature Since 1890* appears on these shelves with the inscription, "Mary C. Ahern, '29." Written by Carl Van Doren and his younger brother Mark Van Doren and published by the Century Co. in New York in 1925, the text contains lengthy discussions of such well-known writers as Robert Frost, Amy Lowell, Frank Norris, O. Henry, Thomas Hardy, H. G. Wells, and J. M. Barrie. One reader, presumably Mary C. herself, has underlined with pencil information she thinks especially pertinent. Additionally, another book belonging to Mary C. and marked "'29" appears in *English Literature during the Last Half-Century* by J. W. Cunliffe. Published by Macmillan in 1928, this text also contains underlining. Cunliffe begins by acknowledging the difficulties of assessing the value of current literature: "Contemporary literature presents at first sight," he remarks, "a spectacle of multifarious and even bewildering activity." That said, he offers a book of over 350 pages attempting to discern and present the main thrust.[141] A final example of literary history appears in *An Introduction to Poetry* by Jay B. Hubbell and John O. Beaty. Also bearing Mary C.'s name and published by Macmillan in the 1920s, these three books probably constitute texts she read in college and considered worthy of keeping. *A Text-Book for the Study of Poetry* by F. M. Connell, published by Allyn and Bacon in Boston in 1913, shows considerable use with marginalia as well as underlining.

*Poetry*

Overall the Aherns reveal a marked interest in poetry. A 1915 abridged copy of Alfred, Lord Tennyson's *The Idylls of the King* bears the inscription "Miss Mary Ahern . . . 9/10/21." A Victorian text *Poems of Pleasure* by Ella Wheeler Wilcox, published by Belford, Clarke in New York in 1888, was quite popular and remains in the library. From Wisconsin, Wilcox rivaled in popularity James Whitcomb Riley, the most popular poet of the time, and Eugene Field, author of such lyrics as "Little Boy Blue" and "Wynken, Blynken, and Nod." Wilcox's *Poems of Passion*, published in 1886, had earlier attracted the attention of the reading public as a text that was quite risqué. More sentimental than sensational, the collection is still remembered for the poem "Solitude," which opens, "Laugh and the world laughs with you / Weep and you weep alone."[142]

Another poet who seems admired by the Aherns is Edgar A. Guest in his text *When Day Is Done*, published by the Reilly & Lee Co. in Chicago in 1921. Guest was prolific and became known as the "People's Poet," although he always called himself a newspaperman and not a poet. He had popularized his poetry in a column he wrote for the *Detroit Free Press*, where he worked for decades.[143] Finally a book of poetry on the best-seller lists in the 1940s appears in *The Lifted Lamp* by Grace Noll Crowell. This first edition, published by Harper & Brothers in New York in 1942, still bears its original dustjacket of blue and white. A Texas poet, Crowell gained a wide audience with her short, rhyming lyrics with thoughtful sentiments. The speaker in the brief title poem states,

"I SHALL light my lamp at faith's white spark / And through this wild storm hold it high; / Perhaps across the utter dark / Its light will glow against the sky, / Steady enough and clear enough / For some lost one to steer him by."[144]

*Children's Literature*

The Aherns' library contains examples of children's literature, including an undated copy of *Mother Goose, or the Old Nursery Rhymes*, published in London by Frederick Warne and illustrated by Kate Greenaway. The text is inscribed "For Anne from Tabby, Dec. 25, 1915," no doubt a Christmas present and possibly a first edition, published in 1881. Greenaway, an English artist and author of children's books, created "sunlit and flower-surrounded children clothed in imaginary" clothing of the eighteenth century. She inspired many imitators and an entire line of clothing.[145] Beginning with her first publication for children in 1879, Greenaway became the rage throughout America and Europe, so popular that her pictures were copied on vases, plates, handkerchiefs, and caskets.[146] The Aherns' granddaughter Eleanor remembers her grandmother and Aunt Ann reading to her in the library from Mother Goose, possibly from this greatly admired edition.

Granddaughter Eleanor may also have been sharing her mother's childhood version of Mother Goose, which remains on these shelves. Published by P. F. Volland in New York in 1921, and illustrated by Frederick Richardson, this first edition contains large pictures in color, including many full-color plates that appeal to young readers. Another Mother Goose that shows considerable use—*Nursery Rhymes from Mother Goose*, illustrated by Grace G. Drayton—was probably shared by granddaughter Eleanor. Published by Charles Scribner's Sons in New York in 1916, this first edition presents a small-sized book but one with the remarkable drawings and some full color plates by the illustrator who went on to create the Campbell Soup Kids, cartoons, paper dolls, and paintings of young women. The daughter of lithographer George Gebbie, sometimes called Philadelphia's first art printer, Drayton studied at the Philadelphia School of Design for Women. Drayton's images of children in this Nursery Rhyme book have the iconic cherubic rosy cheeks and noticeably round eyes that have become part of the Americana of the period. The book is inscribed, "Merry Christmas, Anna, from Miss Tabb."[147]

Another example of children's literature appears in *Hitty, Her First Hundred Years* by US author Rachel Field and illustrated by Dorothy P. Lathrop. First published by MacMillan in 1929, the book won the Newbery Award for fiction in 1930. The narrative follows the adventures of Hitty, a wooden doll, who relates her own adventures of being left in a ship, carried by a crow, encountered by Charles Dickens, and abandoned in a museum. "After all, what is a mere hundred years," she asks, "to well-seasoned mountain-ash wood?"[148] With its flower-printed cloth cover and both black-and-white and full-color plates by Lathrop, the book is an attractive children's book from the 1920s.

First published in 1871 by nineteenth-century Scottish author George MacDonald, *At the Back of the North Wind* is inscribed to "Mary Ahern," with the additional phrase, "A Book that every boy and girl should read." Published by David McKay in Philadelphia without a date, this copy of the novel shows much use, perhaps reflective of the inscription. The novel, which was MacDonald's first work for children, offers a story that is more parable than strict allegory. It follows the adventures of Diamond, the young son of a coachman, who finds solace in difficult times through the voice of the North Wind, ultimately leaving this life to go "back of the wind." Called "remarkable" and a "milestone in children's literature," it combines children's fiction and the fairy tale with a concern for social and moral issues and shows influence from both Charles Dickens and Hans Christian Andersen.[149]

### Best Sellers of the Period

Finally, this library contains a number of best-selling texts of their day that have retained their fame largely through film and other adaptations. One of these, *The Story of the Other Wise Man* by Henry Van Dyke, though not initially marketed for children, must have been read by the entire Ahern family, especially during the Christmas season. This first edition, bound in red cloth with a picture of those following the star of the Christ Child on its front, indicates use by many readers. An American author and clergyman—a learned individual who completed a graduate degree at Princeton Theological Seminary[150]—Van Dyke offers comments about the source of his novel's story in his preface, where he claims the book was sent to him as a gift.[151] In addition to film, the novel has generated many other adaptations, including drama, opera, and visual art.

Other first editions and popular novels of the day housed in this library include *Green Dolphin Street* by British novelist Elizabeth Goudge, published in 1944 with Mary Ahern's inscription; *The Keys of the Kingdom* by Scottish writer A. J. Cronin, published in 1941 (a present from Ann to Mary); *The Black Rose* by Canadian journalist and novelist Thomas B. Costain (with Mary's inscription); and *The Robe* by Lloyd C. Douglas, published in 1942. All of these enjoyed successful movie versions. From a different era, *Daddy-Long-Legs,* published in 1912 by American novelist Jean Webster, also garnered numerous film versions, including early renditions with Mary Pickford and later Shirley Temple playing star roles.

Jean Webster constitutes an intriguing figure in her own right, both as one successful in American letters and as the grand- niece of Samuel Clemens. Taking a degree at Vassar College, Webster was quite self-reliant and seems not to have benefited professionally from her family's relationship to Mark Twain. She traveled the world, financed in part by the money she acquired through publishing fiction. *Daddy-Long-Legs* was successful immediately, and although Mary Ahern was only a child when the book first appeared, the spunk shown by both the novel's orphan protagonist and Webster herself seems very much like the personality of the Aherns' oldest daughter, who chose to pursue a career after college rather than marriage and family. Webster herself traveled and lived in small Italian villages, commuted all over India, visited Japan and China, all while creating sketches of her fellow travelers. Described as "affable and serious in purpose," and possessing a "social conscience," she married in her late thirties and died tragically in 1916 one day after giving birth to a daughter. Webster wasn't quite forty.[152]

Finally, *Paris-Underground*, a 1943 memoir by American writer Etta Shiber, became a popular movie in 1945. A first-hand account (with some names changed or omitted to protect others since World War II was still under way), the memoir must have been particularly compelling reading to the Ahern family since Eleanor's husband became a prisoner-of-war himself. The memoir depicts the efforts of Shiber and others to help British pilots behind German lines in Paris to escape from the Nazis. The widow of William Shiber, the wire chief of both *New York American* and *New York Evening Journal*, Shiber had met her future roommate, whom she calls "Kitty Beaurepos" in the text, in 1925 when Etta and her husband were visiting Paris. After her husband's death, Etta moved to Paris to live with Kitty. They got involved in helping soldiers escape almost by accident, but continued until they were apprehended by the Gestapo. Shiber's status as an American citizen saved her from a death sentence. She got three years of hard labor but was exchanged in May 1942 for a German spy. Her close companion Kitty was sentenced to death. When Shiber's book went to press, she didn't know whether her friend had been able to escape.[153]

## Design and Decoration of the Ahern Library

In designing a room for their book collection, Patrick and Mary provided an ample space that would function both pragmatically and aesthetically, locating the library behind the larger parlor or music room. Pocket doors connect the library to the music room and to the central hallway, acknowledging the room's potential as both a private and public space when needed. H. Hudson Holly, a late nineteenth-century American architect and book lover himself, wrote extensively about the ideal home library, which needed to be connected to a more public area in the home, one that could "serve as a waiting-room for persons whose visits are of a business nature."[154] Additionally, an essential quality of the library, for Holly, was adequate light, particularly effective when the light "falls upon the reader's book while he sits facing the fire."[155] One of Holly's house plans—Design Number 17—suggests that the dimensions of a library might be about 15 by 18 feet,[156] which is in fact the approximate size of the Aherns' room. Holly was also a great advocate for the library's inclusion of a bay-window, which he maintained has an especially pleasing effect and makes a "cozy corner for plants and birds."[157] Ideally, he notes, the bay-window is across from the fireplace,[158] a configuration that the Aherns' library mirrors as well.

Another well-known domestic architect of the nineteenth century, A. J. Downing includes in his *The Architecture of Country Houses* observations on the ubiquitous nature of the library. Downing's importance here lies not so much in his innovations but in his role as a "popularizer" of design.[159] In his descriptions of the largest houses, he maintains that the first floor should offer no less than three or four "good size" rooms in addition to the kitchen. Of these rooms, one permits dining, another "social intercourse," and a third, is "devoted to intellectual culture, or the library."[160]

Home decorator Lillie Hamilton French suggests that "recesses are the charm of libraries." A room that has a few angles achieves better aesthetics.[161] Especially important, the home library must "have power to lift even while it charms," to be what French terms "compelling."[162] American novelist Edith Wharton in her 1914 text *The Decoration of Houses* argues that the decorations in a library may be "splendid" and "richly adorned," but if so, the books themselves must be plentiful enough and of such quality that the décor functions as simply a background for the books, not vice versa. In keeping with the library's dignified atmosphere, Wharton stresses that photographs and other objects be minimal.[163] While Wharton permits some ornamentation, objects should be carefully chosen.

The Aherns' library, which has a single vase on the mantel and few pictures of any kind on the walls, is painted an ivory as are all the rooms in the house. French maintains that while the color should not overpower the hues of the books and that a "bright shining red" was always objectionable, she prefers that the color scheme of the walls match that of the books.[164] Her statements suggest she sees books more as art objects than as repositories of collective learning. Ogden Codman, co-author of *The Decoration of Houses*, sometimes chose a "dark red" for libraries, whereas Wharton preferred "a uniform pink," at least in her own library at Land's End in Newport, Rhode Island. "If the fundamental lines are right" in a room, Wharton and Codman maintain, "very little decorative detail is needed to complete the effect."[165] In her popular book *The House Dignified*, French argues that a library in the home created a positive effect on the family in conjunction with the aesthetics of books: "The colors of the bindings," she wrote, "the solidity of rank and file, the constant play of light upon the lettering, the variety of the upright line combined with a certain regularity, the relief of the horizontal shelf, create in their various combinations surfaces which to some are as alluring as tapestries."[166]

The selection of bookcases concerned owners of residential libraries. For "rooms of any importance," Wharton prefers bookcases built into the wall, favoring French architecture of the period.[167] Critical of the "old bookcases, running eight feet high," Holly favors those which permit space on top for ornaments and above for pictures, and especially likes the style that aligned the height of the bookcase with the mantel's, provided the appearance wasn't too "stiff."[168] Influenced by the Wernicke

System Elastic Book Cases, the Aherns chose the type of moveable bookcases with glass fronts, known today as "barrister cases" because lawyers typically selected these for housing their professional libraries. Otto Heinrich Louis Wernicke had invented this stacking system in 1889 in Grand Rapids, Michigan. Henry C. Yeiser, who had established a furniture factory called the Globe Files Co. in Cincinnati in the 1880s, bought the Wernicke company and in 1892 patented this unusual design under the Globe Wernicke Co. to great success.[169]

The architect's notes for the Ahern house indicate that these bookcases were selected at the time of the house's construction to fit along the walls of the library. Ordered in 1905 from the Globe-Wernicke's factory in Cincinnati, Ohio, and shipped by rail, the bookcases fit perfectly into the corners of the room and along the sides, their height of about 5 feet, matching that of the mantel, as Holly favored. An undated brochure of the Wernicke System titled "Always Complete but Never Finished," circulated by the A. H. Andrews Co. in Chicago, pictures a young boy who claims, "My papa pays the freight."[170] One wonders if the Aherns profited from "free shipping" with their order.

The Wernicke brochure describes the bookcases as a "series of small compartments, each ingeniously designed to interlock with another in vertical and horizontal arrangements" and offers numerous pictures to enable customers to select appropriate sizes in width, depth, and height. It also advertises cases in several kinds of wood and finishes: "plain oak, figured oak, walnut, imitation and genuine mahogany."[171] The Aherns chose oak, with the pattern number 299, a "quarter sawed figured oak, deep rich golden finish" with "highly polished, brass oxidized trimmings."[172] The selection of oak complements the floors, woodwork, and mantel. Although the Wernicke brochure advertises "opaque" glass doors made of either "ground, chipped or stained" glass,[173] Patrick and Mary selected clear glass, by far the most common and practical choice. The Aherns' order of corner bookcases, however, was not common as such cases required not only a special design slanted toward a corner, but also base units that were "mitered for that purpose."[174] Two of the bookcases labeled "Sectional bookcase reference 400836," have three shelves, which accommodate their larger reference works and folios. The other cases have four shelves each and reflect the "Standard D" series, which indicates they are about 11.5 inches deep.[175]

Also uncommon, the library's mantel, made of tiger oak, has columns on both sides of a Grecian Ionic style and traditional Greek detailing. Electing to use a mirror instead of a painting over the mantel, the Aherns appropriated the advice of such decorators as Lillie Hamilton French who suggests the practice of substituting a "wide mirror" for a painting.[176] Integral to the design of the mantel, the mirror has a carved oak-leaf border framing it. Hand-painted imported glazed ceramic tiles from Italy provide a platform for the mantel and encase the Humphrey Radiantfire heater. Opening the General Gas Light Company in Kalamazoo Michigan in 1901, Alfred Humphrey soon invented Radiantfire, a "clean and odorless heating unit for fireplaces."[177] The Aherns' decision to construct a house in 1905 with gas heating rather than a wood-burning fireplace represents a noticeably progressive approach to heating.

In 1893 the Columbian Exposition in Chicago had included various groupings of furniture deemed appropriate for residential libraries, including Ean & Company of Chicago, Berkey & Gay Furniture Company of Grand Rapids, Michigan, and the Furniture Exchange of Rockford, Illinois. By the end of the decade, retail furniture stores began displaying furniture for the library.[178] The Aherns chose a three-piece grouping of settee, lady's chair, and gentleman's chair with tufted backs and brass tacks along the edges of the upholstery. Recovered in the 1940s in a tapestry of French design in red roses with a beige background, the original was probably of a darker hue and more masculine design.[179] This oak furniture reveals the claw-foot of the Victorian period, but its lack of intricate detail marks it as transitional toward the plainer style of the early twentieth-century Arts and Crafts movement. A double-sided oak desk with cabriole legs rests in front of the bay window, which faces south. One of the sunniest rooms of the house, the library is an attractive space and remains the least altered room in the house.

Although initially belonging only to Patrick and Mary, as we have seen, the Aherns' residential library grew into a family library, a place where family members came together to read, to be read to, and to discuss books and the affairs of the day. Granddaughter Eleanor remembers the cheerful atmosphere of the library when she lived in the house as a child. In addition to being read to in the library, she recalls her grandmother's typical rejoinder, "Be careful with the bookcases!"[180] Grandson Brian Horrigan recalls sitting in the library as a youth when he visited the house on many occasions. He "especially liked seeing the old etiquette books" that discussed "how to behave in a men's club or how to receive visitors." "They are a window into the past," he adds, which is "really ... a different country."

Brian also notes that his grandparents used the library for both business work and casual reading. They "would lay out business plans on the table" and conduct "negotiations there." He mentions as well that in later times, the library "was a lovely and intimate spot for conversation." With the room being "circular and compact, people could sit in a circle with nothing between them, in comfortable chairs." The room was quiet, with the doors closed. "It was common to have an after-dinner drink there while conversing," and it wasn't just men in the room. Women in the family joined in the discussions. The room also served as a place for prayer. "Family members would say the Catholic Rosary together in the library after dinner before moving to conversation." Later on, the room grew even more as a place of meditation. With the television relegated to the back wall of the dining room, the latter became a family room as well as a dining room. The library became a place of seclusion.[181]

As with other domestic libraries, the reading lives that transpired in the Ahern home suggest a complexity of motivations—reading as a reverent act, as a practical goal of self-improvement, as a desire to escape from the mundane into the otherness of book-life, as a retreat from boredom, as an act of curiosity, and perhaps even of rebellion.

In *The Social Life of Books: Reading Together in the Eighteenth-Century Home*, Abigail Williams notes that recent scholarship reveals an increasing interest in the history of reading and "a commitment to the idea that how books were used is as important as what's in them."[182] The library-life of the majority of the Aherns' collection shows the use that comes with reading, thumbing passages and mulling over new information and ideas, in being absorbed in another's story and ideas. In the final analysis, the book collection exists both as the collective private selves of the Ahern family and as part of their public personae. In donating their book collection to the Texarkana Museums System, the Ahern family has contributed considerable information to our knowledge of the nature of print culture and home libraries in early Texarkana.

Texarkana's first public library, courtesy of the Texarkana Museums System, Wilbur Smith Research Archive

Bay window in the P. J. Ahern library, Texarkana Museums System, photograph by Doris Davis

Eleanor Horrigan and John Ahern visiting in the library in the P. J. Ahern home, courtesy of Maureen Ahern Leahigh

# 5

# Searching for the Fashionable in Early Texarkana

Women's Clothing in Public and Private Spaces

*I say, beware of all enterprises that require new clothes,
and not rather a new wearer of clothes.*

—Henry David Thoreau,[1] *Walden*

When Mary Olive Lansdale married Patrick Joseph Ahern in 1904 in Washington, DC, and moved to Texarkana, Arkansas, she arrived no doubt with a lot on her mind—helping her husband build their large home in a prestigious section of town called Quality Hill, planning for their family (they would have six children in all), and assuming a prominent role in society in a frontier town only some thirty years old. A young bride in her mid-twenties, she must also have been solicitous about her ongoing procurement of a wardrobe, especially so in a new town of not quite two thousand people and one boasting more saloons than dress shops. As social historian Betty J. Mills argues, even women on the Texas plains in the nineteenth century in "desolate settings were concerned with what they wore and how they looked."[2]

Among the artifacts left in the Ahern home, few seem as exquisite as the four pieces of clothing that comprise part of Mrs. Ahern's wedding trousseau. These intimate, handmade items—her wedding gown, bed jacket, gown and matching robe—emulate the meticulous skill of a

Parisian couturier and attest to the young bride's taste and style and, as her youngest daughter asserted in an interview in 2004, her mother's love of "pretty things."[3] That they are also symbolic of a young woman's emotional rite of passage only heightens their appeal. Anyone looking thoughtfully at their fine quality might wonder how an upper-middle-class bride replenished her wardrobe living in a small, isolated town in the early 1900s. Her success in doing so would personify both her position as a public figure, married to an important man of the town, and her role as a young wife.

Her choice in dress, in fact, would have been read by others as a kind of individualized language, exclusive in her personal selections of design, fabric, color, and style, yet inclusive enough to transmit decipherable texts or signs to her contemporaries. As social critic Katherine Joslin suggests about clothing in general, Mrs. Ahern's choices in dress might be considered a form of "hieroglyphs."[4] Further, "as an imaginative construct," Joslin adds, "dress creates the drama of the body."[5] Just as with her personalized design of her home's architecture and furnishings, Mary Olive's choices in fashion constitute a form of art as she imaginatively constructs public and private images of each. Both the house and the body, thus, will function as a kind of signifying surface.[6]

Clothing historian Valerie Steele proposes that fashion is largely a woman's personal choice within a changing social context of what constitutes beauty or sexual attractiveness. To a degree, a society's sense of beauty is an "artificial construct" that alters from one culture to another.[7] Fashion styles tend to be cyclic, with each period reacting to what has come before, just as in any artistic movement. Mrs. Ahern's selection of dress in 1904 as a young married woman places her in the midst of the lush Edwardian period, which clearly grew out of Victorianism, but even then projected itself toward what would become the style of the slender and youthful flapper of the 1920s.[8] Her selection of clothing in her early married life and beyond records her own society's evolving sense of feminine beauty.

Mrs. Ahern's contemporaries' decoding of the vestimentary meaning of her attire required their understanding of each article of her dress, a knowledge they absorbed from society itself. Her selections of clothing offered a guide to her identity as a woman of means and contained an intrinsic social message. It is a message that Lily Bart, the protagonist of

American writer Edith Wharton's 1905 *The House of Mirth*, understands well. "If I were shabby," Lily says to a young man in the novel's opening scene, "no one would have me; a woman is asked out as much for her clothes as for herself."[9] And clothing carries not only an "external cue" read by others, but also an "internal cue" that influences self-concept and confidence.[10]

As a bride, Mary Ahern would have been judicious in selecting the items of her trousseau. Different from the "hope chest" or "bottom drawer," the trousseau consisted of clothes needed for a wedding, honeymoon, and beyond. In the Victorian period the bride ideally gathered all the undergarments and clothing she required for a period of two or more years. Social historian Ellen M. Plante offers a varied list: "morning dresses, carriage dresses, walking suits, evening dresses and traveling dresses."[11] The trousseau clearly represented a woman's taste, style, and economic level. A woman of means might be extravagant in preparation and want a dozen of everything. Some writers in period journals, though, advised restraint, recommending as necessary only a half dozen of each type of undergarment. By the end of the nineteenth century, some recommended thinking in terms of merely what the woman already owned. Prices ranged from the modest sum of $5.98 from Sears in 1902 for a four-piece bridal set advertised as "a trousseau fit for an American queen," made of "fine cambric," and consisting of "gown, skirt, drawers and corset cover," to lavish sums spent by those of the greatly privileged.[12] We have only four pieces of clothing to judge the young Mrs. Ahern's sense of fashion. Her granddaughter Eleanor remembers that when she lived there as a child in the 1940s, she thought the wedding dress so "beautiful."[13]

The *Washington Post*'s account of the Ahern marriage ceremony indicates yet another trousseau item—a "going-away gown" of "blue broadcloth," with a "two-toned hat to match."[14] Married at St. Aloysius Church in a morning ceremony followed by a nuptial Mass, the Irish Catholic couple were wed by the Rev. John O'Hara, S.J., of Woodstock College, Maryland, who was assisted by the Rev. John Conway, of Georgetown University. Professor Armand Gumprecht, organist of St. Patrick's Church, played the "wedding march" and other selections in a sanctuary "beautifully decorated with white chrysanthemums and palms." The bride was attired in a gown of "white silk Brussels net, over ivory taffeta," wore a "large white picture hat" and a "diamond crescent, a gift of the groom," and "carried a white Prayerbook."[15] The notion of the white wedding dress had been codified in the 1840s when Queen Victoria wore a creamy white Spitalfields silk satin and lace gown" in her wedding.[16] The wedding was a solemn affair, what a 1906 etiquette book *Correct Social Usage* terms "the most important thing in the construction of society."[17]

The US practice of a morning ceremony that the Aherns followed may reflect an earlier British law that had required weddings to take place in the morning until the late 1880s, with the reception often taking the form of a wedding breakfast.[18] After the Aherns' ceremony, their wedding breakfast occurred at the home of the bride's uncle in a house "prettily decorated with cut flowers and palms." The honeymoon—an "extended honeymoon trip North"—necessitated other garments in her trousseau, but what style, color, or fabric remains enigmatic over a century later, allowing only informed supposition. Given that she was a member of an upper-middle-class family in Washington, DC, living relatively close to the center of the US fashion industry of New York, one can guess her trousseau contained other high-end pieces of early twentieth-century clothing made with the skill and fashion of a couturier.

## Replenishing the Wardrobe—through Travel

But the question remains: How did she renew her clothing in a manner indicative of her class? Four possible options include (1) going out of town to procure garments, (2) ordering clothing through the mail, (3) having garments made locally, or (4) buying ready-made attire locally.

With the completion of the railroad in the 1880s, Texarkana citizens could reach urban centers by train. New Orleans, which imported many foreign items, seemed the "Paris of America" to early settlers in Texas.[19] Late nineteenth-century writer Kate Chopin, for instance, depended on the establishment of Madame Olympe, a French-born New Orleans dressmaker who frequently journeyed to France to keep abreast of the latest styles of millinery and clothing.[20] By 1880 dealers of dry goods were plentiful in urban areas such as Dallas, Fort Worth, Houston, and Galveston. Accompanied by a family member or a suitable female companion, Mrs. Ahern might have traveled by rail to New Orleans, Dallas, or Fort Worth. She could have stayed in a hotel and employed the skills of a modiste, "a dressmaker who dealt in fashionable dress."[21]

## Purchasing via Mail Order

Along with other women in early twentieth-century Texarkana, Mrs. Ahern might have elected to buy certain items through mail-order purchases, although initially in the nineteenth century, such patronage was largely done by the working classes. Aaron Montgomery Ward began a mail-order enterprise as early as 1872, and Sears, Roebuck and Company followed suit in 1893. The retail business promoted through the catalog industry soon grew into a vast economic enterprise. [22] One problem that plagued mail-order business early on concerned a garment's lack of proper fit. Soon, though, companies progressed from a one-size-fits-all approach to offering multiple sizes and finally to the intricate measuring charts such as the one provided by Philipsborn's of Chicago in 1928, which even included measurements for hats and shoes. A Texarkana family used this chart in the 1920s. By 1920 Ward's catalog had increased from a mere sheet to a tome of 872 pages with the 1921 Sear's edition boasting 1,064 pages. Historians Stuart and Elizabeth Ewen call Ward's first clothing catalog, "a perfect vehicle for 'Americanization.'"[23] Americanization movements in the 1910s and 1920s aimed to prepare immigrants to participate in American culture, language, and principles to become participatory citizens.

## Employing a Local Dressmaker

Early Texarkana city directories list a number of dressmakers. The 1899 *City Directory* lists nine; the 1901 and 1912, both eight; the 1915–16, 1917–18, 1920, and 1924–25, seventeen, fourteen, seven, and six respectively; and the 1931 and 1940, five and twelve. Most seem to be working out of their own homes. Although the directory lists these tradeswomen as "dressmakers," some may have been closer to being "seamstresses" instead. Dressmakers—more highly skilled and better paid—were sometimes in earlier periods called fitters, as they had the ability to cut and fit a garment. Technically, a seamstress of the nineteenth century sewed pieces after they were prepared by a dressmaker. Such a distinction was important to tradeswomen in the garment industry in the nineteenth and turn-of-the-century clothing industry.[24]

Certainly, a Texarkana dressmaker could have secured high-end fabric in 1904. Early on, a number of Texarkana dry goods stores carried clothing material, some selling better quality of cloth than others. Mary Ahern, the Aherns' eldest daughter, said that her father's store always stocked "top quality fabric."[25] Later during the 1940s, Mrs. Ahern's granddaughter Eleanor said she and her mother bought material for clothing at Ben F. Smith's and Criterion. Among the dressmakers in town, some produced high-quality work. Mrs. E. C. East, with a shop at 214/12 East Broad, gained a reputation for being an excellent dressmaker. Highly regarded for her selection of fine materials and the latest styles, Mrs. East regularly traveled to New York by train to replenish her sartorial supplies.[26] In electing to have her clothing custom-made, Mrs. Ahern would have lessened the likelihood that anyone else in the town had the same outfit she wore. Granddaughter Eleanor remembers that she went with her mother, grandmother, and Aunt Ann during the 1940s to deliver material for dresses at a local dressmaker's who always sewed "beautiful things in her home." She recalls that Aunt Ann liked to have her mother and grandmother along for suggestions when she had to return for adjustments.[27]

Judith Wright—a piano student of Mrs. Ahern's daughter Ann in the 1950s—recalled that her mother, Irene Tibbit, made clothes for the Ahern family during the 1950s and 1960s. She began by making clothes for the Aherns' daughter Ann, and when Ann's sister Mary, who lived in Washington, DC, saw the clothes, she asked her to make clothes for her as well and sometimes shipped material from Washington to her. Mary picked up the clothing when she came home for visits. Mrs. Tibbit worked at McCoy's and at Dot and Anne's Dress Shop in the alteration departments and later had her own shop attached to her home.[28] When Ann could no longer maneuver the stairs easily and moved her bedroom downstairs, she used the long closet that leads to the bathroom downstairs for her clothes. Her music student Ann Nicholas, who took piano lessons in the 1960s, remembers hearing a "rustling" sound with Ann's clothing when she moved or when she walked the length of her closet and touched any of her dresses. "Miss Ann always wore full dresses with long sleeves."[29]

Staying fashionable for a woman in the first decade of the twentieth century would also have included the updating of her hats. Throughout the nineteenth and the early twentieth centuries in America, "[N]o self-respecting woman would appear in public without an artfully trimmed hat."[30] The city directories of the period list several milliners.

The 1899 directory lists seven; the 1912, nine; the 1915–16 and 1917–18, both six. The 1915–16 directory also lists two stores where milliners worked—the Criterion and Ben F. Smith Dry Goods. Early on Mrs. E. F. (Elizabeth) Torrans, with a shop at 206 East Broad, gained an excellent reputation as a milliner and beginning around 1912 advertised throughout most of the 1920s. Another highly regarded milliner of the period, Mrs. Etta Elrod lived on Dudley Avenue on College Hill and advertised for decades in the directories. Even today, a civic and church leader of an earlier period in Texarkana recalls Mrs. Elrod's expertise and popularity.[31] Another civic and fashion leader, Mary Collom Fore remembers that Mrs. Elrod made hats for her mother as well. Mary Fore later modeled clothes at McCoy's and other shops and became a buyer for a large department store, Belk-Jones.[32]

An additional early and leading milliner, Lizzie O'Donnell built the 1895 home known today as the Wadley House, located at 618 Pecan Street, and her daughter worked as a milliner at the Criterion.[33] Milliners typically used ribbons, bows, artificial flowers, and feathers to trim period hats. Like dressmakers, milliners in the nineteenth century created a hierarchy; "makers" actually constructed the body of the hat, whereas "trimmers," better paid, decorated it.[34] One current Texarkana resident recalls her mother and grandmother's fondness for using peacock feathers in their own hat trimmings.[35] Most likely, Mary Ahern would have acquired millinery from one or more of these accomplished tradeswomen. Granddaughter Eleanor remembers "loving her grandmother's hats with their feathers on the right side and tiny veils gracing the hat's edge." She recalls as well her grandmother and aunt going to a hat shop in town that made hats and how as a child she played with her grandmother's hats, although she wasn't supposed to. "My grandmother had the greatest hats ever," she says. "Hats were one of her favorite things."[36]

American novelist Edith Wharton documents well the work of the early dressmaker and milliner in the late nineteenth and early twentieth centuries. Although her novels are set in the East, many of her details are applicable to early Texarkana. Of note, her early works often offer the "juxtaposition of . . . two worlds, one established for the making of garments and the other for the ceremonial display of goods."[37] Her early novel *Bunner Sisters*, written in the 1890s, set in the 1870s, but not published until 1916, depicts the stiff competition among small neighborhood stores, such as the one her protagonists Evelina and her sister Ann Eliza run in which they offer sewing and millinery work and the burgeoning commerce represented by early department stores. The sisters' window displays "artificial flowers, bands of scalloped flannel," and "wire hat-frames."[38] The older sister does mending, and the younger typically carries "bundles to the dyer's and delivers purchases of . . . a bundle of pinking" to clients.[39] Of note, Texarkana's 1899 *City Directory* lists two dyers, one being the Excelsior Dye Works at 322 West Front Street. In lieu of using a commercial dyer, women could also purchase dye.

## Sewing Machines—Time Savers for Dressmakers

Texarkana dressmakers profited immensely from the invention of the sewing machine in the Victorian period. Sarah J. Hale, the highly regarded editor of the well-received fashion and advice magazine *Godey's Lady's Book*, notes the great advantages of having a machine when she estimates that sewing a man's shirt by hand requires "more than twenty thousand stitches."[40] Isaac Merritt Singer, an inventor who built on the works of others before him, replaced the hand wheel of the sewing machine with a treadle and helped create the sewing machine's immense success in the 1850s.[41] He also "pioneered a national and international sales campaign to introduce his machine into the home" while his associate Edward Clark developed the first widespread "hire-purchase plan," very popular even with those who could afford to pay cash. The 1865 Singer New Family machine was vastly popular and sold well into the twentieth century.[42] Between 1910 and 1920 Texarkana's Singer store sat at 210 East Broad Street.

The 1880s trade card advertising the Domestic sewing machine conveys the pragmatic nature of ownership. The young women pictured seem highly pleased perhaps in expectation of new garments. Later in the century, the Texarkana 1899 *City Directory* lists a store promoting the Eckles SE sewing machine, located at 218 West Broad, while the 1904 *City Directory* lists Beasley's store as a retailer of the White Sewing machine. Although no sewing machine remains in the Ahern home, Mrs. Ahern's sewing box, dating from the early twentieth century, contains sewing notions along with bobbins from a sewing machine.

Sewing itself was an activity strongly recommended for all girls to learn in the nineteenth and early twentieth centuries. American writer

Mary E. Wilkins Freeman's famous short story "A New England Nun," published in 1891, offers protagonist Louisa, who is not only skilled in sartorial arts, but relishes their practice. The narrator recounts how "Louisa dearly loved to sew a linen seam, not always for use, but for the simple, mild pleasure which she took in it."[43] Although critics differ in interpretation, some see Louisa as a "high priestess of a dying women's culture."[44] Even when families with money hired dressmakers, the women in the family often sewed a great deal themselves. Emily Dickinson's family employed a number of seamstresses, but her letters with her sister Vinnie indicate that these professionals merely supplemented their own sewing.[45]

Even when a family could afford to hire a seamstress, Victorian social writer Catharine Beecher advised middle-class readers to be conservative and extend the life of their garments through "ripping" various seams and refashioning garments.[46] Refashioning garments remained popular. As late as the 1920s, the Extension Service in Arkansas advocated remaking garments in its publication for 4-H Club Girls. Found among the documents from the C. C. Crawford home, located at R.F.D.1, Texarkana, Arkansas, the Extension Service pamphlet advises, "One looks better in attractively planned and well-constructed clothes of old materials than in cheap ready-wear clothes."[47]

## Dressmaking's Zeal for Patterns and Fashion Books

Any dressmaker that Mrs. Ahern employed in early twentieth-century Texarkana would also have been aided by the commercial dressmaking patterns readily available. *Godey's* sold full-size patterns by Mme Demorest as early as 1854. Ebenezer Butterick, a tailor, began making patterns for women in the 1860s, and James McCall began manufacturing McCall's Patterns in various sizes in the 1870s. By the 1870s *Harper's Bazaar* offered "cut-paper" patterns.[48] Social historian Susan Strasser notes the importance of women's fashion magazines initially publishing patterns for home use. And the "paper patterns partially standardized women's clothes long before women's ready-made clothing appeared in great quantities."[49]

Patterns also became less expensive. By the 1920s Joseph M. Shapiro established the Simplicity Pattern Company, which sold patterns for only 15 cents, as did Advice Patterns, which operated from 1932 to 1964 and seems to have been associated with J. C. Penney with a store in Texarkana located at 303 East Broad. Adding to the competition, Conde Nast, who published Vogue patterns, initiated Hollywood patterns for 15 cents in 1932 and published them until 1947.[50]

Should Mrs. Ahern have wished to have a dressmaker sew a particular pattern or to have informed herself about the latest fashions, she could have read one or more of the fashion periodicals readily available when she moved to Texarkana in 1904. Fashion magazines of the day published articles on the excellence of certain pattern types, while some also included short stories and articles on a variety of topics designed for a female audience. Both *Godey's Lady's Book* and *Peterson's Magazine* published materials beginning in the 1860s and profited financially from women's mail-order subscriptions. Similarly, Butterick's *Delineator*, McCall's *Queen of Fashion*, *Ladies' Home Journal*, and *Vogue* included material on patterns, the latter making high-end style of the well-to-do available to the middle and working classes.[51] The *Texarkana Gazette* published its own brand of patterns—at 15 cents each and in sizes 12 to 20—under the name of Marian Martin Pattern Catalog. A collection of patterns of house frocks, lingerie, and pajamas, the catalog instructed patrons to address all orders for patterns to the "*Texarkana Gazette* Pattern Department, 232 West 18th Street, New York City." An example of a *Gazette* Pattern appeared in 1933 featuring a picture of a jumper, which the ad calls "too fetching for words."[52]

## Purchasing Clothing in Texarkana's Stores

Mrs. Ahern might also have purchased ready-made garments from Texarkana's growing retail market. The nineteenth century saw the increased availability of factory-made garments sold in department stores, a retail model that found origins in mid-nineteenth-century Paris. Such American businesses as Stewart in New York, Wanamaker in Philadelphia, and Marshall Field in Chicago had replicated Parisian models by the 1870s. Famously boasting that his store offered "everything from a pin to an elephant," early store pioneer William Whitely, as did other prominent businessmen, achieved success largely through relatively low margins and high-volume sales made possible in part through the proliferation of factory-made garments.[53]

Despite the iconic nature of such London department stores as Harrods and Selfridges, in the early twentieth century American stores quickly assumed a reputation as innovators and began to influence European enterprises.[54] American novelist Theodore Dreiser depicts the allure of the American department store industry with his character Carrie Meeber in his tragic novel *Sister Carrie*, published in 1900. A naive farm girl from Wisconsin, Carrie is seduced by Chicago's glittering department stores, greatly smitten with their "remarkable displays of trinkets, dress goods, stationery, and jewelry.... The dainty slippers and stockings, the delicately frilled skirts and petticoats, the laces, ribbons, hair-combs, purses, all touched her with individual desire, and she felt keenly the fact that not any of these things were in the range of her purchase."[55] Carrie's enthrallment with the department store industry underscores why early on such stores were viewed by the public as the "exclusive province of women." Additionally, while in the past a customer's entrance into a store typically resulted in a sale, the style of the new department store encouraged browsing.[56]

Certainly Mrs. Ahern shopped for clothing at her family's store, O'Dywer & Ahern, located on Broad Street. Granddaughter Eleanor recalls how both her grandmother and her Aunt Ann repeatedly commented, "What a wonderful store the O'Dwyer & Ahern store was!" Another one of Texarkana's early clothing stores, I. Schwarz, Dry Goods & Clothing opened at 102 West Broad Street by 1910. Although the owner, Isaac Schwarz, had to compete with thirteen other dry goods stores in the downtown section, he must have been successful, as he expanded his business, covering both 102 and 104 West Broad Street by 1920. Texarkana historian Beverly Rowe describes Schwarz's 1926 store, then located at 119 West Broad Street, as a "'modern' department store offering a beauty parlor, barber shop, sewing and alterations department, a mailing department, along with a check room, a public restroom, and an ice water fountain."[57] Despite its initial success, the I. Schwarz department store closed in the early 1930s as did the O'Dwyer & Ahern store, both weakened by the Great Depression. "My grandfather tried to keep it [the store] going," Eleanor Purcell commented. "The Depression was very hard for my family."[58]

During its heyday, I. Schwarz advertised a great deal in Texarkana's early newspapers as did Burton-Peel Dry Goods, located at 119–23

West Broad. In the October 11, 1910, *Texarkana Courier,* Burton-Peel announced a "Musical Program Wednesday Afternoon" that claimed to include the "most interesting style showing of the season." Customers could expect to see "original French Pattern Hats," as well as the complete "Fall Millinery" and "Fine Costumes, Dresses, Suits, and Ready-to-Wear."[59] On December 4, 1910, Burton-Peel advertised its half-price sale of women's "Fine Pattern Hats," slashing original prices of $22.50 to $80 down to $11.25 to $40, but still expensive for most women in the area.[60] In autumn of 1911, they advertised women's coats and tailored suits for $19.95 to $29.75 and "New Fall Dresses in serge, broadcloth and taffeta silk" for $19.95. Their ad claims they "are known to handle only garments of the most satisfactory quality and workmanship."[61]

Another early store that advertised high-quality clothing, Ben F. Smith Dry Goods Company, opened as early as 1907, operating initially at 111–13 and then 118 East Broad Street. In an advertisement in the *Texarkana Courier,* Smith promoted its "Beautiful Evening Dresses" priced from $25 to $50. Pictured among them seems to be a modification of the notorious hobble skirt, popular from 1910–14. French designer Paul Poiret created the hobble style, so-called because it restricted a woman's ability to walk naturally. As one might expect, it elicited much satirical comment.[62] Also mentioned in the ad are "Evening Wraps," and "furs, available in muff, neck piece or hat," in "Siberian Fox" and "Japanese Mink."[63] Another high-quality clothing store of about the same time as Smith's, the Criterion also announced its latest fashions in period papers. Establishing the store initially at 106 East Broad Street around 1910, Ray Kosminsky chose the name Criterion because the word meant "a standard by which others would be judged." Later owned by Harry Munz, the store continued to have an excellent reputation, remembered by many area citizens as being "top quality," and closing only in the 1950s.[64]

The owners of the Criterion enhanced their store's reputation for quality goods through artful window displays of chic fashions. They were among the first in town to use extensive plate glass window displays with lifelike mannequins advertising their latest arrivals. The aesthetic success of their windows appears in an extended postcard featuring their window designs. With electric lights highlighting the figures and garments against a darker background, the mannequins are contextualized as though they might be going for a walk or relaxing in their own parlors. In the double postcard picture, which provides the same windows with different garments on display, several mannequins wear dresses, suits, or winter coats in shades of muted brown, red, blue, and gray, with hem lengths that come down to the ankle. Each sports a hat, mostly of the large picture hat design. The postcard image likely dates from around 1910 and emphasizes the store's opulence and sophistication. The popularity of the postcard suggests that it was probably used by the store to advertise and the city to attract regional visitors to the town's commercial center. The style of the large plate glass store window with artistic design had been promoted initially in a journal called *The Show Window*, established in 1897 by "display technocrat" L. Frank Baum—later the author of *The Wizard of Oz*.[65] The immense growth of the display industry resulted in the tradition of window shopping, both in Texarkana and throughout the United States. Such an appeal would last for decades.

A particularly interesting Criterion advertisement appeared on April 6, 1920, in the Texarkana *Four States Press* that touted the store's "Silken Underwear." The ad assures the "Bride-to-Be" that she can "Select Her Trousseau Here with Unbounded Confidence and Pleasure." Among the garments listed are gowns "in a wondrous variety of style, developed in Crepe de Chine, Washable Satin and Georgette Crepe" ($8.95–$35.00); teddies "in Satins, Georgette, Crepe and Crepe de chine—flesh only" (up to $15.00); "Petticoats in heavy Crepe de Chine, Washable Satin, and Pussy Willow" (up to $15.00); Camisoles "delightfully trimmed in dainty ribbons, rosebuds and laces" (up to $9.50); and "Exquisite Philippine Underwear, Gowns and Teddies, each garment hand-made and hand-embroidered in lovely designs" (up to $12.50). The ad assures potential customers they will not find such a trousseau "rivaled in any way—anywhere."[66]

If a bride-to-be had wanted to purchase five of each of the most expensive garments, as suggested by the writer of an earlier period concerning trousseaus, the total sum of $435 would have represented a sizable amount in 1920. The average net income per tax return in Arkansas in 1920 was only a little over $3,000. Moreover, this average represented only a little over the 2 percent of the population who made enough to file a return.[67] Clearly, the women who shopped at the Criterion in 1920 would have been among Texarkana's elite.

In his analysis of the clothing advertisements in *Vogue*, historian Daniel Delis Hill notes how American fashion design effectively combined an emphasis on mass production—as admired by utilitarian British manufacturers—with the French emphasis on style.[68] An examination of the clothing ads in Texarkana's local papers in the early decades of the century reveals this dual focus on both quality and affordability. Democratizing the acquisition of affordable renditions of haute couture, department stores enabled the middle class to emulate the more socially elite. While clothing at Smith's and the Criterion was above the means of most Texarkana women in the early twentieth century, these stores, nonetheless, advertised quality as coexisting with economy. Their clothing would no doubt have appealed to Mrs. Ahern's sense of fashion.

## Fashionable Styles in the Early Twentieth Century

Aside from how or where Mrs. Ahern might have acquired clothing in the early decades of the century, what would have been the world of fashion she experienced? Born in 1877, she grew to maturity during the late Victorian and Edwardian periods, the so-called Gilded Age. Born too late to have worn the famous hoop and crinoline of mid-century, she would have known in the second decade of her life the extremely popular bustle, which was "worn by women from all classes, as well as by little girls with their short skirts."[69] While some form of the bustle had existed for centuries, the 1870s and 1880s designers emphasized its form. The idea seems to have been, according to nineteenth-century theorist Thomas E. Hill, that while men were supposed to be broad shouldered, women should appear in narrow, tight-fitting tops but with garments accentuating their hips, thus emphasizing their femininity.[70] The bustle became even more exaggerated from 1885 on, with "poufs and drapes over rear appendage" and "trains on skirts."[71]

Although the bustle eventually fell out of favor, the corset remained important throughout the late nineteenth and early twentieth centuries. Thorstein Veblen, author of *The Theory of the Leisure Class* (1899), famously asserted that the corset functioned as "a mutilation undergone for the purpose of lowering the subject's vitality and rendering her permanently and obviously unfit for work."[72] Yet as the price of corsets became more reasonable, women of all classes wore them. And although doctors continued to warn that corsets were dangerous to the health, the use of the garment continued due to the influence of fashion. The September 11, 1910, issue of the *Texarkana Courier*, for example, shows a young woman seemingly quite happily arrayed in the latest style of a Kabo Corset.[73] And even though Parisian couturier Paul Poiret famously claimed the corset dead by the 1920s, fashion historians note it simply morphed into garments with other names such as the girdle.[74] The corset also changed into two parts, with a separate garment for the breasts. By early twentieth century many women began wearing the bra.

American fashion historian Betty J. Mills points out that by 1900 corsets had grown longer and the bustle disappeared. The result was a much more "slender silhouette" with "gored" skirts, tiny waists, and minimized hips.[75] The slender image was heightened by the "narrow sans-centre corset, which squeezed away the belly and gave the body an S-shaped line."[76] The resulting shape helped to create the so-called Gibson Girl effect. The so-named Gibson Girl became symbolic of an ideal feminine form as depicted by the illustrations of artist Charles Dana Gibson spanning a twenty-year period from 1890 to 1910.

When Mrs. Ahern came to Texarkana in 1904, she would certainly have worn shirtwaist dresses, popularized by Gibson with long, sweeping skirt lengths; blouses with high collars; high-buttoned or laced shoes with cloth tops; and suits. The latter was used for business, travel, and recreation. Jackets revealed a more masculine cut generally with lapels and cuffs, and the frock coat at times hung just above the ankle.[77] Garments sewed in "delicate light fabric over color" were especially popular.[78] Mrs. Ahern's choice in her trousseau of a second-day dress in blue broadcloth clearly suggests the fashion then in style as does her wedding dress of white net over ivory taffeta. Her selection of a white picture hat reflects typical millinery choices of her day. Sometimes known as a Gainsborough hat, the picture hat had a wide brim and tended to frame the face.

By 1910, however, much of her clothing selections would have changed. The corset disappeared as such, skirts shot up to reveal the ankle and appeared with contrasting jackets, and the white lingerie dress was in vogue. In fact, colors generally were brighter by 1910, and included blue-green, royal blue, "pale Chinese yellow," and "periwinkle." Popular fabrics offered brocaded taffeta, velvet, "fine" linen, corded silk, and chiffon. Fabrics were often striped or embossed with bold Chinese and Art Nouveau motifs. Garment trims included all kinds of lace as well as "sheer embroidery."[79] And because summer gowns in the first decade of the new century began to be made without linings, underwear became of greater importance.[80]

From about 1912 until World War I broke out, evening garments reflected excitement over a new dance, the Argentine tango. Such evening wear included "gold-embroidered tunics and turbans with upright feathers."[81] But perhaps the most innovative women's wear of the twentieth century—long trousers—occurred during the period of the Great War, inaugurated not by designers but by working women. Following the war, women's work clothing was "mostly borrowed from men."[82]

Such female couturiers as Coco Chanel, Madeleine Vionnet, Nina Ricci, and Jeanne Lanvin rose to prominence during this time and became important to the Aherns as Eleanor, the youngest of Mrs. Ahern's daughters, chose a gown designed by Vionnet for her wedding dress. Women themselves, as well as fashion historians later, could convincingly argue that female designers best understood a woman's new role after the war.

Models' figures now rather ironically denied the feminine curves so popular in previous decades. Rather, they projected slender figures and wore "undergarments that flattened their breasts and stomachs." Dressed in garments with dropped waists, they appeared to have a straight rather than a curved figure. Newspaper and magazine illustrations of the 1920s typically offered surreal and elongated sketches of straight, thin, often androgynous-looking women featuring the famous bobbed-hair style.[83] Shoes also appeared elongated as pictured in an ad from Kennedy's Shoe Store in the 1920s.[84]

Hemlines rose again when in 1924 women began to favor lengths that barely concealed their knees. A 1923 ad from the Criterion, "Wouldn't you like to know—where the new hem-line stops?" indicates women's confusion over hemlines. A 1920s O'Dwyer & Ahern ad, for instance, shows women still wearing ankle-length dresses and suits. The ad touts the store's winter sale of garments for all at "Unrivalled Reductions" and argues that shoppers "can buy garments of remarkable quality and beauty in the most popular models, ready to wear, at less than the cost of materials."[85] In the same issue The Criterion advertises its half-price sale of suits and coats with prices originally being $20 to $100.[86] Their branding motto of "Where Fashion Reigns" effectively marketed their savvy sense of style, while their promise of "Goods Shipped Same Day Ordered" reminds contemporary readers of the buying trends of the twenty-first century. Smith's ad, published on the same day as well, not only announced their winter sale, but also that they had "already received" examples of their "New Spring Millinery."[87] By 1925, an ad for O'Dwyer & Ahern shows "Frocks of Tub silk, printed crepes," and "Plain crepes" with dresses at mid-calf length."[88]

On page 2 of this same edition, Higginbotham's touted its silk teddies and bloomers. "What woman," the ad asks, "does not love beautiful Silk Underwear?" An upscale store, it also carried Hart Schaffner Marx clothes for men. This 1920s newspaper substantiates that discussions of women's undergarments had become more explicit. In the paper's column "Of Interest to Women," the writer claims that "underthings are becoming more fanciful and elaborate every day. The very newest fad for milady's more intimate garments is the use of black lace." The ad features a young woman wearing what seems to be fishnet hose with the headline "Peek-A-Boo Lace 'Undies' New Fad."[89] The tone and wording are a far cry from the Victorian practice of referring to women's underwear in polite society as "unmentionables."

With the mid-1920s fashions encouraging women to show more of their legs, the quality of hosiery became more important as reflected in the 1925 ad placed in the *Daily Texarkanian* by I. Schwarz that touted "Hole-proof Silk Hose" for $1.00 a pair.[90] A few days later the store advertised "Ombre colored Chiffon Hosiery" at $3.50 each, claiming that "Paris, London, and New York are wild over these new shaded hose."[91] A couple of decades earlier Kate Chopin had recorded the allure of silk hosiery in a short story. In her 1890s "A Pair of Silk Stockings," protagonist Mrs. Sommers finds herself drawn to the personal luxuries that an extra windfall of $15 represents. Although she initially considers only the pragmatic purchases of new shoes and clothes for her children, when she inadvertently touches her hand "upon a pile of silk stockings" and sees a sign indicating they are on sale, she loses all self-control, confronted with such luxury.[92]

By the mid-1920s Gabrielle "Coco" Chanel proclaimed her brilliance in haute couture, designing "dresses, jersey suits, and knit jumpers."[93]

"The first war made me," she told others. "In 1919, I woke up famous."[94] In 1926 she revealed the now famous "little black dress," which became a staple in women's evening wear, with a kind of "simple elegance" that is replicated today in women's fashions. With short skirts, women now enjoyed showing their stockings.

## The Age of Makeup Begins

In addition to raising their hemlines, most women—young or old—began to wear makeup in the 1920s. Both at home and in public, women subscribed to "beautifiers" to heighten their appearance. In fact, fashion historians term the decade the "beginning of the present heyday for the manufacture of cosmetics."[95] Women generally used "powder, lipstick, rouge, eyebrow pencil, eye shadow and foundation cream" without appearing scandalous to others. They even made cosmetic "repairs . . . calmly . . . in public." The decade was also marked by the beginning of colored nail polish.[96] Besides makeup, the well-to-do 1920s Texarkana woman might also procure facial treatments to enhance her appearance. The 1925 *Daily Texarkanian* ran an ad for Marinello Beauty Parlor, located within the Criterion, where one could spend "one Hour of Time," and "Banish Ten Years from Appearance." The ad promises female patrons that "the tired look will be removed, the complexion freshened and the brain rested by a Marinello Facial Treatment."[97]

By the opening of the 1930s, fashion once again hugged the outlines of the female body with the waist at mid-level. Of note dresses and jackets sported shoulder pads, wide lapels, and "off the shoulder collars." Hemlines fell all the way to mid-calf length. En vogue as well was the "plunging back décolletage, with wide crisscrossing straps, and a waterfall or sweetheart collar."[98] The shirtwaist dress also remained popular. It had origins in the late nineteenth century in the shirtwaist blouse, "that very early product of the American ready-to-wear industry that emerged as part of the uniform of the New Woman in the 1890s and was one of the most American of fashions."[99] Based on a man's tailored shirt with the addition of a skirt, it appeared as both a one-piece or as matching separates. Extremely versatile, it remained in style throughout the twentieth century up to the present day.[100] Granddaughter Eleanor Purcell recalls her grandmother liking to wear the shirtwaist in the

1940s—usually a one piece and often in "soft" colors. "She always looked nice," Eleanor insisted, "whether wearing ordinary, everyday or nice looking dresses. And she never wore slacks."[101]

## Another Wedding

Fashion, at least in the first half of the 1940s, remained simple and practical, reflecting the need to conserve resources and materials because of World War II. Despite the bleakness of the war, however, the Ahern home was the site of a joyous wedding announcement party for the youngest of the Aherns' children, Eleanor, born in 1917. In attending and graduating in 1939 from Our Lady of the Lake College in San Antonio, Eleanor had met and become engaged to then Lt. William K. Horrigan, a 1937 graduate of West Point. The marriage took place on March 14, 1940, in Manilla, Philippines, where William was stationed. Mrs. Ahern accompanied her daughter to San Francisco where Eleanor set sail on February 9 on the *President Coolidge* for the Philippines.

A description of the announcement party appeared in the society section of the *Texarkana Gazette*, detailing the fashion of family members in attendance. The bride-to-be wore a "white crepe" gown; her oldest sister, Mary, a gown in "aquamarine velvet," another sister Ann, a "club crepe," and her mother, a "blue embroidered taffeta" gown. The newspaper described the festivities as a "beautiful, seated tea on Sunday afternoon," and, in the style of the society pages of the day, provided details of flowers in the house: yellow chrysanthemums and cameo gladioli combined with ferns with hollywood roses adorning the entrance hall. In the dining room, a "large wedding bell" of "pompom chrysanthemums suspended from a floral arch" provided the center of the table. Vases of cadet gladioli appeared in the music room along with a flower arrangement in the form of an airplane in honor of the groom's appointment in what would become the air force. Finally, in the library a doll dressed as a bride with a skirt made of chrysanthemums completed the effect.[102]

The wedding itself seems to have been a grand affair judging from the account later published in the *Texarkana Gazette*. A morning Roman Catholic wedding—like that of Mrs. Ahern's—the ceremony took place at the "Archbishop's Palace in the Walled City," with the uncle of the groom officiating. The bride wore a "Vionnet wedding gown of Venetian lace over ivory satin." Based on "princess lines" the gown had a "long, sweeping train, long sleeves, square neckline, and tiny buttons fastening the back of the bodice." She also wore a short veil of "white tulle ... held in place with a ruffled 'Pancake' of tulle centered with a diadem cluster of orange blossoms carved from mother-of-pearl." A necklace of a "star pendant of pearls diamond-centered," described as a "family heirloom," complemented her attire.

Following the wedding, the traditional wedding breakfast took place again in the midst of many flowers, including Eucharis lilies and sprays of cadenza amor. The bride fittingly cut the wedding cake with the groom's own saber. Afterward, the newlyweds planned a honeymoon trip to Baguio, a city in northern Luzon, an island of the Philippines. As with the description of her mother's wedding, we learn what the young Eleanor would wear as a second-day dress: "a white skirt of angel skin topped by a pleated blouse and fingertip jacket of gay printed chiffon." In all, it seems to have been a glorious affair, indeed.

Watching her daughter Eleanor set sail in 1940 must have been bittersweet for Mrs. Ahern. Her husband had died in 1932, and Mrs. Ahern was not able to attend the wedding of her only daughter who married. Of necessity she would only be able to read of the wedding ceremony as described in the Manila paper and mailed by Eleanor sometime later. Mrs. Ahern turned sixty-three the year of her daughter's marriage, but, based on the rich detail included in the *Gazette*'s account of the announcement tea, she seems to have still been quite interested in fashion and style. She would remain in her home until her death in 1970, but not alone. Because of the war, her daughter Eleanor would soon return from the Philippines with her baby girl and spend the next four or so years in the house, waiting for her husband to return from the conflict. Her daughter Ann would be there as well, teaching piano and hosting various musical events for friends and students. Yet, it's tempting to speculate that no future social event at the Ahern home focused quite so much on fashion or in such a personally meaningful way as the party Mrs. Ahern gave honoring her daughter before she sent her off into the world to assume her place as a married woman.

Mary Olive Ahern's 1904 wedding dress, P. J. Ahern home, Texarkana Museums System, photograph by Doris Davis

Mary Olive Ahern's wedding bed jacket, P. J. Ahern home, Texarkana Museums System, photograph by Doris Davis

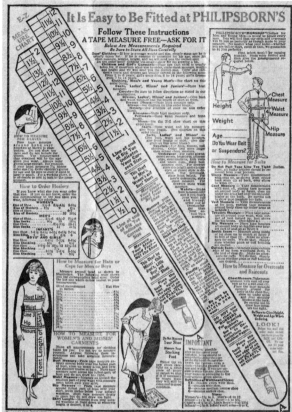

Philipsburg fitting chart, courtesy of Gary Bugh, Crawford materials

The Gold Medal Hat, Mrs. S. E. Camp, *Texarkana Courier*, September 13, 1910, p. 7.

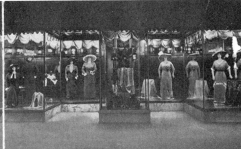

Ad and double postcard from the Criterion, author's collection, photograph by Doris Davis

Ben F. Smith's ad, *Texarkana Courier*, October 7, 1910, p. 3.

A trade card advertising Star Soap shows an early version of the bustle, author's collection, photograph by Doris Davis

1902 girls at Arkansas High School, Texarkana, Arkansas, in the Gibson Girl attire, courtesy of Texarkana Museums System, Wilbur Smith Research Archive

Women in drugstore wearing a version of the picture hat, Texarkana Museums System, Wilbur Smith Research Archive

1920s Texarkana women dressed for beauty pageant, courtesy of the Texarkana Museums System, Wilbur Smith Research Archive

Criterion ad, *Four States Press,* June 4, 1920, p. 5

Eleanor Ahern in her wedding dress, courtesy of the Ahern, Horrigan, and Purcell families

# 6

# The Music Room
## A Space for Family and Song

*If I can't have a Steinway, I don't want any piano at all.*

—Mary Olive Ahern,[1] 1905

Although labeled the larger parlor by the architect's plans, the largest room on the first floor of the Aherns' house by use and reference was always the music room. Linked to the spacious central hall via large, oak pocket doors, the room appears on the left as one walks through the home's front entryway. With the library traditionally claimed by the man of the house, the music room reflected the interest of Mary Ahern, both in terms of music and aesthetics. The Aherns' house design positions the second or smaller parlor across the hall from the music room and mirrors late Victorian architecture's preference for "clearly defined" and separate public and private spaces.[2]

While the smaller parlor signified reserve and public discourse, the music room conveyed warmth and retreat for family and friends. By design and practice, the former space functioned as a kind of holding room for some visitors. As the Aherns' youngest daughter explained, "Guests that mother didn't expect or want to stay long were always taken to the smaller parlor where the furniture was less comfortable and the north wind belted against the house."[3] The two rooms—one cozy and welcoming, the other stiff and formal—offer information on how the Aherns structured their lives as well as their spaces in early twentieth-century Texarkana.

Period home decorators published much on the design and comfort of the parlor. In 1903, designer Lillie Hamilton French maintained the homemaker should create beauty and value in the room. She believed the parlor must produce conviviality but also reveal the extent of cultivation the family had attained.[4] A couple of decades earlier, designer Almon C. Varney had felt so passionately that the home be attractive, he quotes Romantic English poet John Keats: "A thing of beauty is a joy forever." He believed only through combining "domesticity" with "adornment," might one produce "Home Life... [that] radiated with a brighter flow."[5] By 1920, almost fifteen years after the Aherns had completed building their home, designer Frank Alvah Parsons argued that the "artistic" home should not be considered a "luxury." Rather, homemakers had a *duty* to be attuned to aesthetics for the sake of others.[6]

Mary Ahern hardly needed to be reminded to create beauty. Her children knew well her love of "beautiful things" and were taught early on to respect the integrity of their home and the objects in it. Years later a former piano student of Mary's daughter Ann recalls the beauty of the house and room. Such "beautiful rugs," she remembers, "plush," and "Persian style," she adds. "And the antiques ... so lovely."[7] Mary ensured aesthetic appreciation of these beautiful objects by designing an extensive room, anchored at the front toward the east by a Steinway grand piano and along the south side by a bay window across the room from the fireplace.

A family story indicates that sometimes even careful plans go awry. When Mary's grand piano arrived, the piano's bulk and sizable legs wouldn't go through the front door. Instead, the parlor's newly installed front window had to be temporarily removed so the piano could be hoisted through this extra-wide space. In the end, a near catastrophe (at least for a pianist), was avoided, and a beautiful 1905 Steinway claimed its space at the front of the room. It had come a long way, shipped from New York to New Orleans and then by rail to Texarkana.[8] It was always called "mother's piano" by her children, and even decades later, toward the end of her life, daughter Ann still referred to the Steinway as "mother's piano."[9]

The spaciousness of the music room—about 23 feet by 15—allowed not only a grand piano but also the kind of grouping of chairs that decorator

Lillie Hamilton French found most effective. French recommended that the homemaker observe her own parlor as a stranger and then arrange the chairs for comfort and conversation rather than as though one were in a lecture hall. Instead of creating a cozy nook, she should place lamps, tables, and chairs together so that the room might be used for reading, writing, sewing, and conversation, as well as listening to music. Understanding how to do this, French claimed, is the answer to creating a successful parlor.[10]

French also emphasized that flowers and other greenery appear throughout. She envisions "ferns and blossoms in glass bowls," "bunches of laurel in pots on pedestals" and "branches of maple on the mantel."[11] Mary Ahern loved flowers and filled her parlor with her own cut flowers when in season and dried flower arrangements when not.[12] In later years, daughter Ann placed her father's oak roll-top desk at the opposite end of the room from the piano, using the many compartments of this large desk for keeping various records. She still had plenty of space remaining for other furniture and especially the piano, which remained the focal point of the room.[13]

Pianos were of course the centerpiece of many parlors of the day. As nineteenth-century architect A. J. Downing noted, by as early as 1850, the piano had become the typical accoutrement of the parlor in America.[14] In fact, throughout the latter half of the nineteenth century including the early decades of the twentieth, the piano enjoyed an omnipresence in middle- and upper-middle-class homes, a fact that decorators had to consider. Thinking more about the aesthetics of space than sound, period designers were often critical of the shape and size of the piano. In her 1899 study of room décor, American novelist Edith Wharton criticizes the "clumsy lines" of pianos. She especially objects to the piano's bulky legs, which she calls "elephantine supports," recommending instead "slender fluted legs." She also suggests that pianos be "inlaid with marquetry," an art form whereby pieces of veneer are applied to a wooden structure to form a pattern.[15] Architect H. Hudson Holly had suggested the same in 1878, recommending the plainness of the piano be remedied through creating attractive patterns on the piano's surface.[16]

By 1903, French recommended that the piano no longer overpower the parlor.[17] Rather than arranging the piano to showcase the performer's hands, she suggested placing it in a corner with the keys facing the wall. Ideally a small sofa would rest at the piano's end where two might sit comfortably with their back toward the performer and sip their tea by the fire.[18] Whether Mary Ahern knew of French's opinions, her passion for music would have trumped innovative furniture arrangements, and she would never have endorsed such a configuration.

The Aherns' 1905 purchase of a piano occurred in the midst of what musicologist Arthur Loesser calls the "American heyday of the piano." It was a time, he explains, between 1895 and 1914 "when the instrument was most useful, most esteemed, and . . . gave the most substantial pleasure of which it was capable to the greatest number of people."[19] The Aherns' purchase of a piano, thus, mirrored a popular trend found in many middle-class homes throughout America. The only exception was that most didn't have room for a grand nor could they afford a Steinway.

## The Appeal of Steinway and Sons

Mary Ahern's enthusiasm for Steinways wouldn't have surprised anyone who knew about pianos. Steinways were in fact all the rage at the beginning of the twentieth century, and anyone who wanted the best American piano and could afford it bought a Steinway. The piano company's rise to stardom in the competitive world of piano manufacturing had taken place over a few decades' time. While Chickering of Boston had held an undisputed lead in the manufacturing trade at mid-nineteenth century,[20] by 1867 Steinway garnered the first of several gold medals awarded at the Paris Exposition and was soon on its way to surpassing the older piano company.[21]

In 1872 aiming to ensure Steinway's ultimate triumph, William Steinway secured a contract with pianist par excellence of the day, Anton Rubinstein—"the most fiery, most fabulous, and most hypnotic of living pianists, the true inheritor of Liszt's crown." Rubinstein toured the United States, playing only a Steinway piano. Ultimately giving 215 concerts in 239 days (more than six a week), Rubinstein enjoyed a tremendous success. Playing his beloved composers—Bach, Beethoven, Chopin, Schumann—Rubinstein had at last found a piano that matched his speed and power and held up under all his fury. Abetted by the precision and power of the Steinway, in this tour Rubinstein singlehandedly established the "age of the 'classics' in American piano concerts."[22] Indeed, who wouldn't want a Steinway if playing one had the potential for such spectacular results? Great Britain agreed, and on May 29, 1890, through a royal warrant appointed Steinway as the piano manufacturer of the queen.[23] If a Steinway was good enough for the queen, Mary Lansdale Ahern certainly thought it was good enough for her family some fifteen years later.

Whether the young Mary Lansdale knew about Steinway's selection by the British monarchy, certainly she followed the details of the World's Fair in Chicago in 1893 along with thousands of other Americans. That year the extremely popular Polish pianist, Ignacy Jan Paderewski, created something of a scandal over the Steinway. The piano company had decided not to exhibit at the fair because it feared unfair promotion for Chicago-made pianos by organizers. In retaliation, the businessmen forbade any Steinways on the fairgrounds for performances. Their stance was disconcerting for Theodore Thomas, America's foremost symphonic conductor of the period, who had already contracted with Steinway-playing artists, including Paderewski, to perform at this prestigious World's Columbian Exposition. The organizers suggested that Paderewski simply play a Chicago piano. Weren't they just as good? they asked. Then, four days before Paderewski's scheduled concert, the National Commission of the Fair ordered that any Steinway brought on the grounds be "dump[ed] outside the gates." Nevertheless, Paderewski had a Steinway. On May 2 he played a Steinway that had been smuggled onto the grounds having been mislabeled as "hardware" and was a tremendous success. When the affair became public, no piano was "dumped," but the event served instead to promote both the excellence of the pianist and the splendid Steinway.[24] That such an artist had insisted the Steinway alone would suffice had tremendous sway on the purchases of the piano-buying public of the day.

So, what was different about the Steinway that appealed so much to Mary Ahern and set it apart from its competitors? Several things. Earlier, Steinway had begun perfecting what was called "cross-stringing," combining it with a unique "space distribution" on the sounding board. Then they "increased the length of the bridge by curving it more. This adjustment brought it farther from the rim and used more fully the inner sections of the sounding board." Further they "strung the strings in a fan-shaped manner, . . . giving their vibrations . . . more sounding-board space and greatly increased the tension on the frame." Finally, they adjusted the keyboard's action to respond more easily to the pianist's fingers. These modifications took several decades to perfect.

The result was a piano of "matchless strength and sensitiveness."[25] And this was the piano that Mary Ahern wanted and the one she got.

## The Young Mary Olive Lansdale, the National Theatre, and the Piano

Mary Olive Lansdale had been born in 1877 in Washington, DC, into a large Catholic upper-middle-class family. Mary Olive's father was a financially successful builder and listed the value of his real estate and personal estate at $2,000 and $300 respectively on the 1870 census. Of importance, his income would have permitted a piano in the parlor. According to granddaughter Eleanor, all four of the Lansdale sisters excelled at playing the piano.[26] When Mary's older sister Ella married John Kline and moved to Texarkana in 1892, the young couple got a piano for their home. When Mary married Patrick Ahern in 1904, among her earliest requests was for one as well.

The Lansdale sisters came of age at the end of the nineteenth century in the midst of the tremendous popularity of public concerts, including those by pianists. Living in Washington, DC, only a few blocks from the capital's National Theatre, the sisters had access by street car to the artistic performances presented there. Built in 1835, the National Theatre amazed audiences with its "elegant interior" and spectacular performances of music, drama, and other arts forms. A generation before Mary Lansdale's birth, in 1850 the famous singer Jenny Lind performed there presented by the Barnum and Bailey Circus with which she toured.[27] The entire Washington, DC, police force was on hand to protect her and the distinguished guests, including President and Mrs. Millard Fillmore, who attended both concerts, and Senators Daniel Webster and Henry Clay. Webster even sang with the artist during one of her songs. She was a spectacular success, grossing $15,385, with tickets ranging from $3 to $7 each.[28]

Hungarian pianist Rafael Joseffy, who had studied with Franz Liszt and amazed American crowds as early as 1879,[29] appeared at the National Theatre in 1899. By far the most popular pianist of the day, however, one that Mary and her sisters would have arranged to see if at all possible, was Paderewski. He became so popular following his début tour in 1891 and 1892 that one could buy Paderewski candy, Paderewski soap, and even a toy replica of the pianist with a "black frock coat, a white bow tie and a huge head of flame-colored hair, sitting at the piano."[30] These late nineteenth-century male performers were actually the original "matinee idols" in the United States and women helped foster their "cult status."

In 1898 one reviewer observed that women constituted around four-fifths of any matinee performance and three-fifths of evening crowds. One agent noted that women were far greater admirers of music and musicians than men. They "stormed the stage" trying to grab a piece of American pianist Louis Gottschalk's white gloves and hoped to glimpse Paderewski aboard his train as it lumbered across America.[31] Certainly it's possible that Mary Olive and her sisters were in the audience. One girl insisted on getting three autographs from Paderewski, so the narrative goes, "One to frame and hang in my bedroom, one to paste inside the piano to improve its tone, and one to carry with me always." Concert goers believed Paderewski "personified the piano."[32] When he played with the Washington Symphony Orchestra in 1902 at the National Theatre, the audience must have been packed, probably with Mary Lansdale in attendance. In 1905 he played there again, offering the music of Beethoven, Chopin, Schumann, and Schubert, with a large crowd, including Mrs. Theodore Roosevelt.

## Piano Lessons for the Lansdale Girls

Women of course had pursued the piano themselves throughout much of the nineteenth century. In 1810 a reporter for the *Raleigh Star* noted that women generally believed they must learn to play the instrument to secure a husband.[33] Their fathers seemingly believed the same as they spent large sums on lessons for their daughters as compared with that spent on other aspects of their education. The piano apparently enjoyed priority. The preponderance of piano study for young women gave rise to what was termed later in the century as "the piano girl," one who practiced diligently, whether or not talented or interested, for the sake of the comfort of her family before marriage and ideally for her husband and children afterward.[34]

Etiquette manuals prescribed the acceptable style of playing for a young woman as well as the type of music appropriate for the parlor. The "piano girl" of course was not a performer in that she didn't draw attention to herself. Much like Kate Chopin's mother figure Adele in

*The Awakening*,[35] she played only to give pleasure to others, and if she had potential for virtuoso performance, the manuals recommended hiding it or she would be seen as lacking femininity along with the twin virtues of modesty and meekness. An article in *Harper's Magazine* in 1851, addressed to young women readers, indicates typical expectations: "Aim more at pleasing than at astonishing. . . . Never bore people with ugly music merely because it is the work of some famous composer, and do not let the pieces you perform . . . be too long."[36]

Such attitudes, however, were changing by the late nineteenth century when the Lansdale sisters were studying piano. By 1904 James Huneker, a well-known music critic and journalist, in fact, announced the so-called demise of the nineteenth-century stereotype of the "piano girl," writing: "And now at the beginning of the century the girls who devote time to the keyboard merely for the purpose of social display are almost as rare as the lavender water ladies of morbid sensibilities in the Richardson and Fielding novels."[37] By the end of the century, those restrictions forbidding women from pursuing certain professions—such as music—were beginning to erode as well. By 1897 the president of the Music Teachers National Association calculated that at least half of its members were women.[38] Also by century's end some piano students—including women—were pursuing musical studies as an art form instead of only a social accomplishment.[39]

By the latter half of the nineteenth century, some young women had even decided to perfect their musical studies by traveling abroad. In 1869 Amy Fay, originally from Mississippi, went to Europe to study in Berlin. When her letters were published in 1881 with the title *Music Study in Germany*, many young women pursued European studies.[40] Moreover by the end of the century, women pianists had begun to appear on stage in America as instrumentalists.

## Female Concert Pianists

Mary Lansdale and her sisters no doubt followed with interest the news stories featuring female concert pianists. The first female pianist to tour successfully in America, Teresa Carreno was from Venezuela, whom some called "cyclonic" in terms of power.[41] When she began touring in the 1860s, she performed for President Lincoln at the White House, playing his favorite song, "Listen to the Mocking Bird,"[42] a song that

Mary Ahern later selected for her granddaughter Eleanor. By the time Carreno performed at the National Theatre in 1908, Mary Ahern had already married, but she may well have heard her elsewhere.

One of the most successful of women pianists was Fannie Bloomfield-Zeisler, sometimes favorably compared with Rubinstein and Paderewski. She and Paderewski were the two favored pianists at the 1893 Chicago World's Fair.[43] Although she seems not to have performed at the National Theatre, she toured America extensively, playing engagements, for example, at five different Texas towns in 1899.[44] English pianist Ethel Leginska initially toured America in the first decade of the twentieth century. When she made her US debut in Cleveland in 1908, she performed in a vaudeville theater where her concert was sandwiched between acrobats and elephants.[45] She later performed extensively at the National Theatre from 1916 through 1921. And finally American pianist Olga Samaroff, born in 1880 in San Antonio, Texas, and married to the famous English conductor Leopold Stokowski, amazed audiences and became one of the most popular piano teachers of the 1930s and 1940s.[46] She appeared at the National Theatre in 1917, 1919, and 1921, performing with her husband and the Philadelphia Orchestra.

The careers of such successful professional women pianists in the latter half of the nineteenth and early twentieth centuries no doubt encouraged many young women of the period to pursue music for their *own* enjoyment rather than as a social grace and should they have remarkable talent, to develop it fully. Mary Lansdale and her sisters all studied piano during this period probably for a combination of reasons. That Mary and her sister Ella continued to play the piano in Texarkana after their marriages suggests a genuine enjoyment. Granddaughter Eleanor remembers her grandmother playing the piano when she was a child. Her playing was "lovely."[47] That Mary Olive produced two musically talented daughters who considered professional musical careers also points to the serious and artistic attitude taken toward music and the piano in the Ahern home.

## A Musical Education for the Ahern Children

Years later, granddaughter Eleanor remembered her grandmother, whom she called Mamie, playing the song "Listen to the Mocking Bird." "That's your song," her grandmother told her. When Eleanor asked her, she would play and sing it again, in fact as many times as she wanted to hear it.[48]

While she may have begun introductory piano lessons for the children herself, early on Mrs. Ahern relied on the expertise of the teachers at St. Edward School, which had opened in 1908, overseen by the Olivetan Benedictine Sisters. In 1921 Providence Academy was added, which provided more advanced instruction. When the Benedictine Sisters left Texarkana, the Sisters of Divine Providence of San Antonio, Texas, were then in charge of the school.[49] By the time St. Edward School opened in 1908, Mary had two children—Joseph Patrick, born in 1905, and Mary Cecilia, born in 1907. Soon there would be others: Ann Agnes, born in 1910, followed by the twins John William and Catherine Elizabeth, born in 1912, and finally Eleanor, born in 1917. With children spaced so closely together, Mary had practically produced her own children's choir. With a lovely alto voice herself, Mary enjoyed organizing and directing groups of singers, whether her own children or later the church choir at St. Edward Church, which she directed for over half a century.

The yearbooks from Providence Academy housed in the Aherns' library provide some details about the children's musical education. Three of them seem to have excelled in musical study: Mary Cecilia and Ann, or Anna as her friends called her, in piano; and John, in violin.[50] In 1925 Mary Cecilia graduated from the Academy as class Salutatorian and class president. One of her classmates wrote the "Prophesy of the Class of '25" and envisions Mary as a "Prima Donna in the Grand Ormond Opera Company of London, England." This yearbook friend adds, "I am not surprised at that [the prophesy] after the splendid musical recital Mary staged a few weeks before she graduated. Really Mary was always an accomplished girl."[51]

The 1925 Providence annual gives some idea of how extensive teenage Mary's piano repertoire was. As a conclusion to the Seniors' Debate Program in October 1924, Mary performed "Mazurka" by the Russian composer Emil Mlynarski with two violinists. In a recital in November 1924, she played Liszt's "Etude Brilliante" and in December 1924, she performed "Valse Brilliante" by Juan Jose Castro, an Argentine composer and conductor. She offered the concluding performance to a group recital for Class Day in the spring, playing the final movement of "Sonata Eroica" by American composer Edward MacDowell. This sonata, Opus 50, presents MacDowell's interpretation of the Arthurian legend with one critic suggesting the four movements might be called "The Coming of Arthur, Merlin, Guinevere, and The Battle with Modred."[52] The final or presto movement that Mary played is quite fast yet contains lyrical aspects as well.

Mary also wrote the Class Song for her graduating class that year, composing both the music and the words. The final lines of the second verse offer the kind of high-minded charge we associate with graduation day: "Along life's way cause no regret / Let loyalty be our rule, / Stronger then will be our soul, / With faith firm, and courage high / To win success and reach the goal / Ere life glides swiftly by." These lyrics also indicate the personal commitment that Mary had internalized to succeed. The musical score written in A-flat major and 4/4 time and marked "moderato" in tempo seems hymn-like with lyrical moments.[53] Mary clearly had learned part-writing skills in her music theory class at Providence Academy.

Mary's senior recital pieces indicate an impressive technique.[54] She began with Franz Liszt's popular "Dance of the Gnomes," marked by passages of fast finger work in the right hand, repeated chords in the left, and tricky crossing of hands throughout. With its fast tempo and quirky tune, it has remained a popular piece for advanced students. Next, she played Chopin, offering two of the preludes from Opus 28, No. 3 and No. 20. Though marked by brevity, these pieces constitute the mature Chopin, offering brilliant sketches of ideas. The famous musicologist Louis Ehlert calls them "small shooting stars."[55] The first of these, No. 3 in G major, requires fast, strong figures in the left hand, capable of controlling the sound so the melody can soar above, what music scholar Ernest Hutcheson describes poetically as "fairy fingers to compass the sun-kissed ripples of the left hand."[56] The other prelude, No. 20 in C minor, offers an impressive antithesis. In solemn minor chords played in a grand manner, the score seems to Hutcheson to suggest a cathedral.[57]

Mary concluded her recital with "The Chariot Race," an etude of technical study by Danish composer Ludvig Schytte, and "Dr. Gradus ad Parnassum" from Claude Debussy's *The Children's Corner*, dating from 1908. The latter has remained among the standard repertoire for pianists for its beauty, whimsy, and excellence, and perhaps also for its poignant backstory. French composer Debussy wrote this suite of six pieces for his five-year-old daughter Chouchou. "Dr. Gradus ad Parnassum" is a beautiful and charming spoof on the child's piano teacher and perhaps on all who write piano exercises for children.[58] Little Chouchou seemingly plays fast and slow by fits, and then at the end, romps as fast as she can to get her practice completed. The piece amuses and dazzles audiences, and Mary must have made a sensation at the recital.

Years later, in considering her Aunt Mary, Eleanor vowed that she had wanted to be a concert pianist and had gone to Washington DC after high school to pursue such a career. For two years Mary studied at Georgetown Visitation Convent, a high school and two-year college for women operated by the Sisters of the Visitation. The school's motto: *"Labor Omnia Vincit"*—"Work Conquers All" from Virgil's *Georgics*—seems particularly appropriate for Mary's work ethic and determination to succeed. The school's 1927 yearbook, *The Green Gate*, states the following about Mary:

> Besides being one of the best students that Georgetown has ever had, Mary is an accomplished pianist. Many are the delightful evenings that she has afforded the Convent by her concerts! Add to all this a gleaming mass of red hair, a sunny smile, a sweet, generous disposition and a cool determination to win and you will have solved the mystery of Mary's seemingly enchanted existence.

The yearbook also recorded that she played a piano duet—"Valse," Opus 15 by Anton Arensky with another college student for the commencement program.[59] Arensky was a late nineteenth-century Russian composer whose "Valse" or Waltz required two pianos for performance. Hutcheson terms the work "indispensable to the duo-pianist repertory."[60] "Valse" is lengthy and as a waltz moves quickly. It demands pianists with much precision and control. Performing such a piece indicates that Mary was indeed an accomplished pianist. After graduation from Visitation, Mary finished her baccalaureate degree at Trinity College in Washington, DC.

When she graduated, the yearbook editors label her "an artist . . . and scholar." "Hers [is] a deep appreciation of music," they continue. She is one who loves "rhythm and harmony," a "pianist and singer."[61] Her senior yearbook picture shows a self-confident young woman, ready to begin a career. Although Mary ultimately decided not to pursue a career as a concert pianist, she continued to enjoy playing the piano for many years. However, in 1967, she was injured in a serious automobile accident. The damage to one of her wrists was so significant that she could no longer share her love of music through the piano.

The 1925 Providence annual also contains information about Ann Ahern's musical skills at this point. She was a freshman at Providence Academy that year, described by the staff as having a "kind and generous nature" and studious.[62] In the February 1925 recital, Ann performed "Tarantella" by Horvath while Mary concluded the program with an "Etude" by Ludvig Schytte. In May 1925 Ann played "Scherzo" by Schubert and Mary performed the concluding MacDowell mentioned above.[63] The previous fall in December 1924, Ann had played "Consolation" by Theodor Leschetizky, a Polish pianist and composer; and her sister Mary closed the program with the piece by Castro already mentioned.[64]

In the 1926 annual from Providence, now a sophomore, Ann is "talented in school," and "smart" in music. A classmate concludes her poem about her: "And as she's Irish you know she's witty / As well as very, very pretty."[65] On the December 20, 1925, recital, Ann played "Valse" by French composer Benjamin Godard and in February accompanied her brother John, who played "Idilio" by French pianist and composer Théodore Lack. Both Ann and John appear in a picture labeled "Beethoven Division of the Harmony Club."[66] On the May 1925 program, after Ann played Schubert as already mentioned, her younger sister Catherine played a piano duet titled "Gavotte" by the Hungarian composer Ede Poldini, especially known for his short piano pieces. Since the gavotte is a lively folk dance, the performers of this duet created a lilting atmosphere. Listed in this annual as a freshman, John is called "faithful and true" and "kind" by a classmate.[67] John appears in several pictures, one labeled "Artists in the Making." And there's an excellent picture of him, with bow and violin in hand, standing in front of a grand piano, with the inscription "Violinists in the Making."[68] The Aherns' cousin Mary Lansdale also appears in recitals and in some of the photos in both annuals.[69] Based on the pieces students played and the frequency of recitals, Providence seems to have provided an excellent background in music for the Ahern children.

## "Miss Ann," the Piano Teacher

Ann Ahern, or Miss Ann, as she was called by several generations of piano students in the Texarkana area, became a successful teacher of piano, helping students hone their musical skills and develop a solid appreciation of music. She began teaching in the 1930s and continued almost until her death in 1988. It was a career that spanned half a century of lessons, recitals, students, service to the music profession, and, of course, music. Many current residents of the Texarkana area still remember their lessons with "Miss Ann," and often have a favorite story or two to tell about their study. Early on she developed a reputation for a no-nonsense approach. There was no shirking your obligation to practice and learn your pieces if Miss Ann could do anything about it, and she usually could. One student who took lessons from her for twelve years in the 1950s and 1960s decided she wanted to quit when she was a sophomore in high school. When the student's mother relayed the message to Miss Ann, she simply said, "No, I don't give her permission to quit."[70] And that was that. If she saw ability, she didn't allow failure or retreat. You simply recalibrated and stayed on for the duration. According to Miss Ann, you may not be able to control everything that happens to you in life, but you can control how consistently you work. And that would carry you through. Like her sister Mary, Ann also waved labor's banner: "Work Conquers All."

Ann graduated from Providence Academy in 1928 and followed in Mary's footsteps, enrolling at Georgetown Visitation Convent in Washington, DC, the following fall. The 1929 yearbook at Georgetown, called *The Green Gate*, proclaims as its motto: "Learn not for school but for life." Ann internalized this adage as well and determined to learn as much as she could. The annual's student editors call Ann "a saucy red-breasted robin—a shaft of sunlight." She worked on the school magazine, *Red Book*. *The Green Gate* also records that Ann chose the motto "I will be jovial" for a school picture; the editors wrote the following about her:

> Ann won our hearts from the start. Very seldom do we meet a person with such a charmingly consistent good humor. We love to hear her infectious laugh and watch the merry twinkle in her eye. Her natural geniality makes one delight in her companionship for her endless flow of conversation never ceases to amuse and interest. There isn't a living creature for whom Ann would not do a good turn if she possibility could and she is ever the sympathetic listener and comforter when spirits droop and hearts are sad. We know quite decidedly that here is one classmate whom we are never to forget.[71]

In 1930, Ann was back in Texarkana, attending Texarkana Junior College. According to the school's 1931 annual, *The Bulldog*, she was a sophomore. With her father's serious illness (he would die in 1932) and the tremendous financial difficulties caused by the Great Depression, Ann must have come home to be with her family. She simply got to work teaching piano. Her family's "music room" would serve for both teaching and recitals. And eventually she would buy another grand for students to play. Placed side by side in the music room with their keyboards facing toward the library, the pianos stood ready for service for decades.

One of Ann's students who took piano lessons in the 1930s and 1940s remembers playing recitals at the old Texarkana, Arkansas Municipal Auditorium. Another student who took in the 1940s remembers her as "very determined," "tough," and "firm." "If she told you something, you knew what she said," this former student adds. By the 1940s, Ann was also teaching music at Providence Academy, in grades 1–12.[72] Granddaughter Eleanor, who lived in the house during the 1940s, remembers her Aunt Ann as going to different schools to teach piano. Sometimes she would teach until late at night. One student remembers walking from Walnut Street to Texas High School for lessons with Miss Ann. Another student's parent told Eleanor later about a school coach who was supposed to be very strict. The parent says, "After having Miss Ann as a teacher, this coach was a breeze for my child."[73]

Some stories about Miss Ann reveal her wit, at times of a caustic nature. As was her custom, she once asked a student at the beginning of her lesson how her practicing had gone. "Fine," the student assures her. "Did you practice every day?" Miss Ann wants to know. "Oh, yes, ma'am." "Well, have you practiced your piece already today?" "Oh yes, this morning," she replies and smiles. "Well, that *is* strange," says Miss Ann, "because you left your music here last time after your lesson!" The student's rejoinder, if there was one, isn't recorded, but she was clearly caught in her tracks. No doubt she landed in "the practice room," as the smaller parlor grew to be labeled. It was a story shared by students who commiserated with each other about how strict Miss Ann was. Some students even called it "the torture room."[74]

One student who took piano lessons for a few years in the early 1950s remembers trying to trick Miss Ann about her practice. Both she and her older sister took, and at their respective lessons each blamed the other for their having monopolized the piano so much that practicing was impossible. Ann, of course, soon realized the flaw in their stories, as neither showed much evidence of touching the piano. Another time this student thought for sure she would be able to escape—legitimately this time, she believed—the routine of daily practice. When she fell out of a tree in the fourth grade and had her arm in a cast, she imagined that Miss Ann would allow her to rest. Not so! She continued lessons and practiced the best she could.[75]

Woe be to anyone who hadn't learned his or her recital pieces adequately for Miss Ann. With both a Christmas and spring recital and all pieces having to be memorized, students had to be diligent, especially before recital time. Miss Ann wasn't about to let a student's poor performance embarrass her or the parents. The story has survived about a female student who came to a Saturday lesson without practicing her recital pieces adequately. It seems that the little girl's father and one of her girlfriends waited in the car while she had her 30-minute lesson. The father would then drop them off at the movies to have a good time. When his daughter didn't come back to the car after her lesson time was over, the father went into Miss Ann's studio. Miss Ann told him that his daughter wasn't going anywhere because she had to practice. "But we have a guest in the car waiting to go to the movies," the father explains. "Well, just take her home," Miss Ann reportedly says. "Your daughter can't go because she hasn't practiced enough." And that was that. The father evidently did what he was told and at some point several hours later came back for his daughter. If you didn't work hard enough, you didn't deserve to enjoy yourself. That was Miss Ann's philosophy.[76]

Many students remember spending time in the practice room on a Saturday before recitals. As Ann grew older, especially after she had broken both of her wrists, she decided to claim the practice room as her bedroom, which she shared with her mother. The large pocket doors allowed privacy. If you had to go to a practice room in the 1970s, you were sent to the practice piano upstairs, sometimes in the large central hallway and other times in the bedroom leading to the sleeping porch on the south side. Most students landed in one or the other—even the best students, from time to time. Miss Ann could hear you practicing upstairs from the downstairs. She simply called in the next student while you practiced. She called your parents to have them bring toothpaste and pajamas as you would likely be there for some time, certainly until you had learned your music to Miss Ann's satisfaction.[77]

Students soon learned the routine for recitals. You dressed in your best clothes. Girls wore fancy dresses and Sunday school shoes; boys wore slacks and nice shirts. Some girls even wore corsages if their mothers would spring for one. Since some of the recital dresses were strapless, you had to be careful not to get out in the sun in your bathing suit prior to the recital. Miss Ann would not allow anyone to perform with noticeable strap marks on their shoulders.[78] At recitals girls always curtsied and boys bowed following their performances. All waited in the dining room while the other students played. Miss Ann understood what would keep you quiet and get your mind off what was about to happen. She bought an armload of new comic books, which she purchased at the bookstore close to the old McCartney Hotel, and distributed them around the table. You could lose yourself in the antics of Richie or Donald Duck and Minnie Mouse, while your peers performed. Mrs. Ahern sat in the dining room to ensure complete silence if the comic books failed. Meanwhile, Miss Ann waited for you in the hall. She was "notorious for smoothing down your hair, then sending you in to perform."[79]

She had so many students that she always had to have two recitals, two at Christmas and another two in the spring. She never liked to divide the students by gender or age in these recitals, but had a mixture of both, believing that the younger students would be inspired by hearing the older students play. And the recitals were always at night. The old house was lit up with lamps, wall sconces, and chandeliers. In the spring cut flowers graced each room; at Christmas, the lovely seasonal decorations sustained the event's merriment. The audience had recital programs to follow the names of pieces and performers, and afterward, everyone enjoyed lime sherbet punch and brown-edged wafers.

In 1959 Pat Horrigan, Mrs. Ahern's grandson, remembers visiting with his family during one of his aunt's recitals. He especially recalls the "really good punch of lime sherbet and 7-Up," so wonderful that he "never forgot it."[80] Granddaughter Eleanor, or Scamp as everyone called her then, remembers taking piano from her aunt when she was four or five years old in the 1940s and playing in a Christmas recital. "I was so surprised when people clapped," she says. "I didn't think they would because I couldn't even touch the pedals." She remembers worrying the most about not being able to touch either pedal. Her feet just dangled. "Don't waste your energy on that," grandmother Mamie told her.[81]

Miss Ann had plenty of space for her recitals in the home. She had all the pocket doors open and placed folding chairs in the music room, library, and across the hall in the smaller parlor before she decided to use it as her bedroom. Sometimes when students practiced for their recital, she sat back in the library to listen to their pieces, giving the students a sense of audience and allowing herself to judge the quality of their performance from a distance. Although it was crucial to practice well before the day of the recital, Miss Ann instructed all students not to practice the day of the recital. She believed their performance would sound more spontaneous if they followed that dictum.

Although students remember Miss Ann as "very disciplined," they also recall her as an excellent teacher and a loving person. As a student grew older under her tutelage, if lucky, that student then had special privileges. He or she might get to work for her, helping with her record keeping and running errands about town. Some were able to help type recital programs, and some students got to play duets with her. The most gifted became her student teachers, working with other students when they had to go to the practice piano. One student remembers going on errands to buy gifts for the nuns who worked at Providence Academy and elsewhere. She recalls that in selecting their presents, she had to avoid lace (frills evidently forbidden) and to buy only *unscented* lotion. She walked from the house down to Belk-Jones department store on Broad Street and a neighborhood pharmacy for presents.[82]

If you were really lucky, you got to help her decorate her Christmas tree. It was always a tree far larger than any tree you had in your home. It must have been one of the largest Ann could find, easily 8 or 9 feet tall. Miss Ann would send these special students to the attic to get the Christmas decorations and bring them down to the first floor. Some students remember being in awe of the attic because it was so immense. You could stand up and easily walk around in it. They also remember there were antique decorations with glass icicles to attach to the tree, and Miss Ann had a lot of the "old bubble lights" to string on it. They had to be careful placing the angel hair on the mantels, along with the German figurines of children and the bisque ballerinas on the bookcase shelves. Students placed the large, blown-glass Christmas balls on the tree for her. These decorations were larger than softballs and far more delicate and beautiful than those they had in their own homes. She also had fine porcelain bird ornaments that clipped on the branches of the tree. Before the students placed any decorations on the tree, they had to wire each branch carefully to help support the weight of some of the antique decorations. One former student remembers Miss Ann teaching her to "relax when handling them." Granted they were "treasures," but if you were tense, you would be more likely to break one.[83]

Special students often accompanied her in her car, a roomy Oldsmobile with all controls on the steering wheel since she wasn't able to maneuver the pedals with her feet. She'd had polio as a child and throughout her life wore braces on both legs. The determination she showed to succeed as a teacher revealed itself in her approach to other aspects of her life. She wasn't about to feel sorry for herself or limit what she was able to do physically. Students admired her spunk and sense of dignity. Once you got to know Miss Ann, students generally agreed, you really didn't even notice her braces. It was just part of who she was. You noticed the crutches she used, that was all. Several students remember riding around in her car with Miss Ann and going into stores on errands for her.

Occasionally special students even got to spend the weekend with her, helping her with chores and visiting as teacher and friend. On those occasions, Miss Ann and the student might sit on the front porch, visiting, and glance across Laurel Street at the Miller County Courthouse. More than one student mentioned sometimes seeing prisoners housed at the top of the building. The absolute freedom of sitting on this spacious porch flanked by beautiful trees seemed a great distance from the confinement of a jail, but the two worlds met at least by view.[84] Being sent on errands in the house to fetch something was always an adventure although you were not supposed to meander. Miss Ann had two large key rings—and a skeleton style key—that she gave to students when sent on an errand in the house. A lot of cabinets and closets were locked.[85]

Students also remember fondly how Miss Ann would often let you choose the music you wanted to work on, but as one student said, she was a "stickler for classical music."[86] She'd bring a lot of sheet music to lessons and spread it out before you. You sight-read a piece or two that looked intriguing at your lesson. Sometimes she'd play pieces if you especially wanted to hear how a certain one sounded at a performance tempo. Then you could choose which ones you wanted to perfect. She always provided a wide range of pieces from the various musical periods. Most of the pieces appeared on required lists for festivals and various contests, but choosing your own was meaningful. Of course, students also went downtown to Beasley's on Broad Street to buy music from time to time. Sometimes Miss Ann would play recordings of the pieces students were learning or if not the exact piece, she'd play a recording of another piece by the same composer. (Beasley's would later move to a different location on Broad.)

Most former students recall the "red couch" in the central hallway downstairs. Students sat there waiting for their lesson. A large piece of furniture with flat, wooden arms and deep cushions covered in red leather, it reflects the influence of the Arts and Crafts movement. A typical question from former students, "Is the red couch still there?" suggests the ominous character it assumed for some. You waited there, probably wishing you had practiced more, until it was *your* lesson time. You got there early because the student before you might be toted off to the practice room. The couch along with its matching chair remain in the house today, still resting in the central hall. They show the kind of wear that occurs over a long period of time. The couch, or the "long, heavy davenport"[87] as at least one former student terms it, now bears the imprint of the many students who have waited on it. The worn-out springs show themselves through the leather, forming a lumpy and noisy cushion for any would-be recliners today.

Those who took piano lessons from Ann Ahern during their formative years in school typically voice much gratitude toward her for her excellence as a teacher and her extension of friendship. They use such adjectives as *gracious* and *dedicated* in describing her. They remember the house itself as "elegant"—that it seemed to "exude music." One student indicates she owes Miss Ann "everything because of my music"; it has "made her"; "set her on the path" she needed. In the end, she claims Miss Ann was an "angel of music."[88]

## Ann Ahern and the Wednesday Music Club

Ann Ahern was a loyal and enthusiastic supporter of Texarkana's Wednesday Music Club and believed that she grew as a teacher and her students profited immensely from being introduced to this civic group. According to historians Chandler and Howe, the Wednesday Music Club constituted the oldest club in Texarkana, originally created as the Deltheric Club. It changed its name in 1898 when it became part of the Arkansas Federation of Music Clubs. By 1904, it joined the Texas Federation as well.[89] From its inception, the club was guided by the National Federation of Music Clubs (NFMC). A glance at its early presidents as recorded by Chandler and Howe reads like a *who's who* in early Texarkana. Reflecting the social style of the day, their names appear as the embodiment of their husband's prestige: Mrs. George Fouke, Mrs. William Lee Estes, Mrs. W. H. Arnold, Mrs. H. V. Beasley, Mrs. Ben F. Smith, Mrs. Preston Hunt, Mrs. W. L. Wood Jr., and so on.[90] Ann Ahern's name would eventually appear twice on the club's list of presidents.

Ann also served as president of the Arkansas Federation of Music Clubs and Boards. As a long-standing member of the National Federation of Music Clubs, she performed as chair of festivals in Arkansas as well as the acting chair of the National Federation Festival Program.[91] The NFMC had been founded in 1898 to "promote and support American music, performers, and music education."[92] The Arkansas Federation of Music Clubs (AFMC) was established in 1915. During World War I with US military forces stationed in the state, the AFMC in conjunction with the US Army offered musical events for the soldiers in which Arkansas residents and military personnel performed. The AFMC continued after the war, showcasing local talent as well as nationally known musicians during the 1920s and 1930s, and during World War II staged musical events for the hospitals and military camps in the state. Later the AFMC sponsored Inspiration Point Fine Arts Colony in Eureka Springs, contributed toward the Kennedy Arts Center in Washington, DC, and encouraged young musicians in Arkansas through various competitions, festivals, and scholarships.[93]

Ann Ahern's name first appears on the 1936–37 list of members in the Wednesday Music Club handbook,[94] which indicates she served on the Student Loan Fund committee, contributed to current events at the October meeting, and along with Mrs. Roy Baskett and others served as hostess for the December meeting. The topic was Music in Religion. The following year, she continued to serve on the Student Loan Fund committee and served as one of the hostesses for the November meeting where Mrs. W. L. Wood Jr. presented comments on women composers and leaders, including Olga Samaroff, Nadia Boulanger, Amy Beach, and Cecile Chaminade. Ann spoke on current events for the January meeting. By 1939–40, Ann served as treasurer, worked on the Harmony Music Club committee for young musicians, and functioned as a hostess for the November meeting. Ann continued the same duties in 1940–41, but by 1941–42, she served as recording secretary and hostess in February. In April, she attended the club's Music in the Home program with an emphasis on Mrs. W. L. Wood Jr. and daughter Jane, Mrs. Nick Braumiller Jr., and daughters Ann and Betty Jane, and Mrs. Henry Hirsch and daughter Patricia, among others. During the 1943–44 year, she was the "leader" in March of a program on the development of the pianoforte. In 1945–46 and 1946–47, she served as president of the club.

Because some of the yearly club handbooks are missing, it's difficult to record Ann's complete participation in the Wednesday Music Club. At times her name appears under "Semi-Active" members, but by 1964–65 and continuing in 1965–66, she is listed as the president of the Arkansas Federation of Music Clubs and chair of the Junior Festivals. In 1967, she is listed as the Federation Speaker for the Club's September meeting at the Texarkana Country Club where a federation winner performed. In the 1970s, Ann began contributing funds in her mother's name as a "patron," which she continued to do for many years. In 1973–74, Ann hosted the April meeting at 403 Laurel Street; and in 1976 and 1977, the March meetings. In 1984–85, she served as junior counselor.

The NFMC 1960 Club President's Handbook, with Ann Ahern's name on it, remains among the Wednesday Music Club's documents. In addition to a required schedule of events for each month, it denotes the president's responsibilities. Some include: read and answer each club letter the day it is received; know the purpose of all NFMC departments; attend all district and state conferences and meetings of the Council of Club Presidents; adjust your schedule to the National's July 1 through June 30 calendar year; report all Federation matters promptly, ensure newspaper clippings are sent to district and state publicity chairs; and maintain the Junior Festival bulletins. Clearly the office entailed many responsibilities.

In March 1989, the Wednesday Music Club nominated Ann Ahern for the state's Outstanding Service Award for twenty-five or more years' participation.[95] She had died in November the previous year. Among other service records, the form lists fifty-two years of Federation membership, one year as a National Board Member, two as State President, five as State

Committee Member, eleven as a Club Officer, seventeen as a Club Chair, thirty-eight as Club Committee member, and six as Junior Club sponsor. In submitting their nomination, the Wednesday Music Club wrote:

> Ann Ahern always loved music. She consistently wanted to share this love, to share it generously and widely. All musical events of the community had her enthusiastic support. Although childhood polio left her permanently confined to a wheelchair, Ann brought the spiritualizing force of music to countless lives in her community.

Accompanying the application was a letter dated November 22, 1987, addressed to Ann from Fr. David LeSieur sent on behalf of the people of St. Edward Parish, thanking her for her "years of faithful service in the music ministry." Father LeSieur mentioned her work from the early 1940s until the late 1960s, including her teaching at Providence Academy and St. Edward School. "It was you," he writes, "who taught the youth of the parish to sing not only in English, but also in Latin." He further commended her for her work in the school plays and as director of graduation. Finally, he awarded her the Little Rock Diocesan Service Medal.

## The Musical Scores

At Ann's death in 1988, most of her music, her sister Mary's, and her mother's seems to have been left in the house.[96] About half of it consists of scores for choirs, which is not surprising in that both mother and daughter Ann directed choirs, Ann at Providence Academy and the Junior Choir at St. Edward Church and her mother, the adult choir at St. Edward Church. About a fourth of it consists of religious organ music, which was performed by both mother and daughter, and another fourth of the music consists of piano pieces, much of it played by Mrs. Ahern and her daughters. The choral scores are of both a sacred and secular nature and arranged for men's and women's groups. They date from around the beginning of the twentieth century through the 1960s. Additionally, there are musical scores designed to be used in school settings, books that Ann used in teaching music, and piano scores.

Over a dozen examples of popular sheet music remain among the vocal scores, most dating from the second decade of the twentieth century through the 1920s. A World War I song, "Long Boy," with the subtitle

"Good-Bye, Ma! Good-Bye, Pa! Good-Bye, Mule with Yer Old Hee-Haw!" pictures a long-legged, skinny infantryman on the cover with a rifle over his shoulder and a hat on his head leaving the farm. William Herschell's lyrics depict a naïve lad—"When th' war broke out he got right in," and "I may not know what th' war's about, / But you bet, by gosh, I'll soon find out," he croons. "An, O my sweetheart don't you fear, / I'll bring you a King for a souvenir; / I'll git you a Turk an' a Kaiser, too / An' that's about all one feller could do!" In retrospect, of course, the song's lyrics offer an ironic optimism considering the millions of soldiers killed worldwide in the war and the flu pandemic. Another war song of 1918 originating in the English Music Halls—"I'm Glad I Can Make You Cry" pictures a soldier in uniform holding his helmet with his right hand and his girl with his left. While she looks forlorn, he appears content. The lyrics by Charles McCarron and Carey Morgan depict a young soldier happy when he can make his girlfriend jealous.

Songs from the 1920s are brighter. "Pretty Little Cinderella" as sung by the famous Kouns Sisters in G. M. Anderson's *The Frivolities of 1920*, pictures a demure young woman and her suitor. Songwriters Blanche Franklyn and Nat Vincent offer their spin on the traditional story. Two other songs remain popular today: "I Can't Give You Anything but Love (Baby)" by Jimmy McHugh with words by Dorothy Fields, published in 1928, and "Yes Sir: That's My Baby," with words by Gus Kahn and music by Walter Donaldson, published in 1925.

## The Aherns' Musical Recordings

Dozens of recordings of classical works suggest the Aherns' knowledge of and love for music. Granddaughter Eleanor remembers how fond both her Aunt Ann and grandmother were of listening to records. One recording in particular Eleanor remembers hearing a lot as a child is a version of Prokofiev's *Peter and the Wolf*, which her grandmother played over and over again to help her learn the instruments of the orchestra. Numerous recordings in the 78 rpm format offer glimpses of the great performers of the early twentieth century. Examples include the famous Polish American pianist Artur Rubinstein playing Debussy on the Victor Red Seal label, which features "Jardins Sous La Pluie" among others; Rachmaninoff playing his own shorter pieces such as

"Melodie" in E Major Opus 3, No. 3, on the Victor label; Rachmaninoff playing his famous Piano Concerto No. 2 in C minor and his "Rhapsody for Piano and Orchestra on a Theme by Paganini," both conducted by Leopold Stokowski with the Philadelphia Orchestra; the great Russian American pianist Vladimir Horowitz performing Brahms's Concerto No. 2 in B Flat, conducted by his father-in-law Arturo Toscanini with the NBC Symphony Orchestra; and Stravinsky's "The Fire Bird Suite" and Shostakovich's Symphony No. 6, both with Stokowski and the Philadelphia Orchestra on the Victor label. The 33 rpm recordings offer Mozart, Mendelssohn, Franck, Tchaikovsky, Haydn, and many other composers, including Bach played by the renowned Glenn Gould on a Columbia label. Finally, the Aherns' record collection contains recordings of more contemporary pianists—Liberace, Ferrante and Teicher, Roger Williams, Henry Mancini, and others—and such modern classics as Arthur Fiedler's "Wonderful World of Music," a collection published by Reader's Digest in 1974.

## Conclusion

Toward the end of Arthur Loesser's excellent mid-century social history of pianos and the people who played them, he suggests an iconic image, signaling, he believed, the decline and eventual end of a way of life that had been treasured in the home for over a century: the "cozy and warm" conviviality that had revolved around the piano.[97] Loesser points out that by 1910, Steinway and other less prestigious piano companies had altered the physical appearance of pianos, changing the ornately carved legs to "tapered underpinnings." He explains:

> The abandonment of a familiar object's old-fashioned physiognomy suggested a coming break with a previous way of life, the start of a loss of faith in the hitherto robust set of standards. The old legs, lettering, and lattice were visible points of a certain flavor of ostentation; and their frank air of elaborate uselessness was their reason for being.[98]

Soon the piano-buying public began to purchase fewer pianos, some perhaps enamored with the convenience of the player-piano that had come into existence, although in buying one the family lost the prestige of having a daughter who played. Others perhaps became enchanted with the phonograph that appeared on the market along with the rise of the radio. After all, learning to play an instrument required years of work. Wouldn't it be easier simply to have someone else learn and play for you? Even by 1924, Esther Singleton, the editor of *The Antiquarian*, writes that the piano "is in danger of becoming as rare now as a brougham, a phaeton or a dogcart for the banished horse."[99]

Readers of this book born mid-twentieth century or before may be surprised to learn of the piano's decline beginning in the early decades of the century. Most of Miss Ann's students remember what seemed to be a world of friends who took piano lessons, a piano in the homes of many of their acquaintances, and a bountiful number of neighborhood piano teachers waiting in the wings to offer instruction. Today there are few remaining businesses that sell pianos exclusively and fewer and fewer students learning to play piano. And while the popularity of the electronic keyboard has given new life to the keyboard instrument and promotes enjoyment and the sense of belonging to a group, Edward Rothstein, music critic for *The New Republic*, points out several important differences. For one, contemporary culture generally makes less stringent demands for technical perfection on the electric keyboard player than that required in the classical tradition of the acoustic piano. But more importantly, perhaps, because the electronic piano by design is portable, it really isn't a domestic instrument at all. The piano was a fixed anchor in the house that attracted members of the family and friends who gathered in a manner within the home that has all but passed away today.[100]

The music in the Ahern house symbolically died with the death of Ann Ahern in 1988. Mary returned to the house that year but an injury to her wrist prevented her from playing the piano as she once did. As Mary and Joe became elderly in the 1990s, they worried about the fate of the two Steinway pianos. With the approval of other family members, their younger sister Eleanor ultimately found a home for the pianos with Southern Methodist University's School of Music, to be enjoyed by piano majors. There they would be played. Today, decades later, the music room houses two beautiful grand pianos, donated by interested Texarkana citizens.[101] As Mary Olive wished, the music room continues to be filled with melody.

Mary C. Ahern's Class Song, Providence Academy Yearbook, 1926, Texarkana Museums System, Wilbur Smith Research Archive, photograph by Doris Davis

Mary C. Ahern's recital on the Steinway piano in the Ahern's music room, courtesy of Paterson's Studio, Texarkana, Texas and the Ahern, Horrigan, and Purcell families

Desk in music room where Ann Ahern kept her records, part of the Texarkana Museums System's collection, photograph by Doris Davis

Mary Ahern at the piano, surrounded by siblings, courtesy of the Ahern, Horrigan, and Purcell families

# 7

# The Nature of Privacy
## Bedrooms and Beyond

*Oh sleep! it is a gentle thing, Beloved from Pole to Pole!*

—Samuel Coleridge[1]

The Aherns' bedrooms, or chambers as they were often called in earlier periods, are all on the second floor, ensuring the greatest privacy. Had the house been built in the early nineteenth instead of early twentieth century, however, one or more bedrooms might have appeared on the ground floor with doors opening into a reception room. Parents often slept on the ground floor with easy access to prominent social rooms. This configuration of household space generally indicated a position of importance for the head of the household, thus delineating aspects of social rank or class. Children and servants slept in the attic or in outbuilding sleeping areas. By 1850 those of economic means began a continuing trend that placed all bedrooms on the second floor. The Aherns' use of sleeping space mirrors this trend. And because children and servants also slept on the second floor in this new configuration, bedrooms shifted from a status-determined place to a functioned-determined location. This pattern of creating a sleeping area or zone thus privileges privacy over rank and signaled a family's middle-class designation.[2]

As the Victorian era progressed into the Edwardian, rooms increased in size and reflected a designated use. For example, the library was for reading or study, and the bedroom for sleeping. And yet, as social historian David P. Handlin points out, that designation was far too simplistic. The library, for instance, may also be a site for family boardgames. Handlin notes a second level of ambiguity in that Victorian and Edwardian homes often had a network of halls, stairs, and doors including pocket doors that could separate or combine areas in various ways. These possible alterations inherently modified the sense of privacy claimed by rooms, including the bedroom.[3]

In *The Decoration of Houses*, published in 1914, Edith Wharton advocates the French manner of subdividing a bedroom into a suite of two or more smaller rooms. Preferably, a bedroom would have an antechamber that might serve as a sitting room or a more public room that would then open into the sleeping area or bed chamber.[4] The Aherns created a suite of rooms as their principal bed chamber, but they divided the space differently. The larger room is designated as the master bedroom, which opens into a shared bathroom, which in turn connects with the smaller chamber, designated as Mrs. Ahern's. Both chambers have doors that exit into the upstairs main hall, as do all of the other bedrooms. Mrs. Ahern's chamber also connects with the sleeping porch.

Typically, turn-of-the-century parents occupied the main bedroom together although some authorities advocated the practice of sleeping apart intermittently. For instance, some physicians suggested that women sleep separately from their husbands when pregnant, and separate rooms constituted a form of birth control in earlier periods. Other authorities maintained that sleeping in a double bed was not as healthy as sleeping alone, which afforded more privacy and comfort without the inevitable distractions from another person.[5] The 1920s, in fact, saw an increasing popularity of twin beds for married couples who could not afford separate chambers. And in 1934, the Crystal House at the Chicago "Century of Progress" Expositions offered the exclusively modern design of "his" and "her" bedroom suites, each with a separate bathroom.[6] Thus, in designing their sleeping chambers as they did, the Aherns were both in keeping with authorities of the period but also forward thinking.

In addition to the health concerns already mentioned, experts warned against the danger of tuberculosis and advocated that fresh air in sleeping was critical in combatting the disease, sometimes called "The Great

White Plague." Some even warned against kissing one's own kin, the scare of tuberculosis was so immense.[7] The sleeping porch thus in the midst of this scare gained great popularity. In 1918, the Aherns elected to enclose their large balcony on the south side of the house, essentially constructing a sleeping porch. The area has large double-hung windows on three sides of the enclosed space, with each end having two windows and the middle having a "ribbon pattern of windows, with four on each side of the middle column."[8] With the original balcony of wood floors and the original house walls, the space suggests being both outside and indoors.

Sleeping porches gained popularity in the pre-air-conditioned South. Some families, including the Aherns, however, regularly slept on the sleeping porch even in cold weather. The Aherns' youngest daughter, Eleanor, remembered the "wonderful" sleeping porch and indicated that all the children slept out there, whether it was cold or hot. If cold, they took blankets and hot water bottles that they put in the bed. All of them were healthy, Eleanor remembered.[9] The Aherns' grandson Brian recalled that the windows of the sleeping porch were closed during the day to keep out the hot air, then opened at night for a cool breeze. Joe Ahern often checked the screens to ensure mosquitoes couldn't get in. He used cotton to plug in holes.[10]

By 1910, outdoor sleeping and fresh air had become quite popular. Although previously known as a treatment for tuberculosis, these practices appeared good for everything including insomnia and colds. Some even believed that architecture would change to make "night outdoor life" part of a family's experience.[11] Decades earlier in 1869, Catharine E. Beecher and Harriet Beecher Stowe in *The American Woman's Home* had strongly advocated that the mistress of the house ensure fresh air for anyone sleeping. "The debility of childhood, the lassitude of domestics, and the ill-health of families," they wrote, "are often caused by neglecting to provide a supply of pure air."[12]

As mentioned in earlier chapters, most of the original furniture remains in the house. Mrs. Ahern's bedchamber, about 14 by 15 feet, contains a bedroom suite of circa 1905 vintage. Made of oak, the matching dresser and chest of drawers reveal curved drawers, scalloped edges on the top surface, and ornate mirrors of beveled glass. Although the metal bed is not part of the set, its color blends in with the other pieces of furniture. In selecting this bed, Mrs. Ahern may have been following advice from contemporary decorators. During this time, decorators for the middle class thought that iron and brass were more sanitary than wood furniture.[13] In light of the panic over various diseases and the lack of information, Mrs. Ahern may well have chosen what seemed healthier rather than what appeared more aesthetically pleasing.

Mr. Ahern's room, a little over 16 by 16 feet, contains a fireplace mantel and two side-by-side windows to the east and a single window to the south. The largest of the bedrooms, it houses an oak bedroom suite that dates from the 1930s. The dresser has an elongated mirror over two drawers, while the chest of drawers has a small mirror, cabriole legs, and curved drawers. The double bed, also of oak, but not of the same design, reveals an unadorned and relatively short headboard and an even shorter footboard. The matter-of-factness of the bed seems masculine. This room contains the primitive intercom mechanism that connects with the kitchen. The proximity of the room to the front balcony would have allowed Mr. Ahern the opportunity to sit outside on pleasant nights if he were still up after everyone else was asleep. He had easy access to the balcony.

In an era focused on germs and disease, women were understandably concerned with sanitation in the bedroom. Beecher and Beecher Stowe offered detailed suggestions about cleanliness and focus in particular on one aspect of bedroom maintenance. They complain that few young domestics know how to make a bed well and that being able to do so was the hallmark of one trained well in the science and art of housekeeping. The directions are lengthy and specific, involving whether a featherbed and/or another mattress is included, the placement of bolsters, under sheets, blankets, upper sheets, and pillows.[14] "A nice housekeeper always notices the manner in which a bed is made," Beecher and Beecher Stowe argue, "and in some parts of the country, it is rare to see this work properly performed."[15]

## The Children's Rooms

The children's bedrooms are opposite the principal suite of parental rooms, separated by the immense hall that runs the length of the house, mirroring the downstairs main hall. These rooms consist of a bedroom for the boys, one for the girls, and a nursery that also housed a domestic. The boys' bedroom was the end room closest to the front balcony, the girls' was at the other end of the hall, and the nursery, between the stairs and the bathroom. Nurseries were typically located on the second floor in the nineteenth century, as in the case of the Aherns,' and were the epitome of what Victorians perceived to be safe. All of the younger children slept, played, and ate in this one space. The material culture that envelops modern notions of a child's nursery are actually quite recent, developing only in the Victorian period.[16]

Only after 1830 with the beginning of the Victorian period were there specialized materials and goods for children and an attitude that perceived children to be inherently pure. During the colonial period, adults typically saw children as "inadequate creatures, terribly vulnerable to accident and disease, irrational and animalistic in their behavior, and a drain on the family's resources and energy."[17] During this period, the first half of the eighteenth century and earlier, common artifacts consisted of swaddling, which refers to lengthy pieces of linen wrapped tightly around an infant's body to promote straight growth; standing stools that kept an infant in an upright position to encourage walking; and walking stools with wooden wheels but no seats.

The point seems to have been for children to grow into adulthood as quickly as possible. Both genders wore awkward petticoats, lengthy gowns, and firm corsets to enhance posture. Even when out of the nursery, little boys, like little girls, wore long skirts until they were about seven; at which time boys might wear knee breeches.[18] Prior to the Victorian era, children slept wherever they could, with parents, servants, siblings, guests, on the floor or on a pallet. As historian Karin Calvert notes, these sleeping arrangements often resulted in "crowded" rooms.[19]

The Victorians, on the other hand, saw childhood differently. They came to believe that children were inherently innocent and any malfeasance on the part of the child was a result of the child's contact with the sullied adult world.[20] In William Wordsworth's famous nineteenth-century poem "Ode: Intimations of Immortality from Recollections of Early Childhood," the poet concludes the child's soul is born "not in entire forgetfulness . . . But trailing clouds of glory do we come / From God."[21] In other words, the child arrives in a celestial manner, innocent of worldly wiles. Such an attitude inscribed both motherhood and childhood as special states. As guardian and protector of the child, the mother needed special rooms to ensure the child's safety. This attitude influenced the architecture of houses, bringing about the nursery and specialized rooms for children as manifested in the Ahern house.

As mentioned, by the Victorian period, both girls and boys wore bright knee-length frocks or dresses and white trousers or pantaloons. Such attire was shocking to some. Since boys had worn dresses and pantaloons for a long time, the surprise arose in the attire for girls. Never before had they worn trousers or pants, even in the form of underwear. Some worried about the dire effect of girls wearing pants and expressed their concerns in sermons and letters to the editor. They feared it would sully girls and endanger the American family. Nonetheless, the new style stayed in vogue.[22]

Although children's bedrooms sometimes included specialized wallpaper and pictures as well as chairs scaled down for children, including smaller rockers and tables, the first nurseries for children were typically sparsely furnished and often consisted simply of furniture handed down or too shabby to be used in any adult sections of the house. But in *The Decoration of Houses*, Wharton argues that children's rooms should receive the same attention as adults': "To teach a child to appreciate any form of beauty is to develop his intelligence, and thereby to enlarge his capacity for wholesome enjoyment."[23] In the period around the turn of the century when the Aherns built their house, parents, interior decorators, and, in particular, mothers began thinking that children's rooms should look different from adult rooms. They thought that pastel colors best reflected children's rooms, selecting blue for all babies and pink for young children. By the 1920s, they wanted white furniture for children. By 1920, also boys' rooms looked quite different from girls' rooms, the former being rather "spartan" typically with a military theme, the latter being the opposite. Girls' rooms often remained furnished with Victorian pieces, had more pictures on the wall, and carpets and drapes.[24]

The second half of the nineteenth century housed many items in the children's bedroom that were new to middle-class families. The cradle with its rocking structure—so ubiquitous in colonial days—was no more. It was replaced by the metal or wooden crib, a taller object with tall, moveable sides. In an 1890 volume of *The Upholsterer*, an author notes that a cradle was nowhere to be seen. He challenges readers to visit a contemporary furniture store in search of the cradle. They will find only "cribs, perambulators, hammocks, and bassinets."[25] Most artifacts that originated for children in this era had a dual purpose: they protected the children from hurting themselves but also protected the house from the energetic actions of children. These new artifacts included the jumper, which could be secured to any doorway and allowed children to jump and swing but also curtailed their movements. Another new artifact, the highchair with its secured tray, prevented children from eating inappropriate foods on the adult table but also protected the dining room dishes from the exploits of young hands.[26]

The Ahern children left behind a number of artifacts from childhood. For instance, the oldest son, Joseph, donated several: a solid oak baseball bat circa 1910 with matching baseball, a vintage Erector Set dating from the 1920s, and various boardgames. A number of baby beds—cribs of cast iron—and other small cast iron youth beds indicate the presence of children in the house at one time.

A couple of decades before the Aherns' marriage, parents of young children began to accept a philosophical position promoted by scholars and child-rearing authorities and realized in such fictional works as *The Adventures of Tom Sawyer* by Samuel Clemens. According to this view, misbehaving was "natural, normal, and healthy especially in the development of young boys."[27] With this attitude as a backdrop, parents then accepted works of make-believe, such as *Peter Pan* and *Winnie-the-Pooh* as harmless forms of entertainment.[28] The Aherns' library reflects this endorsement of fantasy books.

With the change in attitude about children's development suggesting a more robust nature came the more disturbing notion of childhood sexuality, something that Victorians had not considered in grouping the youngest children in the nursery until they were about seven. Late nineteenth- and early twentieth-century parents decided that the nursery was a place for only the most recent baby in the house and moved relatively young children into a room typically shared by their older siblings of the same gender.[29] The Aherns' upstairs configuration of nursery, boys' room, and girls' room reproduces this new pattern.

In the Ahern house, the boys' bedroom on the northeast side is a spacious room, measuring about 15 by 16.5 feet. A bright room, it displays a fireplace mantel and three windows, one on the north side, and two side by side facing east. As with the closet in the nursery, this chamber has a closet that extends upward in a staircase configuration that appears visually to meet in an arc over the stairs. The two closets do not provide a connecting path to each other but with additional support they might have. Instead, the arc may have been Mrs. Ahern's solution to her concern that without this structural device these two closets would simply hang in the air.[30] At some point after everyone was grown, this room became eldest son Joe's bedroom. The room contains a set of white 1930s French, Marie Antoinette–style bedroom furniture that reflects the fondness for the color white throughout the 1920s, '30s, and '40s. The dresser has two long and three short drawers; on top of these rests the mirror. The chest of drawers has both drawers and a cabinet. An additional part of the set is a small white desk with a design on the front and a single drawer beneath the desk. The set evokes a lightness of spirit.

This room also housed the Horrigan grandsons when they came for visits. An added intrigue for them was that their Aunt Ann kept the older comic books she used with her music students in the closet in this room. Patrick Horrigan calls it a "treasure trove of comic books," where they "binged on *Superman, Batman, Archie* and *Jughead*." The boys' room took on new energy with their visits and promised hours of satisfied reading.[31]

## The Bathrooms

The two and a half bathrooms in the Ahern house indicate its upper-middle-class status and the wealth of the owner. Social historian Thomas J. Schlereth points out that it was not until the opening decades of the twentieth century that the bathroom evolved into a special area of the house containing a tub, toilet, and sink. The Aherns' construction date of 1905–06 indicates the early modernity of the structure. Prior to the twentieth century, only wealthy individuals had designated rooms for bathing. And if they had a toilet, it would have been housed in a closet or some other storage facility. Each of these items—sink, toilet, and tub—migrated from some other place, inside or outside of the house. The sink finds origin in the bowl and pitcher that was placed on a washstand in the individual bedchambers. The toilet migrated from the chamber pot placed in the bedrooms and the outdoor privy. The tub originated in the "portable tin-plated or wood tubs of the kitchen."[32]

As a room, the bathroom was sometimes found in the kitchen, basement, utility area, or bedroom. Because the bathroom depended on a consistent supply of water, architects of new construction during the period generally ensured it was close to the plumbing system. In addition to being innovative in constructing two and a half bathrooms, the architectural plans call for the master bathroom to be constructed on the south side of the house above the music room, apart from the plumbing on the north side involving the other upstairs bathroom and the kitchen. The plumbing in the master bathroom connects with the plumbing in the cellar, where the original laundry room was located. The Ahern house was quite upscale in creating these two areas for indoor plumbing.

Writers of advice manuals on building and cleaning houses had long advised the need for indoor plumbing. Catharine Beecher was one of the early advocates of indoor plumbing, initially endorsing the earth closet, which could be moved to any location in the house and did not depend on a water supply.[33] But it was the water closet, based on a network of underground pipes and a municipal sewer system or underground septic tank that eventually became the standard. By the first decade of the twentieth century, Sears, Roebuck advertised plumbing fixtures that could be purchased separately or as a suite. The tubs had claw-feet and the sinks could be attached to the wall or freestanding. Bathroom fixtures came in standard sizes and were appropriately marketed under the brand name of American Standard.[34] The Ahern house contains original plumbing fixtures in the upstairs bathroom off the main hall. That spacious room has a utility closet, a sink attached to the wall that rests on two legs, a claw-foot tub, and a toilet with the tank attached to the wall. In its day, it represented the state of the art in terms of bathroom hygiene, aesthetics, and convenience.

## The Attic

Traditionally the attic—or garret as it was called in some areas—had been an indoor play area for children. Of course, it was also an area that typically housed a family's various outgrown or seasonal items, as well as providing a large, unencumbered spot for the robust play of children. There they generally would not be able to hurt themselves or to mar the furniture or the immensity of the bric-a-brac of the Victorian period.

The Ahern attic, however, does not fall into this general category because of the nearly complete architectural design and construction of the space. With a ceiling height of about 10 feet and measuring about 40 feet across, the attic has a finished floor of pine and inner walls that decrease the perimeter of the area for aesthetic reasons. The room's design eliminates those spaces shortened by the roof's slope. Eighteen steps lead up into the attic from a door in the upper hallway. The top of the area is encased by a railing to ensure safety. The Aherns clearly had at one time intended to use the room as part of their household space because vestiges of an expensive gold-leaf wallpaper decorate the walls and corner protectors appear throughout and windows brighten the area. The youngest daughter, Eleanor, remembers dances in the attic.[35] This practice of owners of large homes inviting young people to come dance on their premises was common in Texarkana during the early twentieth century. A few individuals still remember dances at the large Buchanan house in Texarkana, Arkansas. Mrs. Ahern loved to dance as did all her children. Unfortunately, Mr. Ahern—though he loved to travel—did not like to dance.

# 8

# Dining in Early Twentieth-Century Arkansas

From Garden to Kitchen

*Grandmother was such a meticulous person. She was ahead of her time in keeping everything healthy and clean.*

—Eleanor Purcell,[1] 2018

The Ahern kitchen measures about 9 by 18 feet, and, as with most kitchens of its type built in the first few decades of the twentieth century, contains various work stations where food was prepared, cooked, and served. With four doors at the front of the kitchen leading to the back stairway, cellar, butler's pantry, and dining room, and one in the rear leading to the backyard, Mrs. Ahern designed a workspace that focused on ready access to the rest of the house. Her design of space reflects the philosophy of the new century as summarized by social historian Ellen M. Plante: "By the year 1900, three key words best described the focus for kitchens of the new century—convenient, economical, and sanitary."[2] By the second decade of the twentieth century, Emily Holt, author of one of the most popular guides on housekeeping, claims that "convenience" in the kitchen "has come in large measure to spell human progress."[3]

Like the majority of kitchens of the period, the Aherns' kitchen is located at the rear of the house on the ground floor with a laundry room in the cellar. Period theorists believed that kitchen walls should ideally be "tile or vitrified brick walls" or hard plaster and white-washed or painted white yearly, and the floor should be tile if affordable, or linoleum, if not.[4] Decades earlier in *The American Woman's Home* Catharine E. Beecher and Harriet Beecher Stowe noted that if parents wished their daughters to acquire domestic skills, they should attempt to make the kitchen cheerful and bright, above ground and preferably with flowers and shrubs surrounding the door and windows, with whitewashed walls to suggest neatness and fresh air.[5] They also told how to make a floor covering out of oilcloth, which was used before linoleum, and suggested it be painted yellow. The sink should be scalded each day, sometimes with lye.[6] The colors white, yellow, and green appeared in turn-of-the-century kitchens, all of which emphasized brightness, cleanliness, and clarity. In 1972, over a century after Beecher and Beecher Stowe published this work, historian Molly Harrison terms their text a "revolutionary book," because it proposed the kitchen as the center of the home with organized services, around which the other rooms gravitated. Harrison maintains that their ideas remain influential.[7]

Probably it was personal preference that led Mrs. Ahern to select linoleum for her kitchen floor, as they could have afforded tile if she had wanted it. The original linoleum remains in the house, a pattern of black, brown, red, and yellow. The sink was built in and remains on the southeast wall of the room, with built-in cabinets surrounding it. With a drawer containing a metal compartment for flour and another one for meal, the cabinet space also has a dough board and more room for storage. On the outer wall, across from the sink and stove, another built-in cabinet hugs the wall. This is probably not original to the house but added later. It has two dough boards and more shelves for storage.

By the 1940s when granddaughter Eleanor helped her grandmother Mamie in the kitchen, the room had changed, not structurally, but in the convenience of modern equipment. In 1910, the icebox had been considered a necessity.[8] First introduced in the 1860s, the icebox had grown in popularity. The placement of the Aherns' icebox on the back wall, as with most iceboxes of the period, allowed ice to be placed inside by the iceman, who delivered the ice routinely and kept the appliance in good condition, ensuring that a drainage pipe carried the melting water outdoors or into a pan.[9] By the 1920s, however, the electric refrigerator appeared, and by 1929 General Electric marketed one with space for a freezer and vegetables and in 1933 offered adjustable shelves.[10]

In addition to updates in the icebox, the Aherns' kitchen stove would have changed considerably. When Eleanor helped Mamie can during the summer months of the 1940s, she recalls "all of the burners going at once on the gas stove." Her grandmother would "take over the kitchen," instructing the two or three women who helped her lift the really heavy pots, which she was unable to do by herself. Everyone wore a "canning apron," including little Eleanor, who also had her own pretend pans. The canning procedure, which Eleanor calls an "ordeal," would take several days. Mrs. Ahern loved canning and would can for a long time. Mr. Ahern had a large vegetable garden along the south side of the house, close to the sidewalk and back steps. His interest in gardening may well have originated in his boyhood in Ireland. Eleanor remembered stories about how her grandfather had been an excellent and enthusiastic gardener and that in his garden grew all kinds of summer vegetables, including squash, okra, tomatoes, beans, peppers, onions, and garlic. Mr. Ahern liked to get up at five o'clock in the morning to work in his garden. Eleanor's Uncle Joe sometimes went out to adjacent farms and peach orchards, bringing back vegetables and fruit for his mother to can and for the cook to prepare fresh.

Mr. Ahern also planted several rows of annual flowers in his garden that bloomed all summer. Mrs. Ahern liked to bring in fresh cut flowers of zinnias, marigolds, sunflowers, and white yarrow, or whatever was in bloom. Blue and pink hydrangea and gardenia bushes no doubt graced the yard and would have been part of her bouquets. Mamie loved beautiful things, which included flowers. John's children recalled hearing about their grandfather's love of cannas and their father's consternation about the time-consuming chore of beating the seeds from the canna stalks every year. Mamie especially loved the roses that grew along the fence. Both Mr. and Mrs. Ahern liked the fig preserves that she made from the large number of figs their backyard fig tree produced.[11] Eleanor recalls the time that she fell out of the fig tree and her grandmother had Uncle Joe cut off the limb she fell from. Grandson Brian remembers fondly the fig tree and how much all "enjoyed those preserves on pancakes on many occasions."[12] The fig tree still exists today though it is much smaller.

The Aherns designed a large cellar that housed Mrs. Ahern's canning jars on designated shelves. Granddaughter Eleanor recalls that her grandmother was always solicitous about labeling jars with dates of canning and ingredients. Eleanor considers the "shelf after shelf" of jars that her grandmother prepared and categorized in the cellar, and she remembers that her grandmother was always concerned about germs and cleanliness. She was especially careful in ensuring the wholesomeness of whatever she preserved.

Although Eleanor was not allowed to go down into the cellar by herself because the steps were too steep, nor was she supposed to come into it from the entrance in the backyard, the cellar always held a certain charm for her when she accompanied Mamie down the steps into the area. She recalls it as cool but always dry, which was important for all the items stored there. With electric lights in the space, no one had to grope in the dark to try to find an item. The gardener also kept his tools in the cellar.[13]

The Aherns' first kitchen stove was no doubt a gas model, although coal stoves were available in 1905 as well as dual-fuel stoves, whereby the home's mistress could burn coal in the winter with the added bonus of heating the house and burn gas in the warmer months to avoid heating up the kitchen and adjacent rooms. But when gas stoves became available, they rapidly grew in popularity. For example, the 1895 Montgomery Ward catalog allotted seven full pages to display various types of stoves, but only part of a page to advertise iceboxes.[14] Mrs. Ahern must have had the latest version of a gas range. Some gas ranges even had six burners and two ovens. But electric stoves became available even before 1920; the Edison Electric Appliance Company displayed an electric model during the infancy of electric stoves, which began to catch on with housewives by the 1930s. Many homemakers thought of electric appliances as more modern, and they wanted to be up to date.[15] Mrs. Ahern, however, was not convinced that electric stoves were superior, and she elected to keep a gas stove in the kitchen.

Social historian Ellen M. Plante notes that in the 1920s, the term *housewife* rather than *housekeeper* began to appear in women's journals, signaling the changing attitudes toward the role of the wife as more of a "mate."[16] In 1920, Elsie De Wolfe had written, "It is the personality of the mistress that the home expresses. Men are forever guests in our homes, no matter how much happiness they may find there."[17] Such a comment must have buoyed women's sentiments, yet the seemingly endless cleaning remained, and cleaning in the kitchen was crucial, especially the sink. Kitchen sinks were made of porcelain or enameled iron and typically stood on legs. The earlier practice of leaving the space under the sink open for sanitary reasons continued throughout the 1920s. Ideally, the sink also had a backsplash and a built-in drainboard so that dirt couldn't collect in the crevices.[18] The 1922 *Good Housekeeping's Book of Menus, Recipes, and Household Discoveries* offers advice from a reader, Mrs. J. A., in Oklahoma on keeping the sink spotless:

> Soap jelly, which is made by dissolving a large bar of soap in two quarts of boiling water and two tablespoonfuls of kerosene, is a great aid in keeping a white, shining sink. I keep a glass of soap jelly on the sink shelf, and when I have finished my dishes, I put a little on a cloth which I keep especially for that purpose, and clean the sink. Then I wash the sink out with clean, hot, sudsy water, and the result is well worth the effort.[19]

So much time spent on the kitchen sink evidently proved successful.

At one time the Ahern kitchen may have included a version of the so-called Hoosier cabinet, which was a forerunner of the modern built-in cabinet and open shelves. One of the earliest and most successful to sell the cabinet, the Hoosier Manufacturing Company in New Castle, Indiana, supplied the generic term for this type. Hoosiers offered all-purpose work centers, including cupboards for cooking utensils, dishware, storage of flour and sugar, and a space to knead dough and prepare a meal. Their emphasis was on convenience, saving time and energy for the kitchen worker.[20] An advertisement from 1919 shows a young bride talking to a friend in front of a Hoosier cabinet, saying, "The Hoosier will help me to stay young."[21]

Mrs. Ahern's design of the butler's pantry added extra storage space for cooking supplies and dishware. While the top shelves are open and offer easy access for bowls, glassware, and cooking utensils, the bottom two shelves are enclosed with glass and provide protection for fine glassware and dishes as does the floor-to-ceiling built-in cabinet in the dining room. The five open shelves of the pantry extend almost to the height of the ceiling. The pantry measures about 8.5 feet in length, 6 feet in depth, and 10 feet in height and requires a stepladder to reach the top storage shelves. At some point Mrs. Ahern added additional shelving at the end of the pantry, creating a cabinet of about 3.5 feet wide. Provided the new cabinet's door remained closed, both doors to the pantry worked well.

Granddaughter Eleanor recalls that her grandmother did a lot of baking and she always preferred Gold Medal flour. As a child, Eleanor said, she thought that her grandmother seemed to be "sifting flour" a lot in the kitchen, perhaps reflective of *Good Housekeeping*'s 1922 "How to Use the Recipes": "Always sift flour once before measuring, then at least once again with the other dry ingredients."[22] While the Aherns had a cook who was responsible for the family meals, Mamie liked to bake. She baked a lot of pastry—birthday cakes and fruit pies. John's children recall that every Christmas she sent his family three large cakes—fruit cake, nut cake, and pound cake—along with her signature plum pudding, and every July she sent John his favorite cake—yellow with chocolate icing—for his birthday.[23] Sometimes Eleanor's Aunt Ann and Mamie made chocolate candy, or in the summer, they often made homemade ice cream. Eleanor recalls the ice cream maker that her grandmother had in the early 1940s. Although Mamie always tried to provide homemade desserts for each dinner, she also focused, Eleanor insists, on eating healthy, wholesome food.

Eleanor remembers the small kitchen worktable, which was set fairly close to the front part of the kitchen. With an enameled top, it was perfect for various jobs she watched her grandmother perform in the kitchen. Part of the benefit of the table was that it could be easily moved to another part of the kitchen if needed.[24] Today the worktable still resides in the house. Along with enameled tabletops, housewives continued to like enameled cooking pots better than cast iron because they were easier to clean and could be purchased in speckled shades of red, green, and blue, which added color to the kitchen.[25]

## Mrs. Ahern's Recipes and Notes

A handwritten copy of a cookbook remains in the house in the form of a small notebook, which measures 6 by 3.5 inches. The lined pages are sewn together with thread. The cover and possibly other pages are missing. Although Mrs. Ahern did not write her name in the notebook, notes and comments in the text strongly suggest that she is the compiler of the information. The notebook seems to date from the earliest period of the Aherns' marriage before the last child, Eleanor, was born in 1917. Early in the notebook, Mrs. Ahern applies her interest in math to the cost of meals for a family of seven. For every $10 spent on food, she determines that $2.50 should be spent on grains, $2.00 on milk, $2.00 on eggs, meat, and fish, $2.00 on fruits and vegetables, and $1.50 on sweets and fats. She lists a yearly income of $1,200 and seems to suggest $75 is allotted for meals per year.[26] Finally, she determines that she'll need to prepare 630 individual meal plates per month for a family of seven.

The handwritten cookbook allows us to see the types of recipes that Mary Ahern collected in her early married life. There are recipes for sweets, as one would expect from someone who liked to bake, but there are recipes for other food groups as well. Sweet foods include fudge, puffed rice candy, crisp oatmeal cookies (a recipe she indicated coming from *Good Housekeeping*), bran muffins, white cake, icing, chocolate pie filling, black chocolate cake, cinnamon buns, pastry dough, apple fritters, mock charlotte (a type of dessert or trifle, also called an icebox cake), caramel custard, orange soufflé and sauce, and devil cake (a recipe she received from a Mrs. Beauchamp of Baltimore, Maryland). Aside from these recipes, the notebook lists recipes for meat and vegetable dishes. These recipes include meat cannelloni, cream soup, egg rolls, cornbread, Honolulu ham, French dressing, Swedish salad, Russian dressing, a turnip and cabbage dish, shrimp canapé, cutlets, eggplant, glazed carrots, Hollandaise sauce, stuffed cabbage and sauce, spaghetti, and a sauce for peppers. Her recipe for ice cream calls for scalding one half of the cream; after it is cold, add the other cream; then add eight ounces of sugar for each quart of cream; finally add fruit (a pint of strawberries put through the colander) to the mixture after it is frozen.

The handwritten notebook includes approximate times for cooking meats: lamb mutton, 2.5 hours; beef, 3.5 hours, ham, 5 hours, and so on. In addition, in one area appears at least part of a menu: cream soup with croutons of whole wheat, salad with French dressing, lentils, lima beans, tomato oyster, and cream pie. The meat may have been cannelloni with a brown sauce. The point is that Mrs. Ahern took the preparation of meals seriously, both for her own family and for entertaining. Mrs. Ahern's grandnephew Dr. Frank Loda believed that his Aunt Mamie always "had charge of the kitchen." She always had a cook, but "she would get in there and help and set an example with others working around her." He adds that she "was always proud of working hard." That Mamie included a recipe she'd gotten from a Mrs. Beauchamp of Baltimore is reminiscent of the tradition women practiced of sharing recipes. A family saying about Mamie's sister Ella was that you could always tell where she had been by the recipes she collected. For instance, she'd gotten a recipe for plum pudding when she stopped at Virginia Beach. Aunt Ella could recite the exact menus of various places where she had eaten.[27]

## The Importance of Efficiency

With the early twentieth-century model of convenience and economy of time and space, many theorists offered opinions on efficiency. One of the most popular writers was Christine Frederick, who wrote copious articles first published in *Ladies' Home Journal* and later collected in books. Her *Journal* articles were also illustrated with the "most up-to-date improvements."[28] She noted changes in such domestic machinery as washing machines, vacuum cleaners, and the pressure cooker, and claimed that all the latest electronic appliances were necessary for efficient management of a home. Her most important message was that "electricity could be the household's 'modern servant.'"[29]

One of Mrs. Ahern's "modern servants" was a mangle or presser. Originally the device was used to wring water from wet laundry; later the mangle pressed sheets, kitchen towels, tablecloths, and pieces of clothing that required little delicate work. Mrs. Ahern had an Ironrite mangle that dates from the late 1930s. The brand was popular and saved the homemaker time that could be allotted to other tasks.

Frederick and other writers such as Florence Nesbitt, who wrote a housekeeping text for poor women, were influenced by the efficiency model promulgated by Frederick Winslow Taylor in his scientific management theory of workflow and labor productivity in business. Nesbitt writes, successful housekeeping "requires no less thought, study and work than the merchant or mechanic gives to his business."[30] The term *efficiency* was very much in vogue in the early decades of the twentieth century, giving rise to such book titles as *Increasing Home Efficiency*, *Efficiency in the Household*, and *The Efficient Kitchen*, most of which, using a factory analogy, equated *efficiency* with the word *good*.[31]

## The Dining Room

In her turn-of-the-century text, *The Decoration of Houses*, Edith Wharton notes that the concept of the dining room as we know it today actually developed from the Elizabethan dining-parlor, so recently, she insists, that a generation before hers typically took their meals in a room where they habitually sat. An English house of the eighteenth century of the truly wealthy generally had a large dining room intended for state entertainment and another for family.[32] The family dining room was "simply a plain parlor, with wide mahogany sideboards or tall glazed cupboards for the display of plate and china."[33] For the dining room floor, Wharton prefers stone or marble, but should a rug be used, it should not be nailed down. She ends her discussion with the English invention of the "ugly extension-table with a central support," which can never compete aesthetically with the old round or square one-piece dining tables previously used.[34]

In his analysis of the changing aspects of everyday life in America in the late Victorian and Edwardian periods, social historian Thomas J. Schlereth notes the duality of the dining room as both a private and public space. It was private when family alone gathered, but public when "the family enacted mannered rituals of dining with guests."[35] For the latter, the family had opportunity to display their table linen, china, stemware, and silver. Middle-class families used their dining room tables a lot, serving ample portions of beef, fruits, and vegetables. Salad, as a meal course, stemmed from French cuisine and gained popularity with the middle class. Head lettuce became available in 1903, when a type known as iceberg appeared by way of long-distance travel. Working-class homes sometimes had dining rooms but usually did not use them more than perhaps twice a year. Rural families typically had their meals in the kitchen all the time, often preferring the kitchen as a sitting room even over the parlor.[36]

All the Aherns' meals—breakfast, lunch, and dinner—were taken in the dining room, which is a large room, about 15 feet wide and 20 feet long. Both the kitchen and butler's pantry have doors that open into the dining room, which permitted the servant to serve meals through the butler's pantry rather than through the workspace of the kitchen. The dining room also has a door leading to the back porch, and it connects with the long central hall, separated from it by a large pocket door. As already mentioned, it has an ample, built-in china cabinet.

The dining room table was large enough to seat twelve. Daughter Eleanor Horrigan recalls the large Thanksgiving dinners that her mother served each holiday. She said it always seemed as if they had other people eating with them, holiday or not, which she liked. On holidays, the Aherns had large, formal dinners and typically invited the Kline family next door. Then the next holiday, the Klines would invite them to dinner. Dr. Frank Loda, Mrs. Ahern's grandnephew, recalls what dinner was like at the Aherns in the 1940s. First, they all had before-dinner drinks, usually bourbon and water. Then everyone would talk for at least an hour in the library. Mary would have come back from Washington for the Christmas holiday. Ann always presided at the table. Frank liked that they had both Irish potatoes and sweet potatoes, homemade cranberry sauce and dressing, and wine to drink. After dinner they went into the music room and Mary played the piano, and they sang while drinking liqueurs. In all, the evening lasted about five hours.[37]

Grandson Brian Horrigan recalls how his grandmother and Aunt Ann made Christmas special for him as a youth in the 1960s. They "made fresh fruit cake, pound cake, nut cake, and plum pudding, and shipped them to us at Christmas as Christmas gifts. . . . Fruit cake has a bad reputation these days, but that is because of cheap ingredients in commercial cooking. A fresh homemade fruit cake is a joy, and I think a southern specialty." Brian also remembers his Uncle Joe making fresh eggnog after Christmas Evening Mass, a tradition he maintained until the end of his life. He used raw eggs and raw milk—secured from local farmers. Although Brian's mother worried about the raw ingredients, he reasons, "After Joe spiked it liberally with Bacardi 151, you may be assured that there were no living bacteria left in the eggnog." Since Joe Ahern lived to be ninety-seven, his penchant for raw milk seems not to have harmed him and his insistence on Mrs. Ahern preparing the fresh fruit and vegetables he got from local farmers was probably a mitigating factor as well.[38]

An amusing story involving granddaughter Eleanor and her grandmother occurred in the dining room. As a child, Eleanor hated eating breakfast, which she was supposed to do each morning before she walked down the street to the Catholic school with her cousin, Frank Loda. One time she decided she wasn't going to eat the oatmeal anymore that her grandmother gave her each morning. When Mrs. Ahern went back to the kitchen, Eleanor dumped the contents of the bowl of oatmeal under a back part of the dining room buffet. She evidently thought this an excellent solution to her problem, and as she didn't get caught, she did so for several days. Well, eventually her grandmother and others started smelling something in the dining room, something putrid, and they found her stash of rancid oats. Eleanor thought everyone would be angry, but they didn't punish her, she recalls. They simply laughed and laughed.[39]

## The Cellar

The cellar, or basement as it was sometimes called, is a large area directly below the kitchen and other rooms in the back part of the house. With a concrete floor and a dimension of about 25 feet in width and 33 feet in length, it functioned largely as a storeroom. It has four large concrete pillars to support the weight of the house and small windows that allow some daylight into the area. With a thick concrete floor, thick concrete walls, and an overhead of 8 feet, the room originally was a dry area where materials could be protected from the elements. With a door that led to the yard and another door that led to the kitchen, the cellar provided ready access to the various items placed there.

Among those items stored in the cellar, Mrs. Ahern's preserves held an important place. Mr. Ahern had carpenters build a storage area underneath the stairway leading down into the cellar. The storage has shelves of about 3 feet wide on the backside of the stairs and 3 feet on the side. Mrs. Ahern filled the shelves with all kinds of preserved vegetables and fruits. She had other large shelving areas in adjacent parts of the cellar as well.

Also stored in the cellar were all the gardening items that the gardener or yardman needed to keep the grounds in good condition. Although Mr. Ahern liked to garden in the summer, the Aherns also had a gardener who took care of the lawn and flowerbeds, which allowed Mr. Ahern to focus on his business and other affairs of the day. The original lawnmower is still in the cellar as are other tools used in the yard.

Since the cellar door stayed locked when not in use, the area was not only safe from the elements but also secure, which was important. The Aherns had a large metal vault stored in the cellar where they kept some of their money. Families of means in early twentieth-century America rarely had all of their money in banks as they thought it expedient to have funds readily available. Besides which, the Aherns lived in an era when banks failed and investors lost money. They evidently practiced the old adage "Don't put all your eggs in one basket." With cash on hand and money invested in land and oil, as well as stocks, they hoped they were safe from any catastrophe.

Ahern dining room decorated for Eleanor Ahern's wedding announcement party, courtesy of the Ahern, Horrigan, and Purcell families

# Conclusion

This book grew from my interest in American domestic architecture and in particular the house located at 403 Laurel Street, Texarkana, Arkansas. Its stately presence impresses any passerby with its sense of grandeur and charm. Current visitors are surprised by its opulence and character and the pride that went into the craftsmanship evident in the structure. Guests marvel over the individualized mantels, beautiful light fixtures, beveled glass windows, and fine woodwork. Many are surprised as well to learn that the house represents the life of a single, extended family—that of the Aherns.

In visiting this house in 1978, *Texarkana Gazette* city editor Sally Kirby offered an image that resonates today. In describing the house's aura, she wrote, "The morning sun chases colored lights across the hallway of [the Ahern] home on Laurel Street. With its leaded glass windows surrounding an oak door the day could be in 1906."[1] Twenty-first-century visitors experience similar revelations of the house's atmosphere. The various artifacts used and presumably loved by the family sustain the appeal.

That day in 1978, Sally Kirby interviewed Ann Ahern, Patrick and Mary's daughter who lived her entire life at the residence. She described her home as a "one-time thing. I couldn't replace it," she said.[2] Ann Ahern's truism concerning the irreplaceable nature of her home remains as accurate today—perhaps even more so—as it was in 1978, as the skilled craftsmanship, materials, and ingenuity that went into her home are no longer available. The Arkansas virgin pines and oaks are gone that created the Aherns' floors and woodwork, and the city's glassworks factory that supplied windows of beveled glass shut down decades ago. All who labored to construct the house's unique concrete blocks are gone as well, as are the people whose experiences were shared here.

In fact, for a few years the house was vacant, seemingly left to the vagaries of fortune. Without heat, the house was subject to temperature changes and fluctuating levels of humidity. The plastered walls began to crack, old pipes corroded, and uninvited rodents felt encouraged to nest within. But in 2011 the Ahern family rescued the old structure that had protected and nourished their family members for over a century. With the installation of a new ductless heating and air system designed for historic homes, the house was on the road to recovery. Workers replastered walls, painted rooms beige, and refurbished the old woodwork. The Texarkana Museums System oversaw the cataloging of books, furniture, and other artifacts and began the process of the house once more functioning as a house of worth.[3]

The Ahern family wanted the house to be used by the community for music programs, lectures, games, retreats—for whatever provided information and entertainment. When interviewed in 1978, Ann Ahern had said, "This is a house that has been enjoyed."[4] Today the house stands as a place of enjoyment, intrigue, and mystery, filled as it is with the history of a past era, an important part of Texarkana history, and a reminder of a former prominent family. Although Patrick Ahern has been gone now for almost a century, his gift to his young bride, Mary, remains. The house serves now as a writing retreat, music center, and setting for historical presentations, among other uses.

Now reborn, the house functions as a gift to all to enjoy as long as it is maintained. While the house itself took about a year and four months to build, it takes a community's commitment to survive. All of us admirers of the house and students of history owe a debt of gratitude to those who have been instrumental in saving and preserving this home—the extended Ahern family and the Texarkana Museums System.

A Columbus Day celebration float, showing the dirt roads and side of the house, courtesy of the Ahern, Horrigan, and Purcell families

# Appendix

Ahern House Floor Plan
and Ahern–Lansdale Family Tree

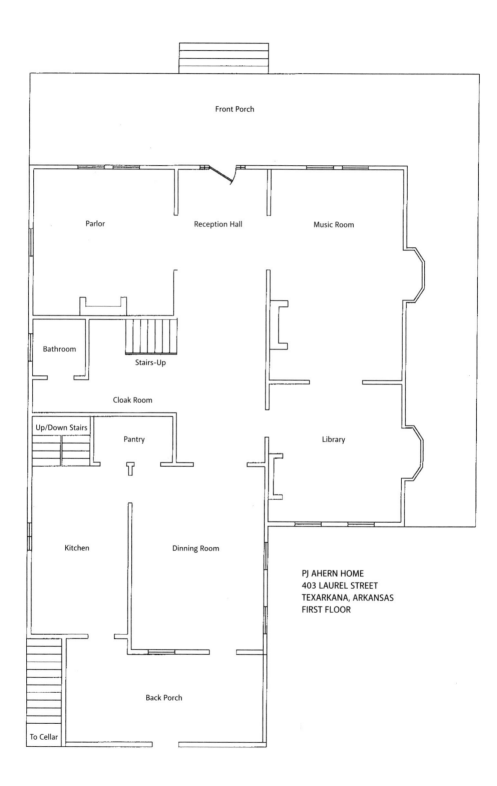

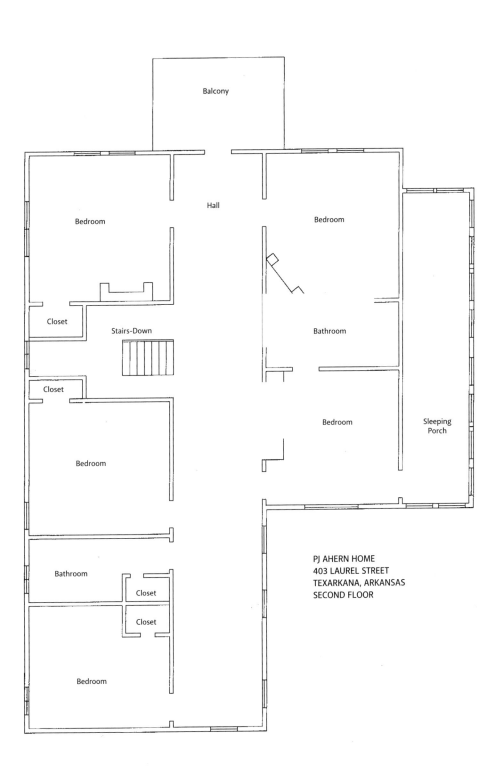

# Patrick Joseph Ahern and Mary Olive Lansdale
## Family Tree

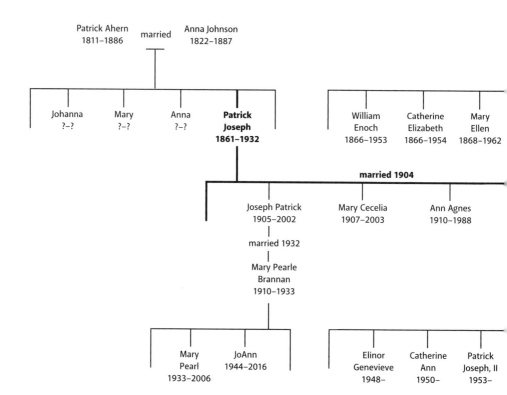

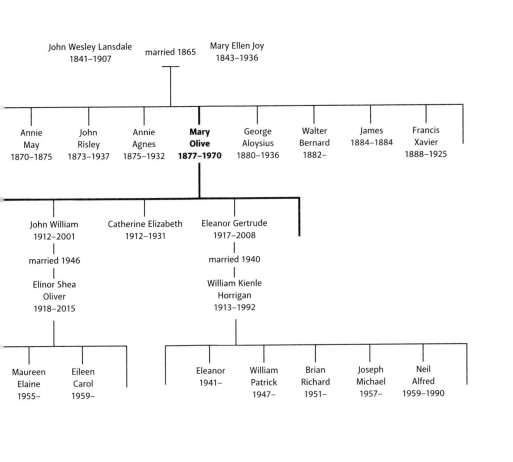

# Notes

**Preface**

1. Sally Kirby, "Time Leaves Homes Untouched through All the Years," Life, sec. C, *Texarkana Gazette*, April 2, 1978, 1.
2. Ibid.

**Chapter 1**

1. Jamie Simmons, interview with Eleanor Horrigan, 2004, 2005.
2. Brian Horrigan, "The Ahern and Lansdale Family History" (unpublished manuscript, June 21, 2018), 5.
3. Ibid., 6–7.
4. Ibid., 8.
5. Barbara Overton Chandler and J. Ed Howe, *History of Texarkana and Bowie and Miller Counties, Texas-Arkansas* (Shreveport, LA: J. Ed Howe, 1939), 227.
6. William D. Leet, *Texarkana: A Pictorial History* (Norfolk, VA: Donning, 1982), 27.
7. Beverly J. Rowe, *Historic Texarkana: An Illustrated History* (San Antonio, TX: Historical Publishing Network, 2009), 5.
8. Ibid., 5.
9. Beverly J. Rowe, *Once upon a Time in Texarkana* (self-pub., 2005), 8.
10. Doris Davis, interview with Sister Miriam Miller, July 31, 2017.
11. Rowe, *Once upon a Time*, 9.
12. Simmons, interview with Eleanor Horrigan, 2004–2005.
13. Horrigan, "The Ahern and Lansdale Family History," 10.
14. Simmons, interview with Eleanor Horrigan, 2004, 2005.
15. Doris Davis, interview with Dr. Frank Loda, June 19, 2018.
16. Chandler and Howe, *History of Texarkana*, 279.
17. Davis, interview with Eleanor Purcell, June 3, 2018.
18. Simmons, interview with Eleanor Horrigan, 2004, 2005.
19. Horrigan, "The Ahern and Lansdale Family History," 11.
20. Chandler and Howe, *History of Texarkana*, 264.
21. Horrigan, "The Ahern and Lansdale Family History," 6.
22. Doris Davis, interview with Dr. Frank Loda, June 15, 2018.
23. Ibid.

24. Notes provided by Cathy Ahern and Maureen Ahern Leahigh.
25. Doris Davis, interview with Brian Horrigan, June 29, 2018.
26. Patrick Horrigan, emails to Doris Davis, August 22, 2019, and May 3, 2022.
27. Doris Davis, interview with Mike Naples, May 9, 2018.
28. Jason Beaubien, "Chasing Down Polio," *All Things Considered*, NPR News, October 15, 2012.
29. Patrick Horrigan, email to Doris Davis, August 22, 2019.
30. Chandler and Howe, *History of Texarkana*, 225.
31. Rowe, *Historic Texarkana*, 122.
32. Horrigan, "The Ahern and Lansdale Family History," 17.
33. Christus St. Michael Health System, *100 years of Healing*, 10. 2016.
34. Horrigan, "The Ahern and Lansdale Family History," 17.
35. The author heard this story from several sources although no one wanted his/her name attached as a source. It is her understanding that the story was also related at the funeral of one of the Aherns. It is a problematic narrative, however, as explained in the text.
36. Rowe, *Historic Texarkana*, 122.
37. Horrigan, "The Ahern and Lansdale Family History," 19.
38. Rowe, *Historic Texarkana*, 29.
39. saintedwardstexarkana.com
40. Horrigan, "The Ahern and Lansdale Family History," 14.
41. Ibid., 14.
42. Ibid., 14.
43. Cathy Ahern and Maureen Leahigh, emails to Doris Davis, January 30, 2020.
44. Jamie Simmons, interview with Eleanor Horrigan, 2004, 2005.
45. Horrigan, "The Ahern and Lansdale Family History," 11.
46. Ibid., 32.
47. Simmons, interview with Eleanor Horrigan, 2004, 2005.
48. Horrigan, "The Ahern and Lansdale Family History," 15.
49. Ibid., 32. The three-mile-limit refers to a territorial jurisdictional limit of a country's authority along its coast; hence, prohibition only extended that far.
50. Doris Davis, interview with Frank Loda, June 19, 2018.
51. Horrigan, "The Ahern and Lansdale Family History," 8–9. Unfortunately, as far as the author could ascertain, all materials pertaining to the store were destroyed before the Texarkana Museums System began to manage the property at 403 Laurel Street.
52. Irwin Unger and Debi Unger, *Twentieth Century America* (New York: St. Martin's Press, 1990), 210–11.
53. Ibid., 220.
54. For a discussion of married women's property rights in Arkansas, see Michael B. Dougan, "The Arkansas Married Woman's Property Law," *Arkansas Historical Quarterly*, 46, no. 1 (Spring 1987): 3–26. Although territorial Arkansas had passed the nation's first married woman's property law, the law was not

retained when Arkansas became a state in 1836. Arkansas's 1874 constitution mandated that a married woman's property "shall not be subject to the debts of her husband" (Dougan, "Arkansas Married," p. 19). Nonetheless, this law was repeatedly challenged in the Arkansas Supreme Court until the turn of the twentieth century and beyond.

55. Horrigan, "The Ahern and Lansdale Family History," 16.
56. Doris Davis, interview with Eleanor Purcell, June 3, 2018.
57. Horrigan, "The Ahern and Lansdale Family History," 33.
58. Doris Davis, interview with Dr. Frank Loda, June 19, 2018.
59. Doris Davis, interview with Rosie Sanderson, August 15, 2017.
60. Horrigan, "The Ahern and Lansdale Family History," 43.
61. Mrs. Ahern, of course, had other daughters who might have married. But Catherine died tragically of tuberculosis at seventeen, Ann's polio probably curtailed her marital choices, and Mary seemed quite content to be independent with a career.
62. Doris Davis, interview with Eleanor Purcell, June 9, 2018.
63. Horrigan, "The Ahern and Lansdale Family History," 43.
64. Davis, interview with Eleanor Purcell, June 9, 2018.
65. Ibid.
66. Unger and Unger, *Twentieth Century America*, 271.
67. Patrick and Michael Horrigan, interview with Col. William K. Horrigan, December 1987.
68. Horrigan, "The Ahern and Lansdale Family History," 44, and Pat Horrigan, email to Doris Davis, February 12, 2020.
69. Unger and Unger, *Twentieth Century America*, 272.
70. Horrigan, "The Ahern and Lansdale Family History," 13.
71. Davis, interview with Eleanor Purcell, June 3, 2018.
72. Simmons interview with Eleanor Horrigan, 2004, 2005.
73. Davis, interview with Eleanor Purcell, June 3, 2018.
74. Davis, interview with Jana Atchison Alexander, May 16, 2018.
75. Davis, interview with Judith Wright, June 5, 2018.
76. Davis, interview with Ann Nicholas, May 12, 2018.
77. Davis, interview with J. T. Smith, June 7, 2018.
78. Horrigan, "The Ahern and Lansdale Family History," 32.
79. Davis, interview with Teresa Howard Culling, June 18, 2018.
80. Brian and Pat Horrigan, email to Doris Davis, September 2020.
81. Cathy Ahern and Maureen Ahern Leahigh, email to Doris Davis. October 2020.
82. Davis, interview with Sister Miriam Miller, July 31, 2017.
83. Davis, interview with Theresa Howard Culling, June 18, 2018.
84. Davis, interview with Sister Miriam Miller, July 31, 2017.
85. Horrigan, "The Ahern and Lansdale Family History," 35.
86. Davis, interview with Frank Loda, June 15, 2018.
87. Davis, interview with Teresa Howard Culling, June 18, 2018.

88. Horrigan, "The Ahern and Lansdale Family History," 35.
89. Michael Naples, May 9, 2018.
90. Horrigan, "The Ahern and Lansdale Family History," 7.
91. Ibid., 37.
92. Davis, interview with Jana Atchison Alexander, May 16, 2018.
93. Davis, interview with Ann Atchison Nicholas, May 12, 2018.
94. Davis, interview with Theresa Howard Culling, June 18, 2018.
95. Davis, interview with Pat Thomas, summer 2017.
96. Davis, interview with Jana Atchison Alexander, May 16, 2018.
97. Davis, interview with Michael Naples, May 9, 2018.

## Chapter 2

1. Jamie Simmons, interview with Eleanor Horrigan, 2004, 2005.
2. Phyllis Palmer, *Domesticity and Dirt: Housewives and Domestic Servants in the United States, 1920–1945* (Philadelphia: Temple University Press, 1985), 2.
3. Judith Rollins, *Between Women: Domestics and Their Employers* (Philadelphia: Temple University Press, 1985), 48–9.
4. Ibid., 50.
5. Ibid.
6. Quoted in Rollins, *Between Women*, 51.
7. Faye E. Dudden, *Serving Women: Household Service in Nineteenth-Century America* (Middletown, CT: Wesleyan University Press, 1984), 5–6.
8. Rollins, *Between Women*, 54.
9. Evelyn Nakano Glen, *Unequal Freedom: How Race and Gender Shaped American Citizenship and Labor* (Cambridge, MA: Harvard University Press, 2002), 109.
10. Ibid.
11. Doris Davis, interview with Dr. Frank Loda, June 16, 2019.
12. Jamie Simmons, interview with Eleanor Ahern Horrigan, 2004, 2005.
13. Dudden, *Serving Women*, 35.
14. Margaret Watts Livingston, "Servants," in *Correct Social Usage* (New York: New York Society of Self-Culture, 1906), 542.
15. Ibid., 561.
16. Ibid., 562.
17. Susan Strasser, *Never Done: A History of American Housework* (New York: Pantheon Books, 1982), 105.
18. Ibid., 109.
19. Ibid., 113.
20. Ibid., 117.
21. Thomas J. Schlereth, *Victorian America: Transformations in Everyday Life, 1876–1915* (New York: Harper Perennial, 1991), 113.
22. Lorraine Gamman and Sean O'Mara, "Laundry," in *Fads to Nylon*, ed. Valerie Steele, vol. 2, *Encyclopedia of Clothing and Fashion* (New York: Thomson Gale, 2005), 339.
23. Ibid.

24. Jamie Simmons, Curator of the Texarkana Museums System, based on her knowledge of the period, house, and family, 2019.
25. Strasser, *Never Done*, 109.
26. Zora Neale Hurston, "Sweat," in *Spunk: The Selected Stories of Zora Neale Hurston* (Berkeley, CA: Turtle Island Foundation, 1985), 38.
27. Dudden, *Serving Woman*, 30.
28. Ibid., 77.
29. Stephen Steinberg, *The Ethnic Myth: Race, Ethnicity and Class in America*, 3rd ed. (Boston: Beacon Press, 2001), 199.
30. Jamie Simmons, interview with Eleanor Ahern Horrigan, 2004, 2005.
31. Doris Davis, interview with Frank Loda, June 19, 2018.
32. As quoted in Dudden, *Serving Women*, 195.
33. Dudden, *Serving Women*, 225.
34. Jamie Simmons, 2019.
35. Patrick Horrigan, email to Doris Davis, August 22, 2019.
36. Doris Davis, interview with Eleanor Purcell, June 3, 2018.
37. Kimberly Wallace-Sanders, *Mammy: A Century of Race, Gender, and Southern Memory* (Ann Arbor: University of Michigan Press, 2008), figure 12, GA.

## Chapter 3

1. Ralph Waldo Emerson, "The Poet," in *Essays: Second Series, the Selected Writings of Ralph Waldo Emerson*, ed. Brooks Atkinson (New York: The Modern Library, 1940), 320.
2. Gaston Bachelard, *The Poetics of Space* (Boston, MA: Beacon Press, 1958), 47.
3. As quoted in Neil Harris, *Building Lives: Constructing Rites and Passages* (New Haven: Yale University Press, 1999), 7.
4. Mariana Griswold Van Rensselaer, *Accents as Well as Broad Effects: Writings on Architecture, Landscape, and the Environment, 1876–1925*, ed. David Gebhard (Berkeley: University of California Press, 1996), 40.
5. Korydon Smith, ed., *Introducing Architectural Theory: Debating a Discipline* (New York: Routledge, 2012), 4.
6. Adolf Loos, "Ornament and Crime," 1908, in Smith, *Introducing Architectural Theory*, 45.
7. John Ruskin, "The Lamp of Truth," 1849, in Smith, *Introducing Architectural Theory*. Pages 74–83.
8. Smith, *Introducing Architectural Theory*, 10.
9. Robert Venturi, *Complexity and Contradiction in Architecture*, 1966, in Smith, 31.
10. D. S. Hopkins, *Late Victorian House Designs* (Mineola, NY: Dover, 2004), iii. Reprint: D. S. Hopkins, *Houses and Cottages* (Grand Rapids, MI, 1893).
11. Ibid.
12. Ibid.
13. Virginia and Lee McAlester, *A Field Guide to American Houses* (New York: Knopf, 2009), 5–6.

14. Daniel D. Reiff, "Introduction to the Dover Edition," *The Most Popular Homes of the Twenties*, by William A. Radford (Mineola, NY: Dover, 2009), v. Reprint: William A. Radford, *The Most Popular Homes in America* (Chicago American Builder, 1925).

15. See William T. Comstock, *Turn-of-the-Century House Designs* (New York: Dover, 1994).

16. A. W. Cobb, "Suggestions on House Building," in Comstock, *Turn-of-the-Century House*, 12–13.

17. Ibid., 12.

18. Other early architects with offices in town include Ogden Bryant, mentioned in *Gate City News*, January 2, 1875, and the [Texarkana, Texas] *News*, November 3, 1877, and Daniel Dobra, mentioned in the [Texarkana, Texas] *News*, November 3, 1877. I am indebted to Thomas Cutrer for this information.

19. Jamie Simmons, Curator of the Texarkana Museums System, based on her knowledge of the period, house, and family, 2019.

20. Burdsal is buried in Woodlawn Cemetery, Texarkana, Arkansas.

21. National Register of Historic Places, Registration Form, Patrick J. Ahern House, MI0041, 403 Laurel Street, Texarkana, AR 71854, Section 7, 1.

22. Ibid.

23. Atlas Portland Cement Company, *Concrete County Residences: Photographs and Floor Plans of Turn-of-the-Century Homes* (Mineola, NY: Dover, 2003), 5.

24. Ibid., 6–7.

25. National Register, Section 7, 1.

26. Ibid.

27. Jamie Simmons, interview with Eleanor Horrigan, 2004.

28. Brian Horrigan, "The Ahern and Lansdale Family History," unpublished manuscript, June 21, 2018, 11.

29. National Register, Section 7, 4.

30. Jamie Simmons, interview with Eleanor Horrigan, 2004, 2005.

31. Doris Davis, interview with Theresa Howard Culling, June 18, 2018.

32. National Register, Section 7, 3.

33. Candace M. Volz, "The Modern Look of the Early-Twentieth-Century House: A Mirror of Changing Lifestyles," in *American Home Life, 1880–1930: A Social History of Spaces and Services*, ed. Jessica H. Foy and Thomas J. Schlereth (Knoxville: University of Tennessee Press, 1992), 27.

34. Ibid., 31.

35. Gustav Stickley, *Catalogue of Craftsman Furniture* (Eastwood, NY: Craftsman Workshops, 1901), 3, quoted in Foy and Schlereth, *American Home Life, 1880–1930*, 26.

36. Doris Davis, interview with Eleanor Purcell, January 13, 2018.

37. Miller County Report, Parcel 1011920, ID 24182, Property Owner: Ahern Home Charitable Lead, 403 Laurel, Black/Lot: 047/006, 3.

38. Doris Davis, interview with Eleanor Purcell, June 3, 2018.

39. Mark Wigley, *The Architecture of Deconstruction* (Cambridge, MA: MIT Press, 1995), 11.

40. Van Rensselaer, *Accents as Well as Broad*, 282.

41. Volz, "The Modern Look," 35.

42. Ibid.

43. Yi-Fu Tuan, *Space and Place: The Perspective of Experience* (Minneapolis, Minnesota: University of Minnesota Press, 1977), 6.

44. Ibid., 32.

45. Gaston Bachelard, *The Poetics of Space* (Boston, MA: Beacon Press, 1958), 14.

46. Edward Hollis, *The Secret Lives of Buildings: From the Ruins of the Parthenon to the Vegas Strip in Thirteen Stories* (New York: Picador, 2009), 12.

47. Ibid., 13.

## Chapter 4

1. Lillie Hamilton French, *The House Dignified: Its Design, Its Arrangement and Its Decoration* (New York: Putnam's Sons, 1908), 79, quoted in Harold M. Otness, "A Room Full of Books: The Life and Slow Death of the American Residential Library," *Libraries and Culture* 23, no. 2 (Spring 1988): 111.

2. Otness, "A Room Full of Books," 111.

3. Robert Darnton, "Scholarship and Readership: New Directions in the History of the Book," in *Books and Prints, Past and Future* (New York: Grolier Club, 1984), 36, quoted in Linda M. Kruger, "Home Libraries: Special Spaces, Reading Places," in *American Home Life, 1880-1930: A Social History of Spaces and Services*, ed. Jessica H. Foy and Thomas J. Schlereth (Knoxville: University of Tennessee Press, 1992), 95.

4. Kruger, "Home Libraries," 95

5. Barbara Overton Chandler and J. Ed Howe, *History of Texarkana and Bowie and Miller Counties* (Shreveport: J.S. Hyland, 1939), 264.

6. Ibid., 278.

7. Jamie Simons, interview with Eleanor Horrigan, 2004, 2005.

8. Otness, "A Room Full of Books," 123.

9. Jane Austen, *Pride and Prejudice*, ed. Donald Gray, a Norton Critical Edition, 3rd ed. (New York: W. W. Norton, 2001), 76.

10. Charles A. Seavey, "Public Libraries," in *Encyclopedia of Library History*, ed. Wayne A. Wiegand and Donald G. Davis Jr. (New York: Garland Press, 1994), 520-21.

11. Wayne A. Wiegand, "Community Places and Reading Spaces: Main Street Public Library in the Rural Heartland, 1876-1956," in *Libraries and the Reading Public in Twentieth-Century America*, ed. Christine Pawley and Louise S. Robbins (Madison: University of Wisconsin Press, 2013), 23.

12. Benjamin Wyche, "Free Public Libraries in Texas: Ten Years' Growth, 1899-1900," *Texas Libraries* 1, no. 1 (Nov. 1909): 6-7. The dates differ in other documents.

13. Theodore Jones, *Carnegie Libraries across America* (New York: John Wiley and Sons, 1997), 131. All Arkansas libraries are Carnegie. The date refers to the date of the grant.

14. "News Notes of Texas Public Libraries," *Texas Public Libraries* 1, no. 4 (April 1914): 11. The article indicates that if the monument is erected alone, it will be south of the post office, but if together with a library and reading room, then on "State Line Avenue where the six streets intersect."

15. Christine Pawley, introduction to *Libraries and the Reading Public in Twentieth-Century America*, ed. Christine Pawley and Louise S. Robbins (Madison: University of Wisconsin Press, 2013), 4.

16. Jones, *Carnegie Libraries*, 129.

17. Dee Garrison, *Apostles of Culture: The Public Librarian and American Society, 1876–1920* (Madison: University of Wisconsin Press, 1979), 224.

18. George S. Bobinski, *Carnegie Libraries: Their History and Impact on American Public Library Development* (Chicago: American Library Association, 1969), 17.

19. Seavey, "Public Libraries," 521.

20. Jones, *Carnegie Libraries*, 26.

21. Ibid., 29.

22. Ibid., 31–32. At that time, African Americans constituted 30 percent of the population of the area. To be clear, the Carnegie Foundation granted funds to both African American libraries and integrated libraries.

23. Jones, *Carnegie Libraries*, 51.

24. Quoted in ibid., 49.

25. Dee Garrison, *Apostles of Culture*, 224.

26. She was Director of the Texarkana Public Library from March 1981 to October 2012.

27. Chandler and Howe, *History of Texarkana*, 199–200.

28. Beverly Rowe, *Once upon a Time in Texarkana* (self-pub., 2005), 128.

29. John Fooks, "Centenarian Reflects on Her Good Life, Days Gone By . . . " *Texarkana Gazette*, Metro/State, 5A, February 19, 2005.

30. Joanne E. Passet, "Reaching the Rural Reader: Traveling Libraries in America, 1892," *Libraries & Culture* 26, no. 1 (Winter, 1991): 100–101.

31. "Traveling Libraries for Texas," *Texas Libraries* 1, no. 5 (July 1914): 1–2.

32. Passet, "Reaching the Rural Reader," 113.

33. Seavey, "Public Libraries," 519–19.

34. Beverly J. Rowe, *Women's Status in Texarkana, Texas in the Progressive Era, 1880–1920*, Women's Studies, vol. 37 (Lewiston, NY: The Edwin Mellen Press, 2002), 97.

35. Chandler and Howe, *History of Texarkana*, 156–57.

36. *Daily Texarkanian*, February 2, 1910, 2.

37. David Kaser, *A Book for a Sixpence: The Circulating Library in America* (Pittsburgh: Beta Phi Mu, 1980), 3.

38. Ibid.,12.

39. Ibid., 15.

40. 1899 *Texarkana City Directory*, 273. Other Texarkana booksellers existed as early as 1875. They include Dale and Robinson Drug Store, Broad Street, west

of State Line Avenue, as mentioned in *Gate City News*, February 16, 1875, and the [Texarkana, Texas] *News*, October 20, 1877, and November 3, 1877; and John "Johnnie" Taylor, as mentioned in *Gate City News*, February 6, 1875, and May 20, 1875. I am indebted to Thomas Cutrer for this information.

41. 1901 *Texarkana City Directory*, 352.
42. Rowe, *Once upon A Time*, 51.
43. *Daily Texarkanian*, October 5, 1905, 8.
44. Michael Winship, "The Rise of a National Book Trade System in the United States," in *Print in Motion: The Expansion of Publishing and Reading in the United States, 1880–1940*, ed. Carl F. Kaestle and Janice A. Radway, vol. 4, *A History of the Book in America* (Chapel Hill: University of North Carolina Press, 2009), 63.
45. *Texarkana City Directory*, 1912, 81.
46. *Daily Texarkanian*, June 10, 1910, 2.
47. Elizabeth Long, "Aflame with Culture: Reading and Social Mission in the Nineteenth-Century White Women's Literary Club Movement," in *Print in Motion: The Expansion of Publishing and Reading in the United States, 1880–1940*, ed. Carl F. Kaestle and Janice A. Radway, vol. 4, *A History of the Book in America* (Chapel Hill: University of North Carolina Press, 2009), 480–81.
48. Long, "Aflame with Culture," 481.
49. Winship, "The Rise of a National Book Trade System," 65–69.
50. John Tebbel, *Between Covers: The Rise and Transformation of Book Publishing in America* (New York: Oxford University Press, 1987), pp. 167–68.
51. Ibid., 167.
52. Winship. "The Rise of a National Book Trade," 67.
53. James L. W. West III, "The Expansion of the National Book Trade System," in *Print in Motion: The Expansion of Publishing and Reading in the United States, 1880–1940*, ed. Carl F. Kaestle and Janice A. Radway, vol. 4, *A History of the Book in America* (Chapel Hill: University of North Carolina Press, 2009), 82.
54. Kruger, "Home Libraries," 97.
55. Ibid., 96–97,
56. Charles Johanningsmeier, "The Industrialization and Nationalization of American Periodical Publishing," in *Perspectives on American Book History: Artifacts and Commentary*, ed. Scott E. Casper, Joanne D. Chaison, and Jeffrey D. Groves (Amherst: University of Massachusetts Press, 2002), 311.
57. Carl F. Kaestle, "Seeing the Sites: Readers, Publishers, and Local Print Cultures in 1880," in *Print in Motion: The Expansion of Publishing and Reading in the United States, 1880–1940*, ed. Carl F. Kaestle and Janice A. Radway, vol. 4, *A History of the Book in America* (Chapel Hill: University of North Carolina Press, 2009), 29.
58. Johanningsmeier, "The Industrialization and Nationalization," 312.
59. *Daily Texarkanian*, October 9, 1905, 1.
60. *Daily Texarkanian*, October 19, 1905, 1.
61. *Daily Texarkanian*, October 23, 1905, 1.
62. "Gazette Roots Run Deep in Texarkana," *Texarkana Gazette*, October

4, 2015. http://www.texarkanagazette.com/news/texarkana/story/2015oct/04/gazette-roots-run-deep-texarkana/406672. Retrieved April 26, 2018.

63. Kaestle, "Seeing the Sites," 38–39.

64. Richard Ohmann, "Diverging Paths: Books and Magazines in the Transition to Corporate Capitalism," in *Print in Motion: The Expansion of Publishing and Reading in the United States, 1880–1940*, ed. Carl F. Kaestle and Janice A. Radway, vol. 4, *A History of the Book in America* (Chapel Hill: University of North Carolina Press, 2009), 102–3.

65. Ibid., 107.

66. *Daily Texarkanian*, February 1, 1906, 3.

67. *Daily Texarkanian*, February 2, 1906, 5.

68. Jamie Simons, interview with Eleanor Horrigan, 2004, 2005.

69. Chandler and Howe, *History of Texarkana*, 264.

70. Francis , "Of Studies," in *The Sixteenth Century & The Early Seventeenth Century*, ed. George M. Logan et al., vol. B, *The Norton Anthology of English Literature*, 8th ed. (New York: W. W. Norton, 2006), 1562.

71. F. Scott Fitzgerald, *The Great Gatsby* (New York: Charles Scribner's Sons, 1925), 45. I am indebted to Brian Horrigan for this observation.

72. "The Making of the Catholic Encyclopedia (1917)," *New Advent* 3, http://www.newadvent.org/cathen/00001a.htm. Retrieved April 5, 2018.

73. The Encyclopedia Press, ed., *The Catholic Encyclopedia and Its Makers*, ed. (New York: The Encyclopedia Press, 1917), iii.

74. Una M. Cadegan, "Running the Ancient Ark by Steam: Catholic Publishing," in *Print in Motion: The Expansion of Publishing and Reading in the United States, 1880–1940*, ed. Carl F. Kaestle and Janice A. Radway, vol. 4, *A History of the Book in America* (Chapel Hill: University of North Carolina Press, 2009), 402.

75. Ibid., 392.

76. Ibid., 404.

77. Ibid., 402.

78. Ibid., 397.

79. *The Catholic Encyclopedia and Its Makers*, iv.

80. "Mozart," in *Mass Music–Newman*, ed. Charles G. Herbermann, vol. 10, *The Catholic Encyclopedia* (New York: Robert Appleton Co., 1911), 624. Emphasis added.

81. "Moliere," in *The Catholic Encyclopedia*, 10:435. Emphasis added.

82. *The Catholic Encyclopedia and Its Makers*, viii.

83. Conde B. Pallen and John J. Wynne, comps. and eds., preface to *The New Catholic Dictionary* (New York: The Universal Knowledge Foundation, 1929), iii. Promoter's edition, #5802.

84. James Doyle, preface to *Lives of the Saints*, by Alban Butler, ed. F. C. Husenbeth (London: Henry & Co., n.d.), iii.

85. Thomas N. Burke, table of contents in *Lectures and Sermons of Father Burke*, vol. 1 (New York: P. M. Haverty, 1872), 7.

86. Mary Elizabeth Blake, "The First Steps," in *Irish Literature*, vol. 1, ed. Justin McCarthy (Philadelphia, PA: John D Morris & Co., 1904), 190–91, lines 5–7. Biographical sketch, 189.

87. Emily Dickinson, Poem 1286, "There is no Frigate like a Book," in *The Poems of Emily Dickinson: Reading Edition*, ed. R. W. Franklin (Cambridge, MA: The Belknap Press of Harvard University Press, 1998), 501.

88. Leo Damrosch, "Books That Matter: *The History of the Decline and Fall of the Roman Empire*." http://www.thegreatcourses.com/courses/books-that-matter-the-history-of-the-decline-and-fall-of-the-roman-empire.html. Retrieved April 6, 2018.

89. Robert McCrum, "The 100 Best Nonfiction Books: No 83—*The History of the Decline and Fall of the Roman Empire* by Edward Gibbon (1776–1788)," *The Guardian*, September 4, 2017. http://www.theguardian.com/books/2017/sept/04/200-nonfiction-books-decline-and-fall-of-the-roman-empire-edward-gibbon. Retrieved April 6, 2018.

90. Edward Gibbon, *Decline and Fall of the Roman Empire*, ed. H. H. Milman, vol. 1 (Chicago: Belford, Clark and Co., n.d.), 27.

91. McCrum, "100 Best Nonfiction Books."

92. Ibid.

93. John Clark Ridpath, *History of the World*, vol. 1 (Cincinnati, Ohio: The Jones Brothers Publishing Co., 1890), 2.

94. Ibid., 5–6.

95. "Ridpath's History of the World." Ohio State University. https://www.ehistory.osu.edu/books/ridpath. Retrieved April 6, 2018.

96. Preface to *The Standard Question Book and Home Study Outlines* (Buffalo, NY: Frontier Press, 1914, no author, no pagination).

97. John R. Musick, "The Plan and Scope," in *The Real America in Romance*, 13 vols. (New York: William H. Wise & Co., 1908), 1:vi–vii.

98. Musick, "The Plan and Scope," ix.

99. Nate Pedersen. "The Magic of Encyclopedia Britannica's 11th Edition," April 10, 2012. https://www.theguardian.com/books/booksblog/2012/apr/10/encyclopedia-britannica-11th-edition. Retrieved April 5, 2018.

100. Donald E. Stewart et al., "Encyclopaedia Britannica," August 18, 2017. https://www.britannica.com/topic/Encyclopaedia-Britannica-English-language-reference-work. Retrieved April 5, 2018.

101. Andrew Lang, "Illusion," in *Encyclopedia Britannica*, 11th ed. (New York: The Encyclopaedia Britannica Co., 1910), 2:209.

102. Donald E. Steward et al., "Encyclopaedia Britannica."

103. *New York Times*, https://www.nytimes.com/1906/08/04/archives/bryan-editing-a-book-is-finishing-introduction-to-the-worlds-famous.html. Retrieved April 5, 2018.

104. *The Commoner*. https://www.newspapers.com/image/49589634/?terms=speeches%20that%20have%20made%20history&match=1. Retrieved April 5, 2018.

105. William Jennings Bryan, preface to *Greece (432 B.C.-324 B.C.)*, ed. William Jennings Bryan, v–ix, vol. 1, *The World's Famous Orations* (New York: Funk and Wagnalls, 1906).

106. Bryan, *World's Famous*, 4:150.

107. Bryan, *World's Famous*, 8:79.

108. Bryan, *World's Famous*, 10:253–62.

109. Ibid., 12–13.

110. Bryan, *World's Famous*, 8:9–13.

111. Ibid., 12–13.

112. Stewart Archer Steger, *American Dictionaries* (Baltimore: J. H. Furst Co., 1913), 83.

113. William Dwight Whitney, preface to *The Century Dictionary: An Encyclopedic Lexicon of the English Language*, 6 vols. (New York: The Century Co., 1902), 1:v.

114. Steger, *American Dictionaries*, 86.

115. *The Century Dictionary*. Undated brochure, found in volume 1 of *The Century Dictionary*.

116. John Milton, *Paradise Lost*, Book II, 287, in *The Century Dictionary*, 1:752.

117. Ibid.

118. C. A. Gaskell, preface to *An Art Edition of the Most Popular Dramas of Shakespeare*, ed. C. A. Gaskell (Chicago: U.S. Publishing House, 1889), 3.

119. Jamie Simmons, interview with Eleanor Horrigan, 2004, 2005.

120. Thomas W. Knox, "Advice to Ladies, by a Lady" in *How to Travel* (New York: G. P. Putnam's Sons, 1887), 63.

121. Jamie Simmons, interview with Eleanor Horrigan, 2004, 2005.

122. Louis C. Elson, preface to *Modern Music and Musicians, Part One: Compositions*, ed. Louis C. Elson. 8 vols. (New York: The University Society, 1912).

123. Ibid.

124. Louis C. Elson, *Modern Music and Musicians*, vol. 2.

125. Martin S. Day, *History of American Literature: From the Beginning to 1910* (Garden City: Doubleday, 1970), 241.

126. Bernard O'Reilly, preface to *The Mirror of True Womanhood: A Book of Instruction for Women in the World* (New York: Excelsior Catholic Publishing House, 1895), v.

127. O'Reilly, *The Mirror*, 407–8.

128. Ibid., 409–19.

129. *Etiquette, Politeness, and Good Breeding* (Glasgow: Dunn and Wright Printers, n.d.), 21.

130. Ibid., 23.

131. Humphrey Carpenter and Mary Prichard, *The Oxford Companion to Children's Literature* (Oxford: Oxford University Press, 1984), 156. Dor is "notable for his grotesque illustrations to English children's books."

132. Ann T. Keene, "Irving Bacheller," in *American National Biography*, ed. John A. Garraty and Mark C. Carnes (New York: Oxford University Press, 1999), 1:830–31.

133. Lina Mainiero, "Willa Sibert Cather," in *American Women Writers* (New York: Frederick Ungar, 1979), 1:319.

134. William Dean Howells, *The Rise of Silas Lapham*, with notes by James M. Spinning (Boston: Houghton Mifflin, 1928), iv, v.

135. Jeanne Campbell Reesman and Arnold Krupat, "William Dean Howells," in *1865–1914*, ed. Nina Baym, vol. C, *The Norton Anthology of American Literature*, 7th ed., ed. Jeanne Campbell Reesman and Arnold Krupat (New York: W. W. Norton, 2007), 913.

136. William Dean Howells, "From Novel-Writing and Novel-Reading: An Impersonal Explanation," in *1865–1914*, ed. Nina Baym, vol. C, *The Norton Anthology of American Literature*, 7th ed., ed. Jeanne Campbell Reesman and Arnold Krupat (New York: W. W. Norton, 2007), 917.

137. Tebbel, *Between Covers*, 182.

138. Martin S. Day, *History of English Literature, 1837 to the Present* (Garden City: Doubleday, 1964), 183.

139. William Makepeace Thackeray, *Vanity Fair* (London: J.M. Dent, 1920), 11.

140. Richard Barickman, Susan MacDonald, and Myra Stark, "Politics of Sexuality," in *Vanity Fair*, by William Makepeace Thackeray, ed. Peter L. Shillingsburg. A Norton Critical Edition (New York: Macmillan, 1994), 841.

141. J. W. Cunliffe, *English Literature during the Last Half-Century* (New York: Macmillan, 1928), 1.

142. Day, *History of America Literature*, 270.

143. Robert L. Gale, "Guest, Edgar Albert," in *American National Biography*, vol. 9, 698–99.

144. Grace Noll Crowell, "The Lifted Lamp," in *The Lifted Lamp* (New York: Harper & Brothers, 1942), 1.

145. Carpenter and Prichard, *Oxford Companion*, 225–26.

146. Susan E. Meyer, *A Treasury of the Great Children's Book Illustrators* (New York: Harry N. Abrams, 1983), 110.

147. McGrath, W. E., "Grace Drayton, a Children's Illustrator Who Also Painted Young Women—a Biographical Sketch," https://web.archive.org/web/20121104014436/http://home.comcast.net/~bluepatch/Biographies/Grace_Drayton_web.htm. 1–5.

148. Rachel Field, *Hitty, Her First Hundred Years* (New York: MacMillan, 1929), 207.

149. Carpenter and Prichard, *Oxford Companion*, 33–34.

150. "Van Dyke, Henry," *Who Was Who among North American Authors, 1921–1939* (Detroit: Gale Research Co., 1976), 2:1445–46.

151. Henry Van Dyke, preface to *The Story of the Other Wiseman* (New York: Harper & Brothers, 1895), viii.

152. Linda Schermer Raphael, "Webster, Jean," in *American National Biography.*, ed. John A. Garraty and Mark C. Carnes (New York: Oxford University Press, 1999), 22:869–70.

153. Karen Abbott, "I Was Looking Forward to a Quiet Old Age," *Smithsonian Magazine*, May 25, 2012. http://www.smithsonianmag.com/history/i-was-looking-forward-to-a-quiet-old-age-106393195. Retrieved May 1, 2018.

154. H. Hudson Holly, *Modern Dwellings: In Town and Country* (New York: Harper & Brothers, 1878), 108.

155. Ibid.

156. Ibid., 112.

157. Ibid., 199–200.

158. Ibid., 199.

159. J. Stewart Johnson, introduction to *The Architecture of Country Houses* by A. J. Downing (New York: Dover, 1969), vii. Reprint: New York: D. Appleton & Co., 1850.

160. A. J. Downing, *The Architecture of Country Houses* (New York: Dover, 1969), 272. Reprint: New York: D. Appleton & Co. 1850.

161. Lillie Hamilton French, *Homes and Their Decoration* (New York: Dodd, Mead, and Co., 1903), 222.

162. Ibid.

163. Edith Wharton and Ogden Codman Jr., *The Decoration of Houses* (Mineola, NY: Dover, 2015), 150. Reprint: New York: Charles Scribner's Sons, 1914.

164. French, *Homes and Their Decoration*, 225.

165. Wharton and Codman, *Decoration*, 104.

166. French, *The House Dignified*, quoted in Otness, 122.

167. Wharton and Codman, *Decoration*, 147–48.

168. Holly, *Modern Dwellings*, 198–99.

169. "Globe-Wernicke Sectional Bookcases for Beautifying the Home." Catalogue No. 122. Digital Collections. Library of Congress. https://www.loc.gov/item/ltf91092406/. Retrieved April 19, 2018.

170. "Always Complete but Never Finished," A. H. Andrews Co., Wernicke System Elastic Book Cases, Chicago, Illinois. No date. Advertising brochure.

171. Ibid., 4.

172. "Globe-Wernicke."

173. "Always Complete but Never Finished," 20.

174. Ibid., 23.

175. "Globe-Wernicke."

176. French, "Homes and Their Decoration." 24.

177. Humphrey Products homepage. http://www.humphrey-products.com/content/humphrey-history-1901-today. Retrieved April 19, 2018.

178. Kruger, "Home Libraries," 100.

179. According to Jamie Simmons, TMS Curator.

180. Doris Davis, interview with Eleanor Purcell, 2018.

181. Brian Horrigan, email to Doris Davis. September 2020.

182. Abigail Williams, *The Social Life of Books: Reading Together in the Eighteenth-Century Home* (New Haven: Yale University Press, 2017) 32.

## Chapter 5

1. Henry David Thoreau, *Walden, or Life in the Woods*, in *American Literature 1620–1820*, ed. Nina Baym, vol. 1, *The Norton Anthology of American Literature*, 3rd ed. (New York: Norton, 1989), 1647.

2. Betty J. Mills, *Calico Chronicle: Texas Women and Their Fashions, 1830–1910* (Lubbock: Texas Tech University Press, 1985), 7.

3. Jamie Simmons, interview with Eleanor Horrigan, 2004, 2005.

4. Katherine Joslin, *Edith Wharton and the Making of Fashion* (Durham: University of New Hampshire Press, 2009),7.

5. Ibid., 6.

6. Valerie Steele, *Fashion and Eroticism: Ideals of Feminine Beauty from the Victorian Era to the Jazz Age* (New York: Oxford University Press, 1985), 47.

7. Ibid., 41.

8. Ibid., 4.

9. Edith Wharton, *The House of Mirth* (New York: Norton, 1990), 12.

10. Michael R. Solomon and Susan P. Douglas, "The Female Clotheshorse: From Aesthetics to Tactics," in *The Psychology of Fashion*, ed. Michael R. Solomon, Lexington Books (Lexington, MA: DC Heath, 1985), 389.

11. Ellen M. Plante, *Women at Home in Victorian America: A Social History* (New York: Facts On File, 1997), 26.

12. *The 1902 Edition of the Sears, Roebuck Catalogue* (New York: Bounty Books, a Division of Crown, 1969), 1067.

13. Doris Davis, interview with Eleanor Purcell, January 13, 2018.

14. Ahern–Lansdale wedding announcement.

15. "[I]n earlier times, the owning and display of such a luxury item as a book would have lent the bride additional status, and frequently formed one of her betrothal gifts." Michelle Nordtorp-Madson, "Wedding Costume," in *Occult Dress to Zoran, Index*, ed. Valerie Steele, vol. 3, *Encyclopedia of Clothing and Fashion* (New York: Thomson Gale, 2005), 427.

16. Nordtorp-Madson, "Wedding Costume," 426.

17. M. E. W. Sherwood "Weddings," in *Correct Social Usage* (New York: New York Society of Self-Culture, 1906), 321.

18. Daniel Pool, *What Jane Austen Ate and Charles Dickens Knew: From Fox Hunting to Whist—the Facts of Daily Life in 19th-Century England* (New York: Touchstone, 1993), 184.

19. Mills, *Calico Chronicle*, 28.

20. Joslin, *Edith Wharton*, 11.

21. Mills, *Calico Chronicle*, 104–5.

22. Jean L. Druesedow, "Ready-To-Wear," in *Occult Dress to Zoran, Index*, ed. Valerie Steele, vol. 3, *Encyclopedia of Clothing and Fashion* (New York: Thomson Gale, 2005), 87.

23. In *Channels of Desire: Mass Images and the Shaping of American Consciousness*, as quoted in Lauren S. Cardon, *Fashion and Fiction: Self-Transformation in Twentieth-Century American Literature* (Charlottesville: University of Virginia Press, 2016), 2.

24. Wendy Gamber, *The Female Economy: The Millinery and Dressmaking Trades, 1860–1930* (Urbana-Champaign: University of Illinois Press, 1997), 14.

25. Doris Davis, interview with Sister Miriam Miller, July 31, 2017.

26. According to Texarkana historian Beverly Rowe in conversation with Doris Davis, August 16, 2017.

27. Doris Davis, interview with Eleanor Purcell, January 13, 2018.

28. Doris Davis, interview with Judith Wright, June 5, 2018.

29. Doris Davis, interview with Ann Nicholas, May 12, 2018.

30. Kathleen Paton, "Trimmings," in *Occult Dress to Zoran, Index*, ed. Valerie Steele, vol. 3, *Encyclopedia of Clothing and Fashion* (New York: Thomson, Gale, 2005), 338.

31. Doris Davis, interview with Rosie Sanderson, August 2017.

32. Doris Davis, interview with Mary Collom Fore, March 18, 2020.

33. According to Texarkana Museums System Curator Jamie Simmons.

34. Gamber, *Female Economy*, 14.

35. Doris Davis, interview with Remica Gray, August 1, 2021.

36. Doris Davis, interview with Eleanor Purcell, December 10, 2017, and January 1, 2018.

37. Joslin, *Edith Wharton*, 66.

38. Edith Wharton, *Bunner Sisters* (New York: Everyman's Library, 2008), 274.

39. Ibid., 280.

40. As quoted in Plante, *Women at Home in Victorian America*, 158.

41. Edward Tenner, "Sewing Machine," in *Occult Dress to Zoran, Index*, ed. Valerie Steele, vol. 3, *Encyclopedia of Clothing and Fashion* (New York: Thomson Gale, 2005), 157.

42. Ibid., 158.

43. Mary E. Wilkins Freeman, "A New England Nun," in *1865–1914*, ed. Nina Baym, vol. C, *The Norton Anthology of American Literature*, 7th ed., ed. Jeanne Campbell Reesman and Arnold Krupat (New York: W. W. Norton, 2007), 630.

44. Elaine Showalter, *A Jury of Her Peers: American Women Writers from Anne Bradstreet to Annie Proulx* (New York: Alfred A. Knopf, 2009), 196.

45. Susan Strasser, *Never Done: A History of American Housework* (New York: Pantheon Books, 1982), 131.

46. Ibid.

47. Extension Circular No. 235 (April 1927), 1. This artifact comes from the Gary Bugh collection.

48. Joy Spanabel Emery, "Patterns and Pattern Making," in *Occult Dress to Zoran, Index*, ed. Valerie Steele, vol. 3, *Encyclopedia of Clothing and Fashion* (New York: Thomson Gale, 2005), 25.

49. Strasser, *Never Done*, 134–35.

50. Ibid.
51. Ibid., 26–27.
52. *Texarkana Gazette*, January 1, 1933, 6.
53. Bronwen Edwards, "Department Store," in *Academic Dress to Eyeglasses*, ed. Valerie Steele, vol. 1, *Encyclopedia of Clothing and Fashion* (New York: Thomson Gale, 2005), 361–63.
54. Ibid., 361–62.
55. Theodore Dreiser, *Sister Carrie*, 2nd ed., ed. Donald Pizer (New York: W. W. Norton, 1991), 17.
56. Bronwen Edwards, "Department Store," 362.
57. Beverly Rowe, *Once upon a Time in Texarkana* (self-pub., 2005), 18. Also see discussion 25–27.
58. Doris Davis, interview with Eleanor Purcell, January 13, 2018.
59. *Texarkana Courier*, October 11, 1910, 7.
60. *Texarkana Courier*, October 4, 1910, 6.
61. *Texarkana Courier*, October 2, 1910, 3.
62. N. J. Stevenson, *Chronology of Fashion: From Empire Dress to Ethical Design* (London: A&C Black, 2011), 82.
63. *Texarkana Courier*, October 27, 1910, 3.
64. Rowe, *Once upon a Time*, 33–34.
65. Jane Audas, "Window Displays," in *Occult Dress to Zoran, Index*, ed. Valerie Steele, vol. 3, *Encyclopedia of Clothing and Fashion* (New York: Thomson Gale, 2005), 434.
66. *Four States Press*, April 6, 1920, 5.
67. IRS.gov: Statistics of Income—Calendar Year 1920, 3.
68. As quoted in Cardon, *Fashion and Fiction*, 2.
69. H. Kristina Haugland, "Bustle," in *Academic Dress to Eyeglasses*, ed. Valerie Steele, vol. 1, *Encyclopedia of Clothing and Fashion* (New York: Thomson Gale, 2005), 204–5.
70. Ibid., 204
71. Mills, *Calico Chronicle*, 177.
72. Valerie Steele and Colleen Gau, "Corset," in in *Academic Dress to Eyeglasses*, ed. Valerie Steele, vol. 1, *Encyclopedia of Clothing and Fashion* (New York: Thomson Gale, 2005), 291.
73. *Texarkana Courier*, September 11, 1910, 2.
74. Mills, *Calico Chronicle*, 177.
75. Ibid.
76. Ingrid Losebek, "Twentieth-Century Fashion," in *Occult Dress to Zoran, Index*, ed. Valerie Steele, vol. 3, *Encyclopedia of Clothing and Fashion* (New York: Thomson Gale, 2005), 348.
77. Ibid.
78. Mills, *Calico Chronicle*, 177.
79. Ibid.
80. M. D. C. Crawford and Elizabeth G. Crawford, *The History of Lingerie in*

*Pictures* (New York: Fairchild, 1952), 15.
  81. Losebek, "Twentieth-Century Fashion," 348.
  82. Ibid.
  83. Cardon, *Fashion and Fiction*, 108–09.
  84. *Four States Press*, June 10, 1920, 6.
  85. *Four States Press*, January 4, 1920, 2.
  86. Ibid., 5.
  87. Ibid., 5.
  88. *Daily Texarkanian*, May 3, 1925, 3.
  89. Ibid., 5.
  90. *Daily Texarkanian*, May 1, 1925, 8.
  91. Ibid., 6.
  92. Kate Chopin, "A Pair of Silk Stockings," in *The Complete Works of Kate Chopin*, ed. Per Seyersted (Baton Rouge: Louisiana State University Press, 1969).
  93. Losebek, "Twentieth Century Fashion," 349.
  94. Quoted in Valerie Steele, *Paris Fashion: A Cultural History* (New York: Oxford University Press, 1988), 246.
  95. R. Turner Wilcox, *Five Centuries of American Costume* (New York: Charles Scribner's Sons, 1963), 163.
  96. Ibid.
  97. *Daily Texarkanian*, May 3, 1925, 3.
  98. Losebek, "Twentieth-Century Fashion," 349–50.
  99. Patricia Campbell Warner, "Shirtwaist," in *Occult Dress to Zoran, Index*, ed. Valerie Steele, vol. 3, *Encyclopedia of Clothing and Fashion* (New York: Thomson Gale, 2005), 162.
  100. Ibid., 162–64.
  101. Doris Davis, interview with Eleanor Purcell, January 13, 2018.
  102. *Texarkana Gazette* announcement, January 1940.

## Chapter 6

  1. Jamie Simmons, interview with Eleanor Ahern Horrigan, 2004, 2005.
  2. Katherine C. Grier, "The Decline of the Memory Palace: The Parlor after 1890," in *American Home Life, 1880–1930: A Social History of Spaces and Services*, ed. Jessica H. Foy and Thomas J. Schlereth (Knoxville: University of Tennessee Press, 1992), 51.
  3. Simmons, interview with Eleanor Ahern Horrigan, 2004, 2005.
  4. Lillie Hamilton French, *The House Dignified: Its Design, Its Arrangement and Its Decoration* (New York: Putnam's Sons, 1903), 191.
  5. Almon C. Varney, *Our Homes and Their Adornments: Or, How to Build, Furnish and Adorn a Home* (Detroit: J. C. Chilton & Co., 1880), vi.
  6. Frank Alvah Parsons, *Interior Decoration: Its Principles and Practice* (Garden City: New York, 1920; Forgotten Books, 2018, rpt.), 227. Emphasis added.
  7. Doris Davis, interview with Jana Atchison Alexander, May 16, 2018.
  8. Jamie Simmons, interview with Eleanor Ahern Horrigan, 2004, 2005.

9. Davis, interview with Alexander, May 16, 2018.

10. French, *The House Dignified*, 195–97.

11. Ibid., 192.

12. Doris Davis, interview with Remica Gray, August 1, 2017.

13. At some point after Ann Ahern began teaching, she added a second grand Steinway piano in the room.

14. A. J. Downing, *The Architecture of Country Houses* (New York: Dover, 1969), 429. Reprint: New York: D. Appleton & Co., 1850.

15. Edith Wharton and Ogden Codman Jr., *The Decoration of Houses* (Mineola, NY: Dover, 2015), 143. Reprint: New York: Charles Scribner's Sons, 1914.

16. H. Hudson Holly, *Modern Dwellings: In Town and Country* (New York: Harper & Brothers, 1878), 201.

17. French, *The House Dignified*, 373.

18. Ibid., 375.

19. Arthur Loesser, *Men, Women and Pianos: A Social History* (New York: Dover, 1990), 548–49. Reprint: New York: Simon & Schuster, 1954.

20. Ibid, 492.

21. Ibid., 513.

22. Ibid., 515–16. Rubinstein's contract stipulated that he play only at suitable venues, i.e., not beer halls or cafes.

23. Loesser, *Men, Women*, 553.

24. Ibid., 559.

25. Ibid., 494–95.

26. Doris Davis, interview with Eleanor Purcell, June 3, 2018.

27. National Theatre: Washington DC History. https://www.nationaltheatre.org/history/history-of-the-national/. Retrieved June 6, 2018.

28. National Theatre: Washington DC History. Timeline: http://thenationalede.org.history. Retrieved June 8, 2018. All references in the chapter to dates and artists performing at the National Theatre are based on this site unless otherwise noted.

29. Harold C. Schonberg, *The Great Pianists: From Mozart to the Present* (New York: Simon & Schuster, 1963), p. 273.

30. Beth Abelson Macleod, *Women Performing Music: The Emergence of American Women as Classical Instrumentalists and Conductors* (Jefferson, NC: McFarland, 2001), 24.

31. Ibid., 25.

32. Schonberg, *Great Pianists*, 291.

33. Candace Bailey, *Music and the Southern Belle: From Accomplished Lady to Confederate Composer* (Carbondale: Southern Illinois University Press, 2010), 92.

34. Judith Tick, "Passed Away Is the Piano Girl: Changes to American Musical Life, 1870–1900," in *Women Making Music: The Western Art Tradition 1150–950*, ed. Jane Bowers and Judith Tick (Urbana: University of Illinois Press, 1987), 335.

35. For a discussion of how piano music functions in this classic novel, see

Doris Davis, "The Enigma at the Keyboard: Chopin's Mademoiselle Reisz," *Mississippi Quarterly: The Journal of Southern Cultures* 58, no. 1–2 (Winter-Spring 2004–2005), 89–104.

36. Quoted in Christine Ammer, *Unsung: A History of Women in American Music* (Westport, CT: Greenwood Press, 1980), 43.

37. Tick, "Passed Away," 325.

38. Ibid., 326.

39. Loesser, *Men, Women*, 537.

40. Ibid., 538.

41. Schonberg, *Great Pianists*, 328.

42. Ibid.

43. Macleod, *Women Performing Music*, 82.

44. Ibid., 87.

45. Ibid.

46. Donna Staley Kline, *Olga Samaroff Stokowski: An American Virtuoso on the World Stage* (College Station: Texas A&M University Press, 1996), xi.

47. Doris Davis, interview with Eleanor Purcell, June 3, 2018.

48. Ibid.

49. St. Edward Catholic Church: Parish History. http://www.saintedwardstexarkana.com/about-us/parish-history. Retrieved May 30, 2018.

50. The youngest daughter, Eleanor, was not old enough to be included in these annuals, and the oldest son, Joseph, had probably already graduated by 1925 or 1926. Catherine Elizabeth is mentioned in the annual, but seems not to have been especially active in music.

51. *Providentia, 1925* (Texarkana: Providence Academy, St. Edward Church), 28.

52. Ernest Hutcheson, *The Literature of the Piano: A Guide for Amateur and Student*, rev. Rudolph Ganz (New York: Alfred A. Knopf, 1964), 380.

53. *Providentia, 1925*, 55.

54. Ibid., 57.

55. Quoted in Hutcheson, *Literature of the Piano*, 234.

56. Ibid., 235.

57. Ibid., 236.

58. Ibid., 312–13.

59. *The Green Gate: Year Book of Georgetown Visitation Convent, 1926*. Vol. 5. (Washington, DC: Georgetown Visitation Convent, 1926), 60.

60. Hutcheson, *Literature of the Piano*, 331–32.

61. *The Trinilogue, 1928* (Washington, DC: Trinity College, 1929), no page number.

62. *Providentia, 1925* (Texarkana: Providence Academy, St. Edward Church, 1925), 52.

63. Ibid., 61.

64. Ibid., 65.

65. *Providentia, 1926* (Texarkana: Providence Academy, St. Edward Church, 1926), no page number. Fellow student Elizabeth Patterson wrote the poem.

66. *Providentia, 1926*, 60.

67. *Providentia, 1926*, no page number.

68. *Providentia, 1925*, 64.

69. Mary Lansdale was the daughter of George Lansdale, Mrs. Ahern's brother, who had moved from Washington, DC, to Texarkana.

70. Doris Davis, interview with Sandra Robertson Albright, May 30, 2018.

71. *The Green Gate: Year Book of Georgetown Visitation Convent, 1929* (Washington, DC: Georgetown Visitation Convent, 1929), 64.

72. Doris Davis, interview with Mary Ellen O'Dwyer Forte, July 31, 2017.

73. Doris Davis, interview with Eleanor Purcell, June 3, 2018.

74. Davis, interview with Albright, May 30, 2018.

75. Doris Davis, interview with Jane Raffaelli Daines, June 6, 2018.

76. Davis, interview with Albright, May 30, 2018.

77. Doris Davis, interview with Jana Atchison Alexander, May 16, 2018.

78. Davis, interview with Daines, June 6, 2018.

79. Davis, interview with Alexander, May 16, 2018.

80. Pat Horrigan, email to to Doris Davis. September 2020.

81. Davis, interview with Purcell, June 3, 2018.

82. Doris Davis, interview with Ann Atchinson Nicholas, May 12, 2018.

83. Davis, interview with Alexander, May 16, 2018.

84. Doris Davis, interview with Delfina McGee Mays, May 14, 2018.

85. Davis, interview with Alexander, May 16, 2018.

86. Davis, interview with Albright, May 30, 2018.

87. Davis, interview with Alexander, May 16, 2018.

88. Davis, interview with Mays, May 14, 2018.

89. Barbara Overton Chandler and J. Ed Howe, *History of Texarkana and Bowie and Miller Counties* (Shreveport: J. S. Hyland & Co., 1939), 209. Chandler and Howe are confusing, however, about the dates of origin for the state clubs. The 1898 date of origin for the Wednesday Music Club relates to the origin of the National Federation of Music Clubs. The Texas and Arkansas Federations both list their date of official origin as 1915. Chandler and Howe must be providing unofficial dates.

90. Chandler and Howe, *History of Texarkana*, 209–10.

91. Ann Ahern, obituary, *Texarkana Gazette*, November 29, 1988, 9A.

92. https://www.nfmc-music.org. Retrieved June 6, 2018.

93. Arkansas Federation of Music Clubs. https://www.arkansasfmc.org/Arkansas. Retrieved June 7, 2018.

94. The Wednesday Music Handbooks mentioned in this section are all unpublished, informal handbooks housed in the P. J. Ahern House as part of the Texarkana Museums System.

95. All information contained in this discussion is now part of the P. J. Ahern's

records of the Wednesday Music Club. They are all unpublished and remain in the house.

96. These musical scores will provide a musicologist with rich information and deserve further investigation.

97. Loesser, *Men, Women*, 563.

98. Ibid., 600.

99. Quoted in Loesser, *Men, Women*, 602.

100. Edward Rothstein, foreword to *Men, Women, and Pianos: A Social History*, by Arthur Loesser (New York: Dover, 1990), xi. Reprint: New York: Simon & Schuster, 1954.

101. As a gift to TMS, Dr. Wilson and Janella Garrett donated a Steinway piano in honor of Jeff Brown, for his contributions to the city. Ragland Piano Company donated a Schaff piano in support of TMS.

## Chapter 7

1. Samuel Taylor Coleridge, "The Rime of the Ancient Mariner," in *The Romantic Period*, ed. Stephen Greenblatt, Deidre Shauna Lynch, and Jack Stillinger, vol. D, *The Norton Anthology of English Literature*, 8th ed. (New York: W. W. Norton, 2006), p. 438, part 5, lines 293–94.

2. Elizabeth Collins Cromley, "A History of American Beds and Bedrooms, 1890–1930," in *American Home Life, 1880–1930: A Social History of Spaces and Services*, ed. Jessica H. Foy and Thomas J. Schlereth (Knoxville: University of Tennessee Press, 1992), 120–23.

3. David P. Handlin, *The American Home: Architecture and Society 1815–1915* (Boston: Little, Brown, 1979), 344–45.

4. Edith Wharton and Ogden Codman Jr., *The Decoration of Houses* (Mineola, NY: Dover, 2015), 169–70. Reprint: New York: Charles Scribner's Sons, 1914.

5. Cromley, "History of American Beds," 124–25.

6. Ibid., 125.

7. Ibid., 134.

8. National Register of Historic Places, Registration Form, Patrick J. Ahern House, MI0041, 403 Laurel Street, Texarkana, AR 71854, Section 7, 2.

9. Jamie Simmons, interview with Eleanor Horrigan, 2004, 2005.

10. Brian Horrigan, email to Doris Davis, February 2020.

11. Cromley, "History of American Beds," 135.

12. Catharine E. Beecher and Harriet Beecher Stowe, *The American Woman's Home*, ed. Nicole Tonkovich (New Brunswick, NJ: Rutgers University Press, 2002), 271. Reprint: Hartford, CT: Harriet Beecher Stowe Center, 1869.

13. Thomas J. Schlereth, *Victorian America: Transformations in Everyday Life, 1876–1915* (New York: HarperPerennial, 1991), 129.

14. Beecher and Beecher Stowe, *American Woman's Home*, 271–72.

15. Ibid., 272.

16. Ellen M. Plante, *Women at Home in Victorian America: A Social History* (New York: Facts On File, 1997), 81.

17. Karin Calvert, "Children in the House, 1890 to 1930," in *American Home Life, 1880–1930: A Social History of Spaces and Services*, ed. Jessica H. Foy and Thomas J. Schlereth (Knoxville: University of Tennessee Press, 1992), 755.

18. Ibid., 76.

19. Ibid.

20. Plante, *Women at Home*, 79.

21. William Wordsworth, "Ode: Intimations of Immortality from Recollections of Early Childhood," in *The Romantic Period*, ed. Stephen Greenblatt, Deidre Shauna Lynch, and Jack Stillinger, vol. D, *The Norton Anthology of English Literature*, 8th ed. (New York: Norton, 2006), pp. 308–12, lines 62–65.

22. Calvert, "Children in the House," 77.

23. Wharton and Codman, *Decoration of Houses*, 174.

24. Calvert, "Children in the House," 86.

25. As quoted in Thomas J. Schlereth, *Victorian America: Transformations in Everyday Life, 1876–1915* (New York: HarperPerennial, 1991), 130.

26. Calvert, "Children in the House," 81.

27. Ibid., 82.

28. Ibid., 85.

29. Ibid., 87.

30. Texarkana Museums System Curator Jamie Simmons suggested this explanation of the arc over the stairs to the author.

31. Pat Horrigan, email to Doris Davis, May 3, 2022.

32. Schlereth, *Victorian America*, 127.

33. The earth closet "operated on the principle of dropping dry earth on human waste to induce rapid fermentation without the generation of noxious gases. The simplest form . . . was a wooden commode equipped with a back hopper filled with earth"; ibid., 128.

34. Schlereth, *Victorian America*, 128–29.

35. Jamie Simmons, interview with Eleanor Horrigan, 2004, 2005.

## Chapter 8

1. Doris Davis. interview with Eleanor Purcell, June 3, 2018.

2. Ellen M. Plante, *The American Kitchen: 1700 to the Present* (New York: Facts On File, 1995), 161.

3. Emily Holt, *The Complete Housekeeper, 1917*, as quoted in Ellen M. Plante, *American Kitchen*, 161.

4. Plante, *American Kitchen*, 162.

5. Catharine E. Beecher and Harriet Beech Stowe, *The American Woman's Home*, ed. Nicole Tonkovich (New Brunswick, NJ: Rutgers University Press, 2002), 272. Reprint: Hartford, CT: Harriet Beecher Stowe Center, 1869.

6. Ibid., 273.

7. Molly Harrison, *The Kitchen in History* (New York: Charles Scribner's Sons, 1972), 126.

8. Plante, *American* Kitchen, 166.

9. Ibid., 146.
10. Ibid., 251.
11. Doris Davis, interview with Eleanor Purcell, 2018.
12. Brian Horrigan, email to Doris Davis, February 2020.
13. Ibid.
14. Plante, *American Kitchen*, 148.
15. Ibid., 217.
16. Ibid., 241.
17. Elsie De Wolfe, *The House in Good Taste*, 1920, as quoted in Plante, *American Kitchen*, 241.
18. Ibid.
19. *Good Housekeeping's Book of Menus, Recipes, and Household Discoveries* (New York: Good Housekeeping, 1922), 250.
20. Ibid., 169.
21. Plante, *American Kitchen*, 209.
22. *Good Housekeeping's Book of Menus*, 6.
23. Cathy Ahern and Maureen Leahigh, email to Doris Davis, August 2020.
24. Doris Davis, interview with Eleanor Purcell, June 3, 2018.
25. Plante, *American Kitchen*, 178.
26. This seems a small amount to budget for food, but may reflect that Mr. Ahern's garden produced many of the vegetables they ate. Since Mrs. Ahern canned a lot of vegetables, the family could eat from the garden throughout the year.
27. Doris Davis, interview with Frank Loda, June 13 & 15, 2018.
28. David P. Handlin, *The American Home: Architecture and Society, 1815–1915* (Boston: Little, Brown, 1979), 419.
29. Ibid., 419.
30. Susan Strasser, *Never Done: A History of American Housework* (New York: Pantheon Books, 1982), 212–13.
31. Ibid., 213.
32. Edith Wharton and Ogden Codman Jr., *The Decoration of Houses* (Mineola, NY: Dover, 2015), 155–57. Reprint: New York: Charles Scribner's Sons, 1914.
33. Wharton and Codman, *Decoration of Houses*, 159.
34. Ibid., 161.
35. Thomas J. Schlereth, *Victorian America: Transformations in Everyday Life, 1876–1915* (New York, HarperPerennial, 1991), 124.
36. Ibid., 124–26.
37. Doris Davis, interview with Frank Loda, June 15 & 19, 2018.
38. Brian Horrigan, email to Doris Davis, February 2020.
39. Doris Davis, interview with Eleanor Purcell, 2018.

## Conclusion

1. Sally Kirby, "Time Leaves Homes Untouched through All the Years," *Texarkana Gazette*, C, April 2, 1978, 1.

2. Ibid., 5.

3. Aaron Brand, "Ahern Project Preserves History by Restoring a Home," *Texarkana Gazette,* C, November 27, 2011, 1

4. Kirby, "Time Leaves Homes," 5.

# Sources

## Chapter 1

Beaubien, Jason. "Chasing Down Polio." *All Things Considered*. NPR News. October 15, 2012.

Chandler, Barbara Overton, and J. Ed Howe. *History of Texarkana and Bowie and Miller Counties*. Shreveport: J. S. Hyland & Co. 1939.

Christus, St. Michael Health System. *One Hundred Years of Healing*. 2016.

Dougan, Michael B. "The Arkansas Married Woman's Property Law." *Arkansas Historical Quarterly* 46, no. 1 (Spring 1987): 3–26.

Horrigan, Brian. "The Ahern and Lansdale Family History." Unpublished manuscript, June 21, 2018.

Leet, William D. *Texarkana: A Pictorial History*. Norfolk, VA: Donning, 1982.

Rowe, Beverly J. *Historic Texarkana: An Illustrated History*. Commissioned by the Texarkana Museums System. San Antonio, TX: Historical Publishing Network, 2009.

———. *Once upon a Time, in Texarkana*. Self-published, 2005.

Unger, Irwin, and Debi Unger. *Twentieth Century America*. New York: St. Martin's Press, 1990.

## Chapter 2

Dudden, Faye E. *Serving Women: Household Service in Nineteenth-Century America*. Middletown, CT: Wesleyan University Press, 1984.

Gamman, Lorraine, and Sean O'Mara. "Laundry." In *Fads to Nylon*, ed. Valerie Steele, 337–40. Vol. 2 of *Encyclopedia of Clothing and Fashion*. New York: Thomson Gale, 2005.

Glen, Evelyn Nakano. *Unequal Freedom: How Race and Gender Shaped American Citizenship and Labor*. Cambridge, MA: Harvard University Press, 2002.

Hurston, Zora Neale. "Sweat." In *Spunk: The Selected Stories of Zora Neale Hurston*, 38–53. Berkeley, CA: Turtle Island Foundation, 1985.

Livingston, Margaret Warrs. "Servants." In *Correct Social Usage*, 542–68. New York: New York Society of Self-Culture, 1906.

Palmer, Phyllis. *Domesticity and Dirt: Housewives and Domestic Servants in the United States, 1920–1945*. Philadelphia: Temple University Press, 1985.

Rollins, Judith. *Between Women: Domestics and Their Employers*. Philadelphia: Temple University Press, 1985.

Schlereth, Thomas J. *Victorian America: Transformations in Everyday Life, 1876–1915*. New York: Harper Perennial, 1991.

Steinberg, Stephen. *The Ethnic Myth: Race, Ethnicity, and Class in America*. 3rd ed. Boston: Beacon Press, 2001.

Strasser, Susan. *Never Done: A History of American Housework*. New York: Pantheon Books, 1982.

Wallace-Sanders, Kimberly. *Mammy: A Century of Race, Gender, and Southern Memory*. Ann Arbor: University of Michigan Press, 2008.

## Chapter 3

Atlas Portland Cement Company. *Concrete County Residences: Photographs and Floor Plans of Turn-of-the-Century Homes*. Mineola, NY: Dover, 2003.

Bachelard, Gaston. *The Poetics of Space*. Boston, MA: Beacon Press, 1958.

Cobb, A. W. "Suggestions on House Building." In *Turn-of-the-Century House Designs*, 9–14. New York: Dover, 1994. Reprint: *Suburban and Country Homes*. New York: W. T. Comstock, 1893.

Comstock, William T. *Turn-of-the-Century House Designs*. New York: Dover, 1994. Reprint: *Suburban and Country Homes*. New York: W.T. Comstock, 1893.

Emerson, Ralph Waldo. "The Poet." In *Essays: Second Series, the Selected Writings of Ralph Waldo Emerson*. Edited by Brooks Atkinson. New York: The Modern Library, 1940.

Harris, Neil. *Building Lives: Constructing Rites and Passages*. New Haven: Yale University Press, 1999.

Hollis, Edward. *The Secret Lives of Buildings: From the Ruins of the Parthenon to the Vegas Strip in Thirteen Stories*. New York: Picador, 2009.

Hopkins, D. S. *Late Victorian House Designs*. Mineola, NY: Dover, 2004. Reprint: D. S. Hopkins. *Houses and Cottages*. Grand Rapids, MI, 1893.

Horrigan, Brian. "The Ahern and Lansdale Family History." Unpublished manuscript, June 21, 2018.

Loos, Adolf. "Ornament and Crime." 1908. In *Introducing Architectural Theory*, 42–47. Ed. Korydon Smith. New York: Routledge, 2012.

McAlester, Virginia, and Lee. *A Field Guide to American Houses*. New York: Knopf, 2009.

Miller County Report. Parcel 1011920, ID 24182. Property Owner: Ahern Home Charitable Lead, 403 Laurel. Black/Lot: 047/006.

National Register of Historic Places. United States Department of the Interior. National Park Service. Registration Form of the Patrick J. Ahern House, M10041. 403 Laurel Street, Texarkana, Arkansas, Miller County, 71854. December 3, 2004.

Reiff, Daniel D. "Introduction to the Dover Edition." *The Most Popular Homes of the Twenties*, by William A. Radford. Mineola, v–viii. New York: Dover, 2009. Reprint: William A. Radford. *The Most Popular Homes in America*. Chicago American Builder, 1925.

Ruskin, John. "The Lamp of Truth." 1849. In *Introducing Architectural Theory: Debating a Discipline*, ed. Korydon Smith, 74–83. New York: Routledge, 2012.

Smith, Korydon, ed. *Introducing Architectural Theory: Debating a Discipline*. New York: Routledge, 2012.

Stickley, Gustav. *Catalogue of Craftsman Furniture*. Eastwood, NY: Craftsman Workshops, 1901. Quoted in "The Modern Look of the Early-Twentieth House: A Mirror of Changing Lifestyles," by Candace M. Volz, 26. In *American Home Life, 1880–1930: A Social History of Spaces and Services*, edited by Jessica H. Foy and Thomas J. Schlereth. Knoxville: University of Tennessee Press, 1992.

Tuan, Yi-Fu. *Space and Place: The Perspective of Experience*. Minneapolis: University of Minnesota Press, 1977.

Van Rensselaer, Mariana Griswold. *Accents as Well as Broad Effects: Writings on Architecture, Landscape, and the Environment, 1876–1925*. Edited by David Gebhard. Berkeley: University of California Press, 1996.

Venturi, Robert. From *Complexity and Contradiction in Architecture*, 1966. In *Introducing Architectural Theory: Debating a Discipline*, edited by Korydon Smith, 27–31. New York: Routledge, 2012.

Volz, Candace M. "The Modern Look of the Early-Twentieth-Century House: A Mirror of Changing Lifestyles." In *American Home Life, 1880–1930: A Social History of Spaces and Services*, edited by Jessica H. Foy and Thomas J. Schlereth, 25–48. Knoxville: University of Tennessee Press, 1992.

Wigley, Mark. *The Architecture of Deconstruction*. Cambridge, MA: MIT Press, 1995.

## Chapter 4

Abbott, Karen. "I Was Looking Forward to a Quiet Old Age." *Smithsonian Magazine*, May 25, 2012. https://www.smithsonianmag.com/history/i-was-looking-forward-to-a-quiet-old-age-106393195. Retrieved May 1, 2018.

"Always Complete but Never Finished." The A. H. Andrews Co. Wernicke System Elastic Book Cases. Chicago, Illinois. No date. Advertising brochure.

Austen, Jane. *Pride and Prejudice*. Edited by Donald Gray. A Norton Critical Edition. 3rd ed. New York: W. W. Norton, 2001.

Bacon, Francis. "Of Studies." In *The Sixteenth Century & The Early Seventeenth Century*, edited by George M. Logan et al., 1561–62. Vol. B of *The Norton Anthology of English Literature*. 8th ed. New York: W. W. Norton, 2006.

Barickman, Richard, Susan MacDonald, and Myra Stark. "Politics of Sexuality." In *Vanity Fair*, by William Makepeace Thackeray, 841–55. Edited by Peter L. Shillingsburg. A Norton Critical Edition. New York: W. W. Norton, 1994.

Blake, Mary Elizabeth. "The First Steps." In *Irish Literature*. Vol. 1. Edited by Justin McCarthy, 190–91. Philadelphia: John D. Morris & Co., 1904.

Bobinski, George S. *Carnegie Libraries: Their History and Impact on American Public Library Development*. Chicago: American Library Association, 1969.

Boorstin, Daniel J. *In Library: The Drama Within*. Illustrated by Diane Asséo Griliches. Albuquerque: University of New Mexico Press, 1996.

"Bryan Editing a Book." *The New York Times*, August 4, 1906. https://www.nytimes.com/1906/08/04/archives/bryan-editing-a-book-is-finishing-introduction-to-the-worlds-famous.html. Retrieved April 5, 2018.

Bryan, William Jennings. Preface to *Greece (432 B.C.-324 B.C.)*, ed. William Jennings Bryan, v–ix. Vol. 1 of *The World's Famous Orations*. New York: Funk and Wagnalls, 1906.

———. *The World's Famous Orations*. 10 vols. New York: Funk and Wagnalls, 1906.

Burke, Thomas N. Table of contents. In *Lectures and Sermons of Father Burke*, 7–8. Vol. 1. New York: P. M. Haverty, 1872.

Cadegan, Una M. "Running the Ancient Ark by Steam: Catholic Publishing." In *Print in Motion: The Expansion of Publishing and Reading in the United States, 1880–1940*, ed. Carl F. Kaestle and Janice A. Radway, 392–408. Vol. 4. of *A History of the Book in America*. Chapel Hill: University of North Carolina Press, 2009.

"Cadence." *The Century Dictionary*, 752. Edited by William Dwight Whitney. Vol. 1. New York: The Century Co., 1902.

Carpenter, Humphrey, and Mary Prichard. *The Oxford Companion to Children's Literature*. Oxford: Oxford University Press, 1984.

*The Century Dictionary*. Undated brochure.

Chandler, Barbara Overton, and J. Ed Howe. *History of Texarkana and Bowie and Miller Counties*. Shreveport: J. S. Hyland & Co., 1939.

Crowell, Grace Noll. *The Lifted Lamp*. New York: Harper & Brothers, 1942.

Cunliffe, J. W. *English Literature During the Last Half-Century*. New York: Macmillan, 1928.

Damrosch, Leo. "Books That Matter: The History of the Decline and Fall of the Roman Empire." https://www.thegreatcourses.com/courses/books-that-matter-the-history-of-the-decline-and-fall-of-the-roman-empire.html. Retrieved April 6, 2018.

Dante, Alighieri. *Dante's Inferno*. Translated by Henry Francis Cary. Illustrated. by M. Gustave Doré. New York: P. F. Collier. n.d.

Darnton, Robert. "Scholarship and Readership: New Directions in the History of the Book." In *Books and Prints, Past and Future*, 36. New York: Grolier Club, 1984, quoted in Linda M. Kruger, "Home Libraries: Special Spaces, Reading Places." In *American Home Life, 1880–1930: A Social History of Spaces and Services*, ed. Jessica H. Foy and Thomas J. Schlereth, 95. Knoxville: University of Tennessee Press, 1992.

Davis, Doris. "The Enigma at the Keyboard: Chopin's Mademoiselle Reisz." *Mississippi Quarterly: The Journal of Southern Cultures* 58, no. 1–2 (Winter-Spring 2004–2005), 89–104.

Day, Martin S. *History of American Literature: From the Beginning to 1910*. Garden City: Doubleday, 1970.

———. *History of English Literature, 1837 to the Present*. Garden City: Doubleday, 1964.

Dickinson, Donald C. "Bibliomania." *Encyclopedia of Library History*, edited by Wayne A. Wiegard and Donald G. Davis Jr., 75–76, New York: Garland Press, 1994.

Dickinson, Emily. Poem 1286. "There is no Frigate like a Book." In *The Poems of Emily Dickinson: Reading Edition*, edited by R. W. Franklin, 501. Cambridge, MA: The Belknap Press of Harvard University Press, 1998.

Doyle, James. Preface to *Lives of the Saints*, by Alban Butler, iii–viii. Vol. 1. London: Henry & Co., n.d.

Downing, A.J. *The Architecture of Country Houses*. New York: Dover, 1969. Reprint: New York: D. Appleton & Co., 1850.

Elson, Louis C. Preface to *Modern Music and Musicians, Part One: Compositions*. Edited by Louis C. Elson. 8 vols. New York: The University Society, 1912.

The Encyclopedia Press, ed. *The Catholic Encyclopedia and Its Makers*. New York: The Encyclopedia Press, 1917.

*Etiquette, Politeness, and Good Breeding*. Glasgow: Dunn and Wright Printers, n.d.

Field, Rachel. *Hitty, Her First Hundred Years*. New York: MacMillan, 1929.

Fooks, John. "Centenarian Reflects on Her Good Life, Days Gone By . . . ." *Texarkana Gazette*. Metro/State 5A, February 19, 2005.

French, Lillie Hamilton. *The House Dignified: Its Design, Its Arrangement and Its Decoration*, 79. New York: Putnam's Sons, 1908. Quoted in Harold M. Otness, "A Room Full of Books: The Life and Slow Death of the American Residential Library." *Libraries and Culture* 23, no. 2 (Spring 1988): 111.

———. *Homes and Their Decoration*. New York: Dodd, Mead, and Co., 1903.

Gale, Robert L. "Guest, Edgar Albert." In *Gilbert–Hand*, ed. John A. Garraty and Mark C. Carnes, 698–99. Vol. 9 of *American National Biography*. New York: Oxford University Press, 1999.

Garrison, Dee. *Apostles of Culture: The Public Librarian and American Society, 1876–1920*. Madison: University of Wisconsin Press, 1979.

Gaskell, C. A. Preface to *An Art Edition of the Most Popular Dramas of Shakespeare*, edited by C. A. Gaskell, 3. Chicago: U.S. Publishing House, 1889.

"Gazette Roots Run Deep in Texarkana." *Texarkana Gazette*. http://www.texarkanagazette.com/news/texarkana/story/2015/oct/04/gazette-roots-run-deep-texarkana/406672. Retrieved April 26, 2018.

Gibbon, Edward. *Decline and Fall of the Roman Empire*. Edited by H. H. Milman. Chicago: Belford, Clark and Co., n.d.

"Globe-Wernicke Sectional Bookcases for Beautifying the Home." Catalogue No. 122. Digital Collections. Library of Congress. https://www.loc.gov/item/ltf91092406/. Retrieved April 19, 2018.

Holly, H. Hudson. *Modern Dwellings: In Town and Country*. New York: Harper & Brothers, 1878.

Howells, William Dean. "From Novel-Writing and Novel-Reading: An Impersonal Explanation." In *1865–1914*, ed. Nina Baym, 915–17. Vol C of *The Norton Anthology of American Literature*. 7th ed. Edited by Jeanne Campbell Reesman and Arnold Krupat. 7th ed. New York: W. W. Norton, 2007.

———. *The Rise of Silas Lapham*. With notes by James M. Spinning. Boston: Houghton Mifflin, 1928.

"Humphrey Radiantfire." Humphrey Products homepage. http://www.humphreyproducts.com/content/Humphrey-history-1901-today.n, Retrieved April 26, 2018.

"Johann Wolfgang Amadeus Mozart." In *Mass Music–Newman*, edited by Charles G. Herbermann, 623–24. Vol. 10 of *The Catholic Encyclopedia*. New York: Robert Appleton Co., 1911.

Johanningsmeier, Charles. "The Industrialization and Nationalization of American Periodical Publishing." In *Perspectives on American Book History*, edited by Scott E. Casper, Joanne D. Chaison, and Jeffrey D. Groves, 311–12. Amherst: University of Massachusetts Press, 2002.

Johnson, J. Stewart. Introduction to *The Architecture of Country Houses*, by A. J. Downing, v–xv. New York: Dover, 1969. Reprint: New York: D. Appleton & Co., 1850.

Jones, Theodore. *Carnegie Libraries across America*. New York: John Wiley and Sons, 1997.

Kaser, David. *A Book for a Sixpence: The Circulating Library in America*. Pittsburgh: Beta Phi Mu, 1980.

Kaestle, Carl F. "Seeing the Sites: Readers, Publishers, and Local Print Cultures in 1880." In *Print in Motion: The Expansion of Publishing and Reading in the United States, 1880–1940*, ed. Carl F. Kaestle and Janice A. Radway, 22–45. Vol. 4 of *A History of the Book in America*. Chapel Hill: University of North Carolina Press, 2009.

Keene, Ann T. "Irving Bacheller." In *American National Biography*, ed. John A. Garraty and Mark C. Carnes, 830–31. Vol. 1. New York: Oxford University Press, 1999.

Knox, Thomas W. *How to Travel*. Rev. ed. New York: G. P. Putnam's Sons, 1887.

Kruger, Linda M. "Home Libraries: Special Spaces, Reading Places." In *American Home Life, 1880–1930: A Social History of Spaces and Services*, edited by Jessica H. Foy and Thomas J. Schlereth, 94–119. Knoxville: University of Tennessee Press, 1992.

Lang, Andrew. "Apparitions." In *Encyclopedia Britannica*, i–xiv, vol 1. 11th ed.. New York: Encyclopaedia Britannica Co., 1910.

Lopez, Manuel D. "Books and Beds: Libraries in Nineteenth and Twentieth Century American Hotels." *Journal of Library History* 9, no. 3 (July 1974): 196–221.

Long, Elizabeth. "Aflame with Culture: Reading and Social Mission in the Nineteenth-Century White Women's Literary Club Movement." In *Print in Motion: The Expansion of Publishing and Reading in the United States, 1880–1940*, ed. Carl F. Kaestle and Janice A. Radway, 476–90. Vol. 4 of *A History of the Book in America*. Chapel Hill: University. of North Carolina Press, 2009.

Mainiero, Lina. "Willa Sibert Cather." In *American Women Writers*, edited by Lina Mainiero, 315–21. Vol 1. New York: Frederick Ungar, 1979.

"The Making of the Catholic Encyclopedia (1917)." *New Advent* 3. http://www.newadvent.org/cathen/00001a.htm. Retrieved April 5, 2018.

McCarthy, Justin, ed. *Irish Literature*. Philadelphia, PA: John D. Morris & Co., 1904.

McCrum, Robert. "The 100 Best Nonfiction Books: No 83—*The History of the Decline and Fall. of the Roman Empire* by Edward Gibbon (1776–1788)." *The Guardian*. September 4, 2017. https://www.theguardian.com/books/2017/sep/04/100-best-nonfiction-books-decline-and-fall-of-the-roman-empire-edward-gibbon. Retrieved April 6, 2018.

McGrath, W. E. "Grace Drayton, a Children's Illustrator Who Also Painted Young Women—a Biographical Sketch." https://web.archive.org/web/20121104011436/http://home.comcast.net/~bluepatch/Biographies/Grace_Drayton-we.htm. Retrieved May 1, 2018.

Meyer, Susan E. *A Treasury of the Great Children's Book Illustrators*. New York: Harry N. Abrams, 1983.

"Molière." In *Mass Music–Newman*, edited by Charles G. Herbermann, 434–35. Vol. 10 of *The Catholic Encyclopedia*. New York: Robert Appleton Co., 1911.

"Mozart." In *Mass Music–Newman*, edited by Charles G. Herbermann, 623–24. Vol. 10 of *The Catholic Encyclopedia*. New York: Robert Appleton Co., 1911.

Musick, John R. "The Plan and Scope," i–xiv. In vol. 1 of *The Real America in Romance*. New York: William H. Wise & Co., 1908.

"News Notes of Texas Public Libraries." *Texas Public Libraries* 1, no. 4 (April 1914): 11.

Ohmann, Richard. "Diverging Paths: Books and Magazines in the Transition to Corporate Capitalism." In *Print in Motion: The Expansion of Publishing and Reading in the United States, 1880–1940*, ed. Carl F. Kaestle and Janice A. Radway, 102–15. Vol. 4 of *A History of the Book in America*. Chapel Hill: University of North Carolina Press, 2009.

O'Reilly, Bernard. *The Mirror of True Womanhood: A Book of Instruction for Women in the World*. New York: Excelsior Catholic Publishing House, 1895.

Otness, Harold M. "A Room Full of Books: The Life and Slow Death of the American Residential Library." *Libraries & Culture* 23, no. 2 (Spring, 1988): 111–34.

Pallen, Conde B., and John J. Wynne, comps. and eds. *The New Catholic Dictionary*. New York: Universal Knowledge Foundation, 1929.

Passet, Joanne E. "Reaching the Rural Reader: Traveling Libraries in America, 1892–1920." *Libraries & Culture* 26, no. 1 (Winter 1991): 100–18.

Pawley, Christine. Introduction to *Libraries and the Reading Public in Twentieth-Century America*, edited by Christine Pawley and Louise S. Robbins, 3–20. Madison: University of Wisconsin Press, 2013.

Pedersen, Nate. "The Magic of *Encyclopedia Britannica*'s 11th Edition." *The Guardian*. April 10, 2012. Retrieved April 5, 2018.

Raphael, Linda Schermer. "Webster, Jean." In *American National Biography*, edited by John A. Garraty and Mark C. Carnes, 869–70. Vol. 22. New York: Oxford University Press, 1999.

Reesman, Jeanne Campbell, and Arnold Krupat. "William Dean Howells." In *1865–1904*, ed. Nina Baym, 913. Volume C of *The Norton Anthology of American Literature*. 7th ed. New York: W. W. Norton, 2007.

Ridpath, John Clark. *History of the World*. Vol. 1. Cincinnati, OH: Jones Brothers Publishing, 1890.

"Ridpath's History of the World." Ohio State University. https://ehistory.osu.edu/books/ridpath

Roosevelt, Theodore. "On American Motherhood." In *America (1861–1905)*, edited by William Jennings Bryan, 253–62. Vol. 10 of. New York: Funk and Wagnalls, 1906.

Rowe, Beverly J. *Once upon a Time in Texarkana*. Self-published, 2005.

———. *Women's Status in Texarkana, Texas in the Progressive Era, 1880–1920*. Women's Studies, vol. 37. Lewistown, New York: The Edwin Mellen Press, 2002

Seavey, Charles A. "Public Libraries." In *Encyclopedia of Library History*, edited by Wayne A. Wiegand and Donald G. Davis Jr., 520–21. New York: Garland Press, 1994.

Sogoyewapha. "Red Jacket on the Religions of the White Man and the Red." In *America (1761–1837)*, edited by William Jennings Bryan, 9–13. Vol. 8 of *The World's Famous Orations*. New York: Funk and Wagnalls, 1906.

*The Standard Question Book and Home Study Outlines*. Buffalo, NY: The Frontier Press Co., 1918.

Steger, Stewart Archer. *American Dictionaries*. Baltimore: J. H. Furst Co., 1913.

Stewart, Donald E., Christopher Hardy Wise Kent, and Others. "Encyclopædia Britannica." https://www.britannica.com/topic/Encyclopaedia-Britannica-English-language-reference-work/Eleventh-edition-and-its-supplements. Retrieved April 5, 2018.

Tebbel, John. *Between Covers: The Rise and Transformation of Book Publishing in America*. New York: Oxford University Press, 1987.

*Texarkana City Directory*, 1899–1900, 1901, 1912, 1915–1916.

Thackeray, William Makepeace. *Vanity Fair*. London: J. M. Dent & Sons, 1920.

"Traveling Libraries." *Texas Libraries* 1, no. 5 July 1914): 1–2.

Van Dyke, Henry. Preface to *The Story of the Other Wiseman*, viii–xiii. New York: Harper & Brothers, 1985.
"Van Dyke, Henry." In *Who Was Who among North American Authors: 1921–1939*, 1445–46. Vol. 2. Detroit: Gale Research Co., 1976.
West, James L. W. III. "The Expansion of the National Book Trade System." In *Print in Motion: The Expansion of Publishing and Reading in the United States, 1880–1940*, ed. Carl F. Kaestle and Janice A. Radway, 79–89. Vol. 4 of *A History of the Book in America*. Chapel Hill: University of North Carolina Press, 2009.
Wiegand, Wayne A. "Community Places and Reading Spaces: Main Street Public Library in the Rural Heartland, 1876–1956." In *Libraries and the Reading Public in Twentieth-Century America*, edited by Christine Pawley and Louise S. Robbins, 23–39. Madison: University of Wisconsin Press, 2013.
Wharton, Edith, and Ogden Codman Jr. *The Decoration of Houses*. Mineola, NY: Dover, 2015. Reprint: New York: Charles Scribner's Sons, 1914.
Whitney, William Dwight, ed. *The Century Dictionary: An Encyclopedic Lexicon of the English Language*. 6 vols. New York: The Century Co., 1902.
———. Preface to *The Century Dictionary and Encyclopedic Lexicon of the English Language*. In vol. 1, v–xvi. New York: The Century Co., 1902.
Williams, Abigail. *The Social Life of Books: Reading Together in the Eighteenth-Century Home*. New Haven: Yale University Press, 2017.
Winship, Michael. "The Rise of a National Book Trade System in the United States." In *Print in Motion: The Expansion of Publishing and Reading in the United States, 1880–1940*, ed. Carl F. Kaestle and Janice A. Radway, 56–77. Vol. 4 of *A History of the Book in America*. Chapel Hill: University of North Carolina Press, 2009.
"The World's Famous Orations." Advertisement. *The Commoner*, June 1916, 29. http://nebnewspapers.unl.edu/lccn/46032385/1916-06-01/ed-1/seq-29.pdf. Retrieve April 5, 2018.
Wyche, Benjamin. "Free Public Libraries in Texas: Ten Years' Growth, 1899–1901." *Texas Libraries* 1, no.1 (Nov. 1909): 6–7.

*Newspapers*

*The Commoner* (Nebraska), June 1, 1916.
*Daily Texarkanian*, October 5, 9, 19, 23, 1905; February 1, 2, 1906; February 2, 1910.

## Chapter 5

Audas, Jane. "Window Displays." In *Occult Dress to Zoran, Index*, ed. Valerie Steele, 434–36. Vol. 3 of *Encyclopedia of Clothing and Fashion*. New York: Thomson Gale, 2005.
Chopin, Kate. "A Pair of Silk Stockings." In *The Complete Works of Kate Chopin*, edited by Per Seyersted, 500–504. Baton Rouge: Louisiana State University Press, 1969.
Cardon, Lauren S. *Fashion and Fiction: Self-Transformation in Twentieth-Century American Literature*. Charlottesville: University of Virginia Press, 2016.

Crawford, M. D. C., and Elizabeth G. Crawford. *The History of Lingerie in Pictures*. New York: Fairchild, 1952.

Dreiser, Theodore. *Sister Carrie*. 2nd ed. Edited by Donald Pizer. New York: W. W. Norton, 1991.

Druesedow, Jean L. "Ready-To-Wear." In *Occult Dress to Zoran, Index*, ed. Valerie Steele, 84–90. Vol. 3 of *Encyclopedia of Clothing and Fashion*. New York: Thomson Gale, 2005.

Edwards, Bronwen. "Department Store." In *Academic Dress to Eyeglasses*, ed. Valerie Steele, 361–63. Vol. 1 of *Encyclopedia of Clothing and Fashion*. New York: Thomson Gale, 2005.

Emery, Joy Spanabel. "Patterns and Pattern Making." In *Academic Dress to Eyeglasses*, ed. Valerie Steele, 25–29. Vol. 1 of *Encyclopedia of Clothing and Fashion*. New York: Thomson Gale, 2005.

Freeman, Mary E. Wilkins. "A New England Nun." In *1865–1914*, ed. Nina Baym, 626–34. Vol. C of *The Norton Anthology of American Literature*. 7th ed. Edited by Jeanne Campbell Reesman and Arnold Krupat. New York: W. W. Norton, 2007.

Gamber, Wendy. *The Female Economy: The Millinery and Dressmaking Trades, 1800–1930*. Urbana-Champaign: University of Illinois Press, 1997.

Haugland, Kristina. "Bustle." In *Academic Dress to Eyeglasses*, ed. Valerie Steele, 204–6. Vol. 1 of *Encyclopedia of Clothing and Fashion*. New York: Thomson Gale, 2005.

Hodges, Bess P. "Home Demonstrations in Clothing for Fourth Year 4-H Club Girls." Extension Service, College of Agriculture, University of Arkansas U.S. Department of Agriculture Cooperating, April 1927.

IRS.Gov. "Statistics of Income—Calendar Year 1920."

Joslin, Katherine. *Edith Wharton and the Making of Fashion*. Durham: University of New Hampshire Press, 2009.

Losehek, Ingrid. "Twentieth-Century Fashion." In *Occult Dress to Zoran, Index*, ed. Valerie Steele, 348–58. Vol. 3 of *Encyclopedia of Clothing and Fashion*. New York: Thomson Gale, 2005.

Mills, Betty J. *Calico Chronicle: Texas Women and Their Fashions, 1830–1910*. Lubbock: Texas Tech University Press, 1985.

*The 1902 Edition of the Sears, Roebuck Catalogue*. New York: Bounty Books, a Division of Crown, 1969.

Nordtorp-Madson, Michelle. "Wedding." In *Occult Dress to Zoran, Index*, ed. Valerie Steele, 425–27. Vol. 3 of *Encyclopedia of Clothing and Fashion*. New York: Thomson Gale, 2005.

Paton, Kathleen. "Trimmings." In *Occult Dress to Zoran, Index*, ed. Valerie Steele, 337–39. Vol. 3 of *Encyclopedia of Clothing and Fashion*. New York: Thomson Gale, 2005.

Plante, Ellen M. *Women at Home in Victorian America: A Social History*. New York: Facts On File, 1997.

Pool, Daniel. *What Jane Austen Ate and Charles Dickens Knew: From Fox Hunting to Whist—The Facts of Daily Life in 19th-Century England*. New York: Touchstone, 1993.
Rowe, Beverly. *Once upon a Time in Texarkana*. Self-published, 2005.
Sherwood, M. E. W. "Weddings." In *Correct Social Usage*, 321–37. New York: New York Society of Self-Culture, 1906.
Showalter, Elaine. *A Jury of Her Peers: American Women Writers from Anne Bradstreet to Annie Proulx*. New York: Alfred A. Knopf, 2009.
Solomon, Michael R., and Susan P. Douglas. "The Female Clotheshorse: From Aesthetics to Tactics." In *The Psychology of Fashion*, ed. Michael R. Solomon, 387–401. Lexington Books. Lexington, MA: D. C. Heath, 1985.
Steele, Valerie. *Paris Fashion: A Cultural History*. New York: Oxford University Press, 1988.
Steele, Valerie. *Fashion and Eroticism: Ideals of Feminine Beauty from the Victorian Era to the Jazz Age*. New York: Oxford University Press, 1985.
Steele, Valerie, and Colleen Gau. "Corset." In *Academic Dress to Eyeglasses*, ed. Valerie Steele, 290–91. Vol. 1 of *Encyclopedia of Clothing and Fashion*. New York: Thomson Gale, 2005.
Stevenson, N. J. *Chronology of Fashion: From Empire Dress to Ethical Design*. London: A&C Black, 2011.
Stoddard, Elizabeth Drew. "Lemorne Versus Huell." In *The Norton Anthology of American Literature*, ed. Nina Baym et al., 2424–37. 4th ed., vol. 1. New York: W. W. Norton, 1994.
Strasser, Susan. *Never Done: A History of American Housework*. New York: Pantheon Books, 1982.
Tenner, Edward. "Sewing Machine." In In *Occult Dress to Zoran, Index*, ed. Valerie Steele, 157–59. Vol. 3 of *Encyclopedia of Clothing and Fashion*. New York: Thomson Gale, 2005.
*Texarkana City Directory*, 1899, 1901, 1902, 1915–1916, 1917–1918, 1920, 1924, 1925, 1931, 1940, 1950.
Thoreau, Henry David. *Walden, or Life in the Woods*. In *American Literature 1620–1820*, ed. Nina Baym, 1635–1808. Vol. 1 of *The Norton Anthology of American Literature*. 3rd ed. New York: Norton, 1989.
Warner, Patricia Campbell. "Shirtwaist." In *Occult Dress to Zoran, Index*, ed. Valerie Steele, 162–64. Vol. 3 of *Encyclopedia of Clothing and Fashion*. New York: Thomson Gale, 2005.
Wharton, Edith. *Bunner Sisters*. New York: Everyman's Library, 2008.
———. *The House of Mirth*. Edited by Elizabeth Ammons. A Norton Critical Edition. New York: W. W. Norton, 1990.
Wilcox, R. Turner. *Five Centuries of American Costume*. New York: Charles Scribner's Sons, 1963.

*Newspapers*

*Daily Texarkanian*, May 1, 3, 1925.
*Texarkana Courier*, October 2, 4, 11, 27, 1927.
*Texarkana Four States Press*, January 4, April 6, June 10, 1920.

## Chapter 6

Armitage, M. Teresa. Introduction to *Junior Laurel Songs*. Boston: C. C. Birchard, 1917.
Ammer, Christine. *Unsung: A History of Women in American Music*. Westport, CT: Greenwood Press, 1980.
Arkansas Federation of Music Clubs. https://www.arkansasfmc.org/arkansas. Retrieved June 7, 2018.
Bailey, Candace. *Music and the Southern Belle: From Accomplished Lady to Confederate Composer*. Carbondale: Southern Illinois University Press, 2010.
*The Bulldog*, 1932–1933. Texarkana: Texarkana Junior College, 1933.
Chandler, Barbara Overton, and J. Ed Howe. *History of Texarkana and Bowie and Miller Counties*. Shreveport: J. S. Hyland & Co. 1939.
Davis, Doris. "The Enigma at the Keyboard: Chopin's Mademoiselle Reisz." *Mississippi Quarterly: The Journal of Southern Cultures* 58, no. 1–2 (Winter-Spring 2004–2005): 89–104.
Downing, A. J. *The Architecture of Country Houses*. New York: Dover, 1969. Reprint: New York: D. Appleton & Co., 1850.
French, Lillie Hamilton. *Homes and Their Decoration*. New York: Dodd, Mead, and Co., 1903.
*The Green Gate: Year Book of Georgetown Visitation Convent*, 1926. Washington, DC: Georgetown Visitation Convent, 1926.
*The Green Gate: Year Book of Georgetown Visitation Convent*, 1929. Washington, DC: Georgetown Visitation Convent, 1929.
Grier, Katherine C. "The Decline of the Memory Palace: The Parlor after 1890." In *American Home Life, 1880–1930: A Social History of Spaces and Services*, edited by Jessica H. Foy and Thomas J. Schlereth, 49–74. Knoxville: University of Tennessee Press, 1992.
Holly, H. Hudson. *Modern Dwellings: In Town and Country*. New York: Harper & Brothers, 1878.
Horrigan, Patrick. Unpublished papers on the Ahern Family, September 4, 2019.
Hutcheson, Ernest. *The Literature of the Piano: A Guide for Amateur and Student*. Revised by Rudolph Ganz. New York: Alfred A. Knopf, 1964.
Kline, Donna Staley. *Olga Samaroff Stokowski: An American Virtuoso on the World Stage*. College Station: Texas A&M University Press, 1996.
Loesser, Arthur. *Men, Women and Pianos: A Social History*. New York: Dover, 1990. Reprint: New York: Simon & Schuster, 1954.
Macleod, Beth Abelson. *Women Performing Music: The Emergence of American Women as Classical Instrumentalists and Conductors*. Jefferson, North Carolina, McFarland, 2001.

National Federation of Music Clubs. https://www.nfmc-music.org. Retrieved June 7, 2018.
National Theatre: Washington DC. History. https://www.nationaltheatre.org/history/history-of-the-national/. Retrieved June 8, 2018.
Obituary: Ann A. Ahern. *Texarkana Gazette*, November 29, 1988, 9A.
Parsons, Frank Alvah. *Interior Decoration: Its Principles and Practice*. Reprint: New York: Garden City, 2018.
*Providentia, 1925*. Texarkana: Providence Academy, St. Edward Church, 1925.
*Providentia, 1926*. Texarkana: Providence Academy, St. Edward Church, 1926.
Rothstein, Edward. Foreword to *Men, Women and Pianos: A Social History*, by Arthur Loesser, vii–xii. New York: Dover, 1990. Reprint: New York: Simon & Schuster 1954.
St. Edward's Catholic Church: Parish History. http://www.saintedwardstexarkana.com/about-us/parish-history. Retrieved May 30, 2018.
Schonberg, Harold C. *The Great Pianists: From Mozart to the Present*. New York: Simon & Schuster, 1963.
Tick, Judith. "Passed Away Is the Piano Girl: Changes in American Musical Life, 1870–1900." In *Women Making Music: The Western Art Tradition 1150–950*, edited by Jane Bowers and Judith Tick, 325–48. Urbana: University of Illinois Press, 1987.
*The Trinilogue, 1928*. Washington, DC: Trinity College, 1929.
*Ultra Modern Library: Collection of Favorite Piano Solos*. Foreword. Chicago: M. M. Cole, 1936.
Varney, Almon C. *Our Homes and Their Adornments: Or, How to Build, Furnish, and Adorn a Home*. Detroit: J. C. Chilton & Co., 1883.
Wednesday Music Club Handbooks. Unpublished annual handbooks, housed in the P. J. Ahern House. Texarkana Museums System.
Wharton, Edith, and Ogden Codman Jr. *The Decoration of Houses*. Mineola, NY: Dover, 2015. Reprint: New York: Charles Scribner's Sons, 1914.

## Chapter 7

Beecher, Catharine E., and Harriet Beecher Stowe. *The American Woman's Home*. Edited by Nicole Tonkovich. New Brunswick, NJ: Rutgers University Press, 2002. Reprint: Hartford, CT: Harriet Beecher Stowe Center, 1869.
Calvert, Karin. "Children in the House, 1890 to 1930." In *American Home Life: A Social History of Spaces and Services*, edited by Jessica H. Foy and Thomas J. Schlereth, 75–93. Knoxville: University of Tennessee Press, 1992.
Coleridge, Samuel Taylor. "The Rime of the Ancient Mariner." In *The Romantic Period*, edited by Stephen Greenblatt, Deidre Shauna Lynch, and Jack Stillinger, 430–46. Vol. D of *The Norton Anthology of English Literature*. 8th ed. New York: W. W. Norton, 2006.
Cromley, Elizabeth Collins. "A History of American Beds and Bedrooms, 1890–1930." In *American Home Life, 1880–1930: A Social History of Spaces and Services*, edited by Jessica H. Foy and Thomas J. Schlereth, 120–41. Knoxville: University of Tennessee Press, 1992.

Handlin, David P. *The American Home: Architecture and Society, 1815–1915.* Boston: Little, Brown, 1979.

National Register of Historic Places, Registration Form, Patrick J. Ahern House, MI0041, 403 Laurel Street, Texarkana, AR 71854, Section 7, 2.

Plante, Ellen M. *Women at Home in Victorian America: A Social History.* New York: Facts On File, 1997.

Schlereth, Thomas J. *Victorian America: Transformations in Everyday Life, 1876–1915.* New York: Harper Perennial, 1991.

Wharton, Edith, and Ogden Codman Jr. *The Decoration of Houses.* Mineola, NY: Dover, 2015. Reprint: New York: Charles Scribner's Sons, 1914.

Wordsworth, William. "Ode: Intimations of Immortality from Recollections of Early Childhood." In *The Romantic Period*, edited by Stephen Greenblatt, Deidre Shauna Lynch, and Jack Stillinger, 308–12. Vol. D of *The Norton Anthology of English Literature.* 8th ed. New York: W. W. Norton, 2006.

## Chapter 8

Beecher, Catharine E., and Harriet Beecher Stowe. *The American Woman's Home.* Edited by Nicole Tonkovich. New Brunswick, NJ: Rutgers University Press, 2002. Reprint: Hartford, CT: Harriet Beecher Stowe Center, 1869.

*Good Housekeeping's Book of Menus, Recipes, and Household Discoveries.* New York: Good Housekeeping, 1922.

Handlin, David P. *The American Home: Architecture and Society 1815–1915.* Boston: Little, Brown, 1979.

Harrison, Molly. *The Kitchen in History.* New York: Charles Scribner's Sons, 1972.

Plante, Ellen M. *The American Kitchen: 1700 to the Present.* New York: Facts On File, 1995.

Schlereth, Thomas J. *Victorian America: Transformations in Everyday Life, 1876–1915.* New York: Harper Perennial, 1991.

Strasser, Susan. *Never Done: A History of American Housework.* New York: Pantheon Books, 1982.

Wharton, Edith, and Ogden Codman Jr. *The Decoration of Houses.* Mineola, NY: Dover, 2015. Reprint: New York: Charles Scribner's Sons, 1914.

# Index

Note: Page numbers in italics indicate illustrative material.

Ahern, Ann Agnes, *34*, *35*, *36*, *38*, *42*; birth of, 6, 142; clothing of, 112; culinary interests, 176, 180; death of, 26, 27; education and music career, 16, 19, 23, 25, 142, 145–55; polio diagnosis, 9–10, 23, 26–27, 151; reading interests, 94–95, 97; remarks on family home, 183, 184; summer road trips, 24–25
Ahern, Catherine ("Cathy") Ann, 23
Ahern, Catherine Elizabeth, *34*, *36*, *38*; birth of, 6, 142; death of, 18; memorial to, 14; musical interests, 145
Ahern, Eileen Carol, 23
Ahern, Eleanor Gertrude. *See* Horrigan, Eleanor Gertrude Ahern
Ahern, Elinor ("Ellie") Genevieve, 23
Ahern, Elinor Shea Oliver, 23, 25, *42*
Ahern, JoAnn, 19
Ahern, John William, *34*, *38*, *41*, *42*, *106*; birth of, 6, 142; and death of Catherine, 18; education, 16; marriage and children, 23, 25; mentioned, 11; musical interests, 142, 145
Ahern, Joseph ("Joe") Patrick, *34*, *35*, *37*, *42*; birth of, 6, 142; character and personality, 24; childhood artifacts, 167; death of, 27; education, 13, 16; eggnog tradition, 180; marriage and children, 18–19, 24; mentioned, 14, 173; and Prohibition, 15–16; reading interests, 93–94; war effort participation, 22
Ahern, Mary Cecilia, *34*, *35*, *38*, *42*; birth of, 6, 142; clothing of, 112; death of, 27; education and accounting career, 16, 25–26; mentioned, 11, 14, 18; musical interests, 25, 142–44, 145, 155, *159*, *160*; reading interests, 94–96, 98, 99
Ahern, Mary Olive Lansdale, *32*, *34*, *42*; background, 4–5, 138; birth of children, 6; character and personality, 5–6, 9, 14, 45–46; church involvement, 14, 19, 155; clothing of, 107–8, 109–10, 112–13, 117, 121, 124–25; culinary interests, 173–74, 176–78; death of, 26, 27; and death of Catherine, 18; family tree, 190–91; musical interests, 14, 19, 70, 91, 138–42, 155; and Prohibition, 15; reading interests, 91–92; summer road trips, 24–25; wedding, 4, *30*, *31*, 109–10, *127*
Ahern, Mary Pearle ("Little Mary"), 18–19
Ahern, Mary Pearle Brannan, 18, 24
Ahern, Maureen Elaine, 23
Ahern, Patrick Joseph (also called "P.J." by friends), *28*, *34*; birth of children, 6; character and personality, 12, 80; church involvement, 13, 14; family tree, 190–91; gardening interests,

## INDEX

173, 181; health and death, 16, 18, 19, 27; hospital establishment, 10–12; Irish background, 1–2, 7, 83–84; mercantile business, 2, 3–4, 5, 6, 17–18, *29*, *30*, 117; and Prohibition, 15; reading interests, 70, 81–90; wedding, 4, *30*, *31*, 109–10
Ahern, Patrick Joseph II, 23
Ahern Home: floor plan, 188–89; legacy, 183–84. *See also* architecture; decor and furnishings; domestic servants; *specific rooms*
Americanization, 111
appliances, kitchen, 172–73, 174, 178
architecture: exterior, *33*, 57–59, *67*, *68*, *185*; floor plan, 188–89; interior, 59–63 (*see also specific rooms*); landscape gardening, 63; styles of, 56–57; theory of, 54–56, 63, 64–65, 100–102
Arensky, Anton, 144
Arkansas Federation of Music Clubs (AFMC), 153, 154
Arkansas library system, 71
*Art Edition of the Most Popular Dramas of Shakespeare, An*, 89–90
attic, 63, 169–70
Austen, Jane, *Pride and Prejudice*, 70

Bachelard, Gaston, 64
Bacheller, Irving, 93–94; *The Light in the Clearing*, 93; *A Man for the Ages*, 93
Bacon, Francis, 80
basement (cellar), 63, 172, 174, 181–82
bathrooms, 62, 168–69
Baum, L. Frank, 119
Beach, Amy, 153
Beaty, John O., *An Introduction to Poetry* (with Hubbell), 96
bedrooms: and architectural trends and theory, 161–63; children's, 48, 164–68; design and decoration, 163–64, 166–68; master suite, 162, 163–64

Beecher, Catharine E., 115, 163, 164, 169, 172
belles-lettres, book sets, 89
Ben F. Smith Dry Goods Company, 112, 113, 118, 123, *129*
Bennett, Arnold, *Old Wives' Tale*, 95
Bertram, James, 72
Black domestic servants, 44–45, 48, 49–53
Blake, Mary Elizabeth, 83–84
Blocker, C. M., 11
Bloomfield-Zeisler, Fannie, 141
Bob (Ahern family dog), 8, 18
book and stationery stores, 74–75
bookcases, 101–2
Book-of-the-Month Club, 77
books. *See* libraries; library (Ahern); print culture
Boulanger, Nadia, 153
Brahms, Johannes, 157
Branch, Mamie, 52
Branch, William, 52
Brenan, Franic, 2
Bryan, William Jennings, 87
Bufford, Theodore, 13
Burdsal, William, 57
Burton-Peel Dry Goods, 117–18
bustles, 120, *129*
Butler, Alban, *Lives of the Saints*, 83
butler's pantry, 60, 61, 175–76
Butterick, Ebenezer, 115, 116

Cable, George Washington, *The Cavalier*, 91–92
Calvary Cemetery, 13
Calvert, Karin, 165
canning and preserves, 173, 174, 181
Carnegie Foundation, 71–72
Carreno, Teresa, 140–41
Cary, Henry Francis, 93
Castro, Juan Jose, 142, 145
Cather, Willa, *Death Comes for the Archbishop*, 94
*Catholic Encyclopedia, The*, 81–83

# INDEX

Catholic Press, 82
cellar, 63, 172, 174, 181–82
central hall, 60, 152
*Century Dictionary, The: An Encyclopedic Lexicon of the English Language*, 88
Chaminade, Cecile, 153
Chandler, Barbara, 70, 72, 80, 152–53
Chanel, Gabrielle "Coco," 123–24
Chautauqua Literary and Scientific Circle (CLSC), 77
child development theory, 165–68
children's literature, 97–98, 167
chimneys, 59. *See also* fireplaces
china cabinet, 61, 180
Chopin, Frédéric, 143
Chopin, Kate, 110, 123; *The Awakening*, 139–40
Christmas, 7–8, 150–51, 180
Churchill, Lawrence K., 21
circulating (subscription) libraries, 70, 73–74, 75
Clarendon, Oliver B., 13, 18
Clark, Edward, 114
classic literature sets, 89–90
Classical Revival, 55, 56. *See also* architecture
Clay, Henry, 138
closets, 61, 167–68
clothing: at department and dry goods stores, 116–20; local production, 111–14; mail-order, 111; patterns and fashion magazines, 115–16; sewing and sewing machines, 114–15; social meaning of, 108–9; style trends, 120–24, *129–31*; at urban centers, 110
Cobb, A. W., 57
Codman, Ogden, 101
Coleman, Alice, 72
Comstock, William T., 56
concrete structures, 58–59
Connell, F. M., *A Text-Book for the Study of Poetry*, 96

Conway, John, 109
cooks, 52, 177–78
corsets, 120–21
cosmetics, 124
*Cosmopolitan* (magazine), 79
Costain, Thomas B., *The Black Rose*, 99
couches, 61, 152
cradles and cribs, 166
Crane, Stephen, *The Red Badge of Courage*, 94
Criterion, 112, 113, 118–19, 122–23, 124, *129*, *131*
Cronin, A. J., *The Keys of the Kingdom*, 99
Crowell, Grace Noll, *The Lifted Lamp*, 96–97
Cunliffe, J. W., *English Literature during the Last Half-Century*, 95–96
Current Topics Club, 74

*Daily Texarkanian* (newspaper), 74, 75, 78, 79, 123, 124
dances, 170
Dante, *Inferno*, 93
Darnton, Robert, 69–70
De Wolfe, Elsie, 174–75
Debussy, Claude, 143–44, 156
decor and furnishings: in bedrooms, 163–64, 166–68; in central hall, 61, 152; for Christmas, 7–8, 150–51; in dining room, 61, 179; in library, 100–103; in music room, 60, 133–36, 147, 158, *159*, *160*; picture rails, 61–62
department stores, clothing at, 116–20
Depression, 17–18, 117
Dewey, Melvil, 73
Dickens, Charles, *Our Mutual Friend*, 95
Dickinson, Emily, 84, 115
dictionaries, book sets, 88
dining room, 60, 61, 179–81, *182*
domestic servants, 43–53; cooks and maids, 51–52, 177–78; employer-

employee dynamics, 45–46; historical overview, 44–46; laundry work, 46–48; nannies, 48–51; rank and uniforms of, 45
Donaldson, Walter, 156
door-to-door book agents, 76
Doré, Gustave, 93
Douglas, Lloyd C., *The Robe*, 99
Downing, A. J., 100, 135
Drayton, Grace G., 97
Dreiser, Theodore, *Sister Carrie*, 117
dressmaking: local, 111–12; patterns and fashion magazines for, 115–16; sewing and sewing machines, 114–15
Du Bois, W.E.B., 44
Dubuis, C. M., 13
Duckett, Mary, 52
Dudden, Faye E., 44–45, 46, 51–52
dyers, 114

East, E. C., 112
Ehlert, Louis, 143
electricity, 60, 173, 174, 178
Elliott, Harry, 52
Elrod, Etta, 113
Elson, Louis C., 91
*Encyclopedia Britannica*, 86–87
*English Belles-Lettres*, 89
Estes, W. Lee, 11
*Etiquette, Politeness, and Good Breeding*, 92–93
etiquette books, 92–93, 104
Ewen, Stuart and Elizabeth, 111

family tree, Ahern, 190–91
fashion. *See* clothing
fashion magazines, patterns in, 115–16
*Father Burke's Sermons and Lectures*, 83
Fay, Amy, 140
Field, Eugene, 96
Field, Rachel, *Hitty, Her First Hundred Years*, 98
Fields, Dorothy, 156

fig tree, 173
Filmore, Millard and Abigail, 138
fireplaces, 60, *67*, 103
First Church of Christian Science, 74
Fitzgerald, Edward, 13
Fitzgerald, F. Scott, *The Great Gatsby*, 81
Flaubert, Gustave, *Salammbo*, 89
floors: linoleum, 172; wooden, 59
Fore, Mary Collom, 113
*Four States Press* (newspaper), 78, 119, *131*
Franklin, Benjamin, 70
Franklyn, Blanche, 156
Frederick, Christine, 178
Freeman, Mary E. Wilkins, 115
French, Lillie Hamilton, *The House Dignified*, 101, 103, 134–36
*French Belles-Lettres*, 89
front door, *66*
front porch, 58, *66*
furnishings. *See* decor and furnishings

Gaines, J. S., 74, 75
garage, 59
gardening and landscaping, 63, 173, 181
garments. *See* clothing
gas heating, 103
gas lights, 60
gas stoves, 173, 174
Gaskell, C. A., 89–90
giant oak trees, 63
Gibbon, Edward, *The Decline and Fall of the Roman Empire*, 84
Gibson Girl style, 121, *130*
Glen, Evelyn Nakano, 45
Godard, Benjamin, 145
*Godey's Lady's Book* (magazine), 115, 116
Gottschalk, Louis, 139
Goudge, Elizabeth, *Green Dolphin Street*, 99
Gould, Glenn, 157

# INDEX

Grant, R. L., 11
Great Depression, 17–18, 117
Greenaway, Kate, 97
Griffin, Appleton Prentiss Clark, 89
Guest, Edgar A., *When Day Is Done*, 96
Gumprecht, Armand, 109

Hale, Sarah J., 114
Halevy, Lodovic, *Abbé Constantin*, 94–95
Halloween, 8
Halsey, Francis, 87
Handlin, David P., 162
*Harper's Bazaar* (magazine), 115
Harrison, Molly, 172
hats and hat-making, 112–14, 118, 121, *128*, *130*
Hayes, Rutherford B., 76
Herschell, William, 156
Hill, Daniel Delis, 120
Hill, Thomas E., 120
holiday celebrations, 7–8, 15, 150–51, 180
Hollis, Edward, 64–65
Holly, H. Hudson, 100, 101, 135
Holt, Emily, 171
Holt, Julia, 52
Hoosier cabinets, 175
Hopkins, D. S., 56
Horowitz, Vladimir, 157
Horrigan, Brian Richard, 23, 103–4, 163, 173, 180
Horrigan, Eleanor Gertrude Ahern, *34*, *41*, *42*, *106*; birth of, 6; character and personality, 19–20; education, 16, 20; marriage and children, 20–21, 23, 25; reflections on home and upbringing, 7–8, 9, 14–15, 16, 18, 50, 59, 133, 163, 170, 180; reflections on parents, 5–6, 9, 14, 46, 70, 80, 90, 108; war effort participation, 22; wedding, 20–21, *40*, 125–26, *132*, *182*
Horrigan, Joseph Michael, 23

Horrigan, Neil Alfred, 23
Horrigan, William ("Bill") Kienle, 20–22, 23, 25, *40*, *42*, 125
Horrigan, William Patrick, 23, 52, 149, 168
Horvath, Géza, 145
hosiery, 123
*House Beautiful*, 70
housewife, as term, 174–75
Howe, J. Ed, 70, 72, 80, 152–53
Howells, William Dean, *The Rise of Silas Lapham*, 94
Hubbell, Jay B., *An Introduction to Poetry* (with Beaty), 96
Humphrey, Alfred, 103
Huneker, James, 140
Hurston, Zora Neale, "Sweat," 48
Hutcheson, Ernest, 143, 144

I. Schwarz, Dry Goods & Clothing, 117, 123
iceboxes, 172–73
*Illustrated Catholic American* (magazine), 79
indoor plumbing, 169
Irish immigration, 1–2, 19
*Irish Literature*, 83–84

Jacobs, A. J., 86
Jeans, James, 86
Jefferson, Thomas, 69–70
Joseffy, Rafael, 138
Joslin, Katherine, 108

Kahn, Gus, 156
Keats, John, 134
Kienle, Alfred, 21
Kirby, Sally, 183
kitchen: appliances, 172–73, 174, 178; and butler's pantry, 60, 61, 175–76; and cellar, 63, 172, 174, 181–82; cooks, 52, 177–78; design, 171–72, 175–76; recipes, 176–78
Kline, Cyril, 8

Kline, John Peter, 5, 7, 8, 11, 18, *32*, 70, 138
Kline, Mary Ellen ("Ella") Lansdale, 5, 7, 8–9, 14, *32*, 50, 138, 141, 178
Kline, Muriel (later Loda), 8–9
Kline, Vivian, 8
Knox, Thomas W., *How to Travel*, 90
Kosminsky, Ray, 118
Krouse, Leo, 11
Ku Klux Klan, 11–12

Lack, Théodore, 145
*Ladies' Home Journal* (magazine), 116
Lamb, Charles and Mary, 89
landscaping and gardening, 63, 173, 181
Lang, Andrew, 86
Lansdale, Annie, 5
Lansdale, Catherine, 5
Lansdale, Francis, 5
Lansdale, George, 5
Lansdale, Mrs. George, 14
Lansdale, John, 5
Lansdale, John Wesley, 5
Lansdale, Mary (cousin), 145
Lansdale, Mary Ellen ("Ella") (later Kline), 5, 7, 8–9, 14, *32*, 50, 138, 141, 178
Lansdale, Mary Ellen Joy, 5, 19
Lansdale, Mary Olive. *See* Ahern, Mary Olive Lansdale
Lansdale, Walter, 5
Lansdale, William, 5
Lapham, Silas, 94
larger parlor. *See* music room
Lathrop, Dorothy P., 98
laundry and laundry room, 46–48, 172, 178
Lee, Rosie, 52
Leginska, Ethel, 141
Leschetizky, Theodor, 145
lexicons, book sets, 88
libraries: home, 69–70, 104, 162 (*see also* library (Ahern)); public, 70, 71–73, *105*; traveling, social, and subscription, 70, 73–74, 75. *See also* print culture
libraries (book sets), 76, 89
library (Ahern), *106*; and architectural theory, 64, 100–102; book collection, overview, 69–70, 80–81; children's literature, 97–98, 167; design and decoration, 60, 100–103; encyclopedias and lexicons, 86–87, 88; etiquette books, 92–93, 104; history books, 84–86; literature and poetry, 83–84, 89–90, 91–92, 93–97; music books, 91; orations, essays, and letters, 87, 89; popular novels and memoirs, 98–100; religious books, 81–83, 94; travel books, 90
Lightfoot, J. A., 11
Lincoln, Abraham, 140
Lind, Jenny, 138
linoleum floors, 172
Liszt, Franz, 138, 142, 143
literature and poetry collections, 83–84, 89–90, 91–92, 93–97
Loda, Frank, 8–9
Loda, Frank, Jr., 7, 8–9, 16, 45, 51, 177–78, 180
Loda, Muriel Kline, 8–9
Loesser, Arthur, 136, 157
Longfellow, Henry Wadsworth, 76
Loos, Adolf, 55

MacArthur, Douglas, 21
MacDonald, George, *At the Back of the North Wind*, 98
MacDowell, Edward, 142–43, 145
MacGeoghegan, Abbe, *The National History of Ireland* (with Mitchell), 85
magazines/newspapers, and print culture, 77–79
maids, 51–52
mail-order purchases, 56, 86–87, 111, 116
makeup, 124

# INDEX

mantels, 60, *67*, 103
Marinello Beauty Parlor, 124
Martha (housekeeper), 52
McCall, James, 115, 116
McCarron, Charles, 156
*McClure* (magazine), 79
McHugh, Jimmy, 156
Meagher, Michael, 10
Mess, Annie Agnes Lansdale, 19
Meynell, Alice Christiana, 86
Michael Meagher Memorial Hospital, 10–12, *38*
Miller Land and Improvement Company, 6
milliners, 112–14, 118
Mills, Betty J., 107, 121
Mitchell, John, *The National History of Ireland* (with MacGeoghegan), 85
Mlynarski, Emil, 142
*Modern Music and Musicians*, 91
Montalembert, Count de, *The Monks of the West*, 83
Morgan, Carey, 156
Morris, John B., 14
*Mother Goose, or the Old Nursery Rhymes*, 97
*Munsey* (magazine), 79
Munz, Harry, 118
music culture: female concert pianists, 140–41; local and national clubs, 152–55; and musical education, 139–40, 141–45; piano social history, 135–38, 139–40, 157–58; public concerts, 138–39
music room: Christmas decorations, 7–8, 150–51; design and decoration, 60, 133–36, *160*; fireplace mantel, 60, *67*; piano lessons and recitals in, 145–50, 151–52; pianos in, 134, 147, 158, *159*, *160*; record collection, 156–57; score collection, 155–56
Musick, John R., *The Real America in Romance*, 85–86

nannies/nurses, 48–51
Nast, Conde, 116
National Federation of Music Clubs (NFMC), 153, 154
National Theatre, 138–39, 141
Nesbitt, Florence, 178
*New Catholic Dictionary, The*, 83
*New York Weekly* (magazine), 79
newspapers/magazines, and print culture, 77–79
Nicholas, Ann, 112
nurseries, 48, 164–67
*Nursery Rhymes from Mother Goose*, 97
nurses/nannies, 48–51

oak trees, 63
O'Donnell, Lizzie, 113
O'Dwyer, Bridget Mary Quillinan, 4
O'Dwyer, Mrs. John C., 14
O'Dwyer, Roger Joseph, 2, 3–4, 17, *28*
O'Dwyer & Ahern Dry Goods Company, *29*, *30*; closure of, 17–18, 117; clothing at, 117, 122, 123; establishment and success of, 2, 3–4; Mary Olive's employment at, 5, 6
Offenhauser, F. W., 11
O'Gara, Mother Teresa, 10
O'Hara, John, 109
orations, book sets, 87
O'Reilly, Bernard, *The Mirror of True Womanhood: A Book of Instruction for Women in the World*, 92
O'Reilly, J. J., 2
ornamentation, architectural, 55
Otness, Harold M., 69
outdoor landscaping and gardening, 63, 173, 181
outdoor sleeping, 163

Paderewski, Ignacy Jan, 137, 138–39, 141
Palmer, Phyllis, 43
parlor (larger). *See* music room
parlor (smaller), 60, 133, 147, 148

*Parochial History of Waterford and Lismore, The*, 85
Parsons, Frank Alvah, 134
patterns, clothing, 115–16
*Peterson's Magazine*, 116
Pettengill, Lillian, 51
Philippines, 20–21
"piano girl" stereotype, 139–40
pianos, social history of, 135–38, 139–40, 157–58
picture rails, 61–62
Plante, Ellen M., 109, 171, 174
plumbing system, 169
poetry and literature collections, 83–84, 89–90, 91–92, 93–97
Poiret, Paul, 118, 121
Poldini, Ede, 145
polio, 9–10, 26
porch, 58, *66*
Post, Josephine Wright, 73
Presbyterian Book Store, 75
preserves and canning, 173, 174, 181
print culture: book and stationery stores, 74–75; door-to-door book agents, 76; early book distribution methods, 73–74; newspapers and magazines, 77–79; publishers' catalogs, 76–77; reading groups, 77. *See also* libraries; library (Ahern)
Prohibition, 15–16
Providence Academy, 13, 142, 143, 145, 155
public libraries, 70, 71–73, *105*
publishers' catalogs, 76–77
Purcell, Eleanor Horrigan ("Scamp"), *41, 42*; birth of, 21; recollections of Ahern family, 5, 20, 24, 97, 103, 109, 112, 113, 117, 124–25, 141–42, 144, 147, 149, 156, 173–74, 176; upbringing in Ahern home, 5, 23, 173–74, 180–81

Quality Hill neighborhood, 59

Rachmaninoff, Sergei, 156–57
Ragland Stationery, 74–75
railroad development, 3
railroad literature, 77
*Rand, McNally & Co.'s Encyclopedia and Gazetteer*, 90
reading groups, 77
"red couch," 61, 152
refrigerators, 173
religious books, 81–83, 94
Ridpath, John Clark, *History of the World*, 84–85
Riley, James Whitcomb, 96
Rind, William, 74
*Rise of Silas Lapham, The*, 94
Roosevelt, Mrs. Theodore, 139
Rothstein, Edward, 158
Rowe, Beverly J., 74, 75, 117
Rowe, John G., *The Romance of Irish History*, 85
Rubinstein, Anton, 136
Rubinstein, Artur, 156
Ruskin, John, 55
Rykwert, Joseph, 54

Sacred Heart Catholic Church, 13
Samaroff, Olga, 141, 153
Schlereth, Thomas J., 47, 168, 179
Schubert, Franz, 145
Schwarz, Isaac, 117
Schytte, Ludvig, 143, 145
servants. *See* domestic servants
sewing machines, 114
Seymour, Mary, 89
Shakespeare, William, 89–90
Shapiro, Joseph M., 115
Shiber, Etta, *Paris-Underground*, 99–100
Shostakovich, Dmitri, 157
Singer, Isaac Merritt, 114
Singleton, Esther, 158
sinks, kitchen, 172, 175
Sisters of Charity of the Incarnate Word, 10–12

## INDEX

slavery, 44–45
sleeping porch, 58, 162–63
smaller parlor, 60, 133, 147, 148
social libraries, 73–74
Southern Furniture Company, 6
square feet measurements, 62
St. Agnes Academy, 13
St. Edward Church and School, 13–14, 37, *38*, *39*, 142, 155
St. Joseph's school, Irish Christian Brothers, 2, 7
staircases, 60–61, *67*
*Standard Question Book and Home Study Outlines, The*, 85
stationery and bookstores, 74–75
Steele, Valerie, 108
Steinberg, Stephen, 50
Steinway pianos, 136–38, 157
Stevick, D. W., 78
Stickley, Gustav, 61
Stokowski, Leopold, 141, 157
stoves, 173, 174
Stowe, Harriet Beecher, 163, 164, 172
Strasser, Susan, 115
Stravinsky, Igor, 157
study rooms, 64
subscription books, 76
subscription libraries, 70, 73–74, 75
*Suburban and Country Homes*, 56–57
Sullivan, Alexander M., *The Story of Ireland*, 85

Taylor, Frederick Winslow, 178
Tennyson, Alfred, *The Idylls of the King*, 96
*Texarkana Courier* (newspaper), 78, 118, 121, *129*
*Texarkana Daily News* (newspaper), 78
*Texarkana Democrat* (newspaper), 78
*Texarkana Gazette* (newspaper), 78, 116, 125
*Texarkana Journal* (newspaper), 78
Texarkana Museums System, 184
Texarkana National Bank, 6

Texarkana Public Library, 70, 71–73, *105*
Texas Cotton Oil Company, 6
Texas library system, 71
Thackeray, W. M., *Vanity Fair*, 95
Thanksgiving, 180
Thomas, Theodore, 137
Thomas à Kempis, *Imitation of Christ*, 83
Tibbit, Irene, 112
Torrans, E. F. (Elizabeth), 113
Toscanini, Arturo, 157
Tovey, Donald Francis, 86
transoms, 62
travel books, 90
traveling libraries, 73
trousseaus and wedding dresses, *31*, *40*, 107–8, 109–10, 119, 121, 125–26, *127*, *132*
Tuan, Yi-Fu, 64
Twain, Mark, 72, 76, 99

undergarments, 122, 123
*Universal Classics Library*, 89

Van Doren, Carl and Mark, *American and British Literature Since 1890*, 95
Van Dyke, Henry, *The Story of the Other Wise Man*, 98
Van Rensselaer, Mariana Griswold, 54, 63
Varney, Almon C., 134
Veblen, Thorstein, *The Theory of the Leisure Class*, 120
vegetable garden, 173
Venturi, Robert, 56
*Village and Farm Cottages*, 56
Vincent, Nat, 156
Vitruvius, 55
*Vogue* (magazine), 116
Volz, Candace M., 64

Wallace-Sanders, Kimberly, 52–53
Ward, Aaron Montgomery, 111

Warren, E. A., 75
Webster, Daniel, 76, 138
Webster, Jean, *Daddy-Long-Legs*, 99
wedding dresses and trousseaus, *31*, *40*, 107–8, 109–10, 119, 121, 125–26, *127*, *132*
Wednesday Music Club, 152–55
Wernicke, Otto Heinrich Louis, 102
Wharton, Edith, 135; *Bunner Sisters*, 113–14; *The Decoration of Houses*, 101, 162, 166, 179; *The House of Mirth*, 75, 109
Wheeler, Henry, 49
Wheeler, Silas, 49
Whitely, William, 116
Whitney, William Dwight, 88
Wiegand, Wayne A., 70
Wigley, Mark, 63

Wilcox, Ella Wheeler, *Poems of Pleasure*, 96
Williams, Abigail, 104
Williams, Hettie, 48–51, *53*
Williams, James, 49
window displays, store, 118–19
woodwork, 59–60
Wordsworth, William, 165
World War I, 153, 155–56
World War II, 21–23, 153
*World's Famous Orations, The*, 87
Wright, Judith, 112
Wyche, Benjamin, 71

Yeiser, Henry C., 102
Young Women's Christian Association (YWCA), 72–73, 74

Other titles in the Red River Books series:

*Beyond Redemption: Texas Democrats after Reconstruction*
    Patrick G. Williams

*Planting the Union Flag in Texas: The Campaigns of Major General Nathaniel P. Banks in the West*
    Stephen A. Dupree

*The Great Southwest Railroad Strike and Free Labor*
    Theresa A. Case

*The Red River Bridge War: A Texas-Oklahoma Border Battle*
    Rusty Williams

*Trammel's Trace: The First Road to Texas from the North*
    Gary L. Pinkerton